JUST PEACE

JUST PEACE
HOW WARS SHOULD END

Mona Fixdal

First published in 2012 by
PALGRAVE MACMILLAN®
in the United States—a division of St. Martin's Press LLC,
175 Fifth Avenue, New York, NY 10010.

Where this book is distributed in the UK, Europe and the rest of the world,
this is by Palgrave Macmillan, a division of Macmillan Publishers Limited,
registered in England, company number 785998, of Houndmills,
Basingstoke, Hampshire RG21 6XS.

Palgrave Macmillan is the global academic imprint of the above companies
and has companies and representatives throughout the world.

Palgrave® and Macmillan® are registered trademarks in the United States,
the United Kingdom, Europe and other countries.

ISBN: 978–0–230–60034–8

Library of Congress Cataloging-in-Publication Data

Fixdal, Mona.
    Just peace : how wars should end / Mona Fixdal.
        p. cm.
    ISBN 978–0–230–60034–8 (hbk.)
        1. War—Case studies. 2. Peace—Political aspects. 3. Peace-building.
    4. Politics and war. 5. War—Moral and ethical aspects. 6. Strategy. I. Title.

U21.2.F59 2012
303.6'6—dc23   2012004991

A catalogue record of the book is available from the British Library.

Design by Newgen Imaging Systems (P) Ltd., Chennai, India.

First edition: August 2012

10 9 8 7 6 5 4 3 2 1

Printed in the United States of America.

For my parents,
with gratitude and love

CONTENTS

Acknowledgments

My parents, Eva and Jan Fixdal, grew up during the Second World War in German-occupied Norway. When we were little, my siblings and I heard stories of excitement about the war—for instance, about how my father acted as a messenger for the Norwegian resistance, delighting in outsmarting the Germans by hiding secret papers in the handlebars of his bicycle. As we grew older, we slowly came to understand more of the trauma that the occupation had brought. My mother was not far away when a bomb blew up on a tram in Oslo. My parents had been cut off from their families—my father's father was imprisoned, his older brothers were in hiding, and my mother was sent away to live with strangers on a remote mountain farm. In writing this book, their experiences of war and peace have never been far from my mind. I am grateful for their continuous, unconditional support and for the many loving ways in which they take part in my life.

This book is based on a dissertation I wrote for the department of political science at the University of Oslo. I owe a great debt of thanks to Raino Malnes, my adviser, whose remarkable ability to unsnarl tangled logic more than once saved me from getting lost in my own argument. As I first started thinking about the subject of just peace, I was helped by conversations with Dan Smith, then the director of the Peace Research Institute Oslo. He carefully read early drafts of my work and offered suggestions that reflected his unique perspective as both a researcher and a practitioner of conflict resolution.

In the past few years, I have been lucky to be part of a research project on the Norwegian peace tradition, hosted by the history department at the University of Oslo. The department has been nothing but supportive of my inquiries, however untraditional they seemed as history. I am grateful to its members and to my peace project colleagues, in particular Helge Pharo, who with wisdom, grace, and humor has managed to be at once a friend, an intellectual partner, and a boss. I have also been helped along the way by Paul Kahn, Ian Shapiro, Robert Huseby, Greg Reichberg, Elizabeth Cousens, and Henrik Syse. Anne Julie Semb deserves special thanks for helping me to find the right track when I was floundering. I have been fortunate, too, to have had the help of James Turner Johnson, who generously read and commented on several chapters and took the time to discuss a number of questions related to just war and just peace. I am indebted to Pablo Kalmanovitz for valuable comments on drafts. In the final stages of completing the manuscript I benefited from the help of Nayma Qayum, who made many suggestions, both large and small, for ways it could be improved.

At Palgrave Macmillan, Sarah Nathan, and Farideh Koohi-Kamali have guided me gently and expertly through the process of making the manuscript ready for publication.

For their enthusiasm and unwavering support, I thank my parents-in-law, Jane and George Silver. Vigdis Cristofoli, Yvonne Dehnes, Cleo Godsey, Benedicte Hoff, Line Lillevik, Danielle Otis, and Tone Sollien have been loyal, wonderful friends. Hilde Nagell deserves extra thanks for helping me to cope with academic life. Weekly runs and wide-ranging conversations with Lori Troilo have been a badly needed, and very enjoyable, distraction. And I am hugely thankful for the companionship of my brothers, Martin and Jon, and of my sister, Trude, without whom life would not be half as good or half as fun.

My husband, Peter, and Celia and Tessa, our daughters, have lived closer to this project than anyone—perhaps closer than they would have wished, however seldom they complained. Peter listened patiently each time I needed to iron out a difficult passage in the text, taking up endless questions of grammar and style. More important, he offered me the blend of inspiration, encouragement, and comfort that I needed to finish the project. Celia, Tessa, and Peter have together given me more joy and affection than any one person can reasonably ask for, and for that I am truly grateful.

1

INTRODUCTION

How should a war end? This book is an attempt to answer that question, and my answer has several parts. In the broadest sense, I hold that any morally acceptable outcome to a war must strike a balance between the goals of justice and of peace. The war should end in a "better state of peace," a peace that is more just and stabler than that which held before it began.[1] To assert this, is to recognize that both justice and peace have inherent, obvious worth and importance—neither can be established to the exclusion of the other.

At the core of any conception of postwar justice must also be an account of what we should consider just terms of peace. Wars reflect a disagreement between adversaries on some fundamental question. In Sri Lanka, for instance, the Tamils fought a long and bloody war for independence against the Sinhalese-dominated government. The question of statehood was at stake, too, in Bosnia-Herzegovina, Kosovo, and South Sudan, to take some other examples. Territorial disagreements have dominated a number of conflicts—as in the war between Argentina and Great Britain over the Falkland Islands and the long standing conflict between Israel and the Palestinians. And arguments about political institutions and kinds of regimes are as explosive as ever, as recent conflicts in Iraq, Libya, and Syria have shown. A war reflects a disagreement of great importance, and we cannot begin to define justice at its end without putting those disagreements at the very heart of our analysis.

As a war ends, other moral questions arise as well. Contemporary discussions of *jus post bellum*, or justice after wars, have focused particularly on questions of war termination, reparations, war-crime trials, postwar reconstruction, and occupation. These studies ask: When should a belligerent terminate a war? Does a defeated state have a responsibility to pay the damages inflicted by war? Does a victorious state have a responsibility to rebuild the political institutions of a defeated one? How should violations of the laws of war be punished? What are the rights and duties of an occupying state? These are important questions, but they do not alone define the scope of *post bellum* justice. In order to judge whether a war ended justly, we also have to look at the point of contention between the adversaries and to ask whether their disagreement found a morally acceptable result.[2]

Because I am interested in a war's issue, or central problem, I look both at international wars and internal ones, as well as those that do not fit comfortably into either category. A conflict over statehood is an internal war if the secessionist group is prevented from seceding, but it will become an international conflict once other states recognize the secessionist's claim to statehood. Conflicts over territory usually take place between two sovereign states, but the administrative boundaries within a state can also be contested. When it is the political system that is under dispute, the conflict is usually internal, but as recent experiences in Iraq show, other states might have strong stakes in the resolution of such a conflict. Thus, the discussion in this book is limited neither to international nor to internal wars.

How can we judge what is a morally acceptable outcome to a war's issue? Especially considering that the belligerents themselves often fight about what justice requires, how are we to go about answering this question? An evaluation of a war's outcome has to consist of three main elements. First, in order to directly take up the arguments that the belligerents make, we must ask what gives rise to valid claims to statehood, territory, and political rights. Here we must look to contemporary political theories for help. The reason is this: say that a substate group wishes to secede, and fights a war to that end. In order to judge whether the war in fact should end with a new state for the secessionists, we have to ask under what conditions a substate group has any right to statehood. Political theories of secession try to spell out the circumstances under which a secessionist struggle should succeed. Similarly, when two belligerents argue over a piece of territory, they will each offer reasons why they have the better claim. In order to assess these claims, we will have to engage with those reasons and explore what gives rise to a valid territorial claim. Moral theories of territorial rights are useful exactly because they investigate when a group has a claim to territorial sovereignty over a particular piece of land. Finally, a number of studies have sought to understand what type of political system is best for a postconflict society. These theories can provide the first step in determining how conflicts over government should end. In other words, we have to base any considered judgment of just peace terms on an underlying moral theory. This first step will help to develop our baseline position on the issue in question.

The second element in a judgment of postwar justice is to look at what I call war-specific considerations. This step takes into account that we are judging the outcome to a conflict that has turned violent, with all the theoretical messiness violence brings. Postwar justice is in some respects unique. War-specific considerations are by and large backward looking: they derive from the war that has just taken place. In particular, war-specific considerations refer to the just war idea that a war should be initiated for the right reasons (*jus ad bellum*) and fought in a morally acceptable way (*jus in bello*). Some contemporary scholars, as I will discuss further below, argue that postwar justice to a large degree can be defined by these war-specific considerations. *Jus post bellum* is, in their view, determined by the rightness of how the war was started and fought. But contemporary scholars have exaggerated the importance of the war-specific considerations. We cannot hope to find the principles of postwar justice in the concepts and principles offered by the just war tradition. That said, the war's outbreak and conduct are not irrelevant to our judgment of its outcome either. The just war tradition might help us clarify some moral issues at the end of war, but not others.

The third step is to consider what kinds of outcomes are likely to bring about stability. Peace is a moral value in its own right. Some peace terms might seem acceptable if judged solely by principles of justice, but do not promote long-term stability. This final step demands that we think seriously and explicitly about how secure and stable an outcome is likely to be. As my discussion will show, a multiplicity of factors come into play here, depending on the type of conflict we are evaluating. The dilemma between peace and justice presents itself in other ways too, perhaps most strikingly when belligerents have to make a choice between either accepting a peace agreement or continuing the fighting. But how peace is best

promoted must enter into our discussions before the belligerents get
to that point. Thus, I have written this book assuming throughout
that it is important to tackle the possible conflict between peace and
justice head-on. It is only by considering and weighing each of these
three kinds of considerations that we can hope to say what the best
outcome to a war is.

My aim in this book is not to try to provide a blueprint for a just
peace, or to design a checklist or lay out a set of criteria that particular peace agreements ought to be measured against. Nor am
I attempting to describe the process by which a just peace can be
reached, or how best to get the parties to a conflict to come to an
agreement on the war's issues. War endings are simply too complicated for that, as are the processes by which peace is achieved. My
primary goal is more modest: I wish to untangle the different elements that must make up any judgment of a war's outcome. This
is not a small goal, because it is only by being transparent about
one's underlying assumptions and the premises of one's argument,
that we can possibly hope to have a reasoned conversation about
justice at war's end. I also hope to contribute substantive views
on what we should regard as a just outcome to, for instance, a
war fought over territory. These substantive judgments consist of
general moral principles, war-specific considerations, and considerations of stability, as well as a judgment about the relative importance of them.

My argument, therefore, is both procedural and substantive. I
want to suggest what I think is the best way to go about judging
a war's outcome by separating the different elements that such
a judgment has to take into account as well as offer substantive
assessments. Thus, although I certainly hope my readers will find
every part of my argument to be equally persuasive, it would be
perfectly possible to take issue with my substantive conclusions,
while still agreeing with the way that I suggest we go about making these kinds of judgments.

In the rest of this chapter, I will discuss how contemporary
scholars have defined *jus post bellum*, and what they believe should
be the most important moral considerations in the transition from
war to peace. By and large, these discussions define the topic of
jus post bellum as the rights and duties of a victorious state that has
fought a just war. But, as I will argue, it is problematic to confine
a just peace discussion only to wars of this sort. In many wars it is

impossible to define a clear victim and a clear aggressor, and often they end in stalemate or a negotiated settlement rather than victory. I also explain why the just war tradition, while important, cannot be our only moral guide when we analyze *jus post bellum*. But first I will address an argument that, if accepted, would undermine my claim that justice is an important goal at the end of war.

Peace or Justice?

Justice, one might say, is inherently desirable, and so it is those who argue for injustice who have the burden of proof. But despite the ingrained value of justice, one could argue that working for a just peace is not always the right thing to do. That is the argument of Yossi Beilin, an Israeli politician, who believes a just peace can be a dangerous goal. The problem is that the goal of justice can lead people to reject peace proposals that in hindsight seem better than any alternative. In 1937, for instance, a British commission led by William Wellesley Peel, first earl Peel, came up with a solution to the conflict between Jews and Arabs in Palestine. It implied dividing the land into two parts. One part, about 20 percent of the total area, would go to the Jews in order that they could establish their own state. The remaining area would be given to the Palestinian Arabs.[3] The plan met with resistance among many Jews, who felt it provided them too little land, but they reluctantly accepted it. Representatives of the Arab states flatly turned down the plan, however, because they saw it as the alienation of the Arabian homeland.[4] Had the plan been accepted, Beilin writes, much suffering could have been avoided. By providing a safe haven for Jews, it might have significantly reduced the magnitude of the Holocaust, and it would have avoided the great number of Palestinian refugees who fled during the 1948 war between Israel and her neighbors. In Beilin's view, this is one of the clearest examples of a settlement lost.[5] By striving for justice, instead of agreeing to peace when the opportunity arises, adversaries might prolong suffering and commit an even greater injustice. As Beilin rhetorically asks, "What can be less just than taking young lives under the excuse that Just Peace has yet to be achieved?"[6]

We cannot really know how the conflict between Israel and the Palestinians would have played out under Lord Peel's plan.[7] But leaving that aside, Beilin illustrates the problem that the perfect can get in the way of the good, and that peace can be in conflict with the value of justice. Others have pointed to the same problem. One anonymous writer has argued that the desire for justice, especially on the part of outside negotiators, significantly prolonged the war in the former Yugoslavia. During this conflict, the goal of justice was pursued both through the kinds of peace agreements that were deemed acceptable and in the quest to prosecute and punish war crimes. But, argues Anonymous, had there not been this insistence on justice, the war could have ended much sooner, and many lives would have been saved. The writer concludes that the "quest for justice for yesterday's victims of atrocities should not be pursued in such a manner that it makes today's living the dead of tomorrow."[8]

The importance of peace is obvious, but is it so important that it should always trump justice? I think not. There is no doubt that peace is an important value in its own right, and that there will be situations where the most important goal is to end the violence rather than seeking justice. That said, I do not believe that in seeking peace we should disregard considerations of justice altogether. On the contrary, there are a number of reasons why it is important to try to define what justice in the aftermath of war is, and why working for it is necessary.

To being with, it is important to examine what a just peace is, simply because it is a topic so many people care about. The call for a just peace is made continually by belligerents, civilians, and outside interveners alike. And in many cases, considerations about what is the right outcome to a conflict are entries into the process that eventually will bring about a peace plan.[9] The period leading up to the Peel Plan illustrates this point. Before he issued his recommendation for peace, Peel toured Palestine and held many meetings. After careful consideration, he concluded that both the Jewish and the Arab sides had valid claims. The conflict was "not one of right against wrong but that of right against right."[10] In trying to consider the interests of both adversaries, Peel had thought about fairness. We might disagree with his interpretation of what fairness was in this instance, but the fact is that Peel sought to find an outcome that would not only end the conflict, but end it in a morally acceptable way. The pursuit of justice is not confined to the battlefield. It takes place at the negotiating table, too.

Since the Cold War ended, wars between established states have become much less common. On the other hand, intrastate wars have become more frequent. These wars are increasingly terminated by negotiated settlements, not military victory.[11] Outside states invest a significant amount of time and resources in helping adversaries come to an agreed end to their conflict. This trend has contributed to a proliferation of peace treaties. According to Christine Bell, an astonishing 646 documents that can be classified as peace agreements were signed between 1990 and 2007.[12] For third parties involved in finding a negotiated solution to a conflict, it is vital to ask which principles such settlements should be based on. What can be considered a morally acceptable outcome to the war will also determine the policy that third parties pursue while the war is still going on.

While many share the goal of justice, there is no agreement on what justice after war is. Belligerents naturally fight about it, and, as I will show more fully below, there is no clear conception of what a just peace is among scholars either. But if we agree in principle that some war endings are better, that is, more morally justified, than others, then it is critical that we think through what makes them better. We cannot only ask, "Should we continue fighting this war to achieve a better peace?" We have also to ask, "What, at a minimum, does justice require for the peace to be morally acceptable?" If we are to reject justice at any given crossroads, we should know what we are rejecting.

Second, I do think there are situations where justice is more important than peace. Imagine, for instance, that Peel had proposed a plan where the Palestinian or Jewish claims were disregarded completely. Had this been the case, it would not be difficult to understand a rejection of the deal. What this suggests is that the dismissal of the Peel Plan does not seem unreasonable because it was a rejection of peace, but because it was a rejection of a reasonably just peace. Had the peace plan been grossly unjust, we might not have lamented its abandonment. In other words, it is difficult to understand how one can make an argument for always choosing peace. If one believes that war on occasion is a justified way of achieving a goal, then one cannot also argue that peace always has to be chosen over justice. One can discuss on each specific occasion the trade-off between peace and justice, but it is difficult to make a principled argument that peace always has priority. The cost of peace can be too high. The argument that it is sometimes wrong to choose justice over peace does not, therefore, lead to the conclusion that we should not think through what justice requires at the end of war.

Finally, it is wrong to assume that the relationship between peace and justice is always one of conflicting trade-offs. While peace and justice are sometimes at odds, often they are not. Some level of justice is probably a precondition for peace. While it is a simplification to say so, war can be viewed as a political instrument, as a means to achieve a goal. On this understanding, which comes from Carl von Clausewitz's influential study *On War*, certain political circumstances will lead one or more groups to conclude that only armed struggle can produce the kind of political order that they deem acceptable.[13] Such groups might feel that the state in which they live does not sufficiently represent their interests and that they deserve more autonomy or a state of their own. Or they might believe that the current regime is not governing in an acceptable way. Injustice, or what would-be belligerents perceive as injustice, is one of the reasons why wars begin in the first place. If, at the end of a war, one of the adversaries has been denied their basic rights to territory, to self-determination, or to political representation, the chances are that the war will start up again. As Adam Roberts points out, "In the Middle East, as elsewhere, some concept of justice...is and will remain an essential precondition of any lasting peace."[14] Kalevi Holsti agrees. In a wide-ranging study, he finds that "those peace settlements that were not considered legitimate by the vanquished and other states were soon threatened or overthrown."[15] As long as people care about justice and fairness, we simply cannot ignore what justice means at the end of war.

JUS POST BELLUM AND THE JUST WAR TRADITION

Most contemporary discussions of *jus post bellum* take place within the just war tradition, so we cannot begin to understand these discussions without having some basic knowledge of this way of thinking about war and peace. The just war tradition is a diverse tradition, made up of contributions from a variety of scholars, including theologians, philosophers, military strategists, and jurists. It spans many centuries and historical circumstances. It is common to say that Saint Augustine, who wrote in the fifth century AD, marks the start of the tradition, but it is sometimes traced back to classical philosophers such as Plato and Aristotle.[16] A systematic and coherent conception of just war began to emerge with the work of canonists, legalists, and theologians of the late twelfth century, and was clearly expressed by Thomas Aquinas in the late thirteenth century.[17]

The just war tradition is still highly relevant today, and it continues to inform current debates about when and how military force should be used. Most discussions of when a military intervention is the right response to a humanitarian catastrophe, for instance, explicitly or implicitly draw on the just war framework.[18] But present-day theories of just war differ considerably from the medieval and early modern conceptions. Whereas the early conceptions developed primarily within theology and focused on the moral obligations of government set by natural law, contemporary conceptions often begin from an assumed basis of underlying human rights and reason about the morality of war from that perspective. The just war tradition, then, is not a static theory of when war is justified. It has evolved over the centuries in response to the changing character of government and warfare. The tradition continues to be revised today as contemporary philosophers, military strategists, legal scholars, and political theorists grapple with the moral challenges of contemporary warfare.

What unites just war thinkers is the presumption that while war always brings about destruction and human suffering, it can under the right conditions be morally acceptable.[19] The just war tradition sits in that way between the pacifist view that war is never justified, and the realist view that the conduct of war cannot be constrained by moral principles. Just war thinkers are united too by the view that the moral acceptability of force depends on the reasons for going to war and the way the war is being fought. As the influential philosopher Michael Walzer has said, "War is always judged twice, first with reference to the reasons states have for fighting, secondly with reference to the means they adopt."[20]

The scholastic theologian Aquinas set the tone for how we should judge the reasons for war when he said that three things are necessary for a war to be just: it has to be fought by the right authority, for a just cause, and with the right intentions.[21] For Aquinas, it was the prince who had the right to wage war, and the right belonged to him because he was God's minister on earth.

When philosophers in the early modern era asked the same question, the religious element became less important, and they saw the prince's authority deriving instead from the community. With the Dutch legal scholar Hugo Grotius, the specifically religious element largely disappeared. For him, the prince was a guardian of his people, whose job was to protect his nation.[22] With Grotius, then, the criterion of right authority was transformed into an acceptance of state sovereignty. Sovereignty, that is, was no longer defined as the right to rule, but in terms of "specific territories inhabited by a particular populace, possessing their own traditions and laws."[23] When this idea was absorbed by international law, it changed from an ethical concept to a legal and political one.[24] Grotius also placed new emphasis on the conduct of war, in the effort to limit conflicts among states through common traditions and rules.[25]

Just war scholars believe that a just cause is a response to an injustice or harm. According to Augustine, "It is the injustice of the opposing side that lays on the wise man the duty of waging war."[26] For Aquinas, too, it is the responsibility of the sovereign to remedy injustice, for instance by recovering lost territory and punishing wrongdoing.[27] Writing at the time of the European discovery of the Americas, the Spanish theologian Francisco de Vitoria claimed that, "The sole and only just cause for waging war is when harm has been inflicted."[28] Grotius, whose work is in many ways a synthesis of earlier just war thinking, argued, "No other just cause for undertaking war can there be except injury received."[29] Wars to avenge injuries and to push out an invading enemy were therefore permissible, but wars for vengeance, for enlarging empire, for religious conversion, or for the personal glory of the prince, were not.[30] Today, self-defense is the most widely accepted reason for a state's going to war, and the only one unambiguously embraced by positive international law.[31] There is growing recognition that this right applies not to sovereign states but more precisely to the individuals and groups that inhabit them. Thus there has also been a trend towards accepting the use of military force to prevent or halt massive violations of human rights.[32]

It is common among philosophers in the just war tradition to follow the lead of Augustine and maintain that the ultimate goal of a just war must be a just peace.[33] This demand, that the intention of the war should be a just peace, provides a bridge

between the start of the war and its end. Some just war philosophers have elaborated on this argument and claimed that the
postwar phase is so integral to the war that it must be considered
its third phase. The Spanish philosopher Francisco Suárez held,
for instance, that we must distinguish among three stages of the
war: "its inception; its prosecution, before victory is gained; and
the period after victory."[34] But Suárez did not develop any concept of *jus post bellum*, and contemporary scholars who focus on
this idea go well beyond what these earlier just war philosophers
had in mind.

The conduct of war has been defined by two principles.
According to the principle of *discrimination*, noncombatants must
be given immunity and protection. It is, for instance, not accept
able to make women, children, the sick, or the wounded targets
of war. According to the principle of *proportionality*, the good
of the military action must outweigh its negative consequences.
There has to be a reasonable correlation between the military utility of acts of warfare and the negative consequences they have.
These two just war principles were later absorbed and elaborated
on by international treaties on warfare, such as the Geneva and
Hague conventions.[35] The 1977 Geneva Protocol I, in particular,
explicitly requires that armed forces distinguish those involved in
combat from noncombatants, and also refers to the principle of
proportionality.

Contemporary Discussions of *Jus Post Bellum*

While the category of *jus post bellum* is often acknowledged, just
war theorists have not given the postwar phase the same amount
of attention they have given the *ad bellum* and *in bello* categories.
In fact, although recent years have seen somewhat of a proliferation of discussion of this topic, it is fair to say that *jus post bellum*
is still largely ignored.[36] As Charles Kegley and Gregory Raymond
point out, "While scholars have argued for centuries about the
conditions under which it is just to wage war, far less thought has
gone into how to craft a just peace."[37] Those who have discussed
jus post bellum have focused primarily on the following five aspects
of the topic: war termination, punishment of war-related crimes,
reparations, and postwar reconstruction, including occupation.[38] In
the following brief survey, I most often make reference to Walzer,

simply because of his compelling and authoritative reasoning about questions of war and peace.

When and how should a war end? At what point should an adversary stop the fighting?[39] One way to answer this question is to connect the termination of war to the rightful reasons a state had to start fighting in the first place. That is what Walzer does when he says,

> The goals that can rightly be aimed at...will also be the limits of a just war. Once they are won, or once they are within political reach, the fighting should stop. Soldiers killed beyond that point die needlessly, and to force them to fight and possibly die is a crime akin to that of aggression itself.[40]

The 1991 Gulf War can serve as an example: many will agree that the US-led coalition had a just cause when it responded to Iraq's invasion of Kuwait—it was a war initiated in response to the territorial aggression of Iraq. The war should consequently have ended when Kuwait's prewar borders had been restored. This was the position President George H. W. Bush and National Security Advisor Brent Scowcroft took. As they write, "When we had achieved our strategic objectives (ejecting Iraqi forces from Kuwait and eroding Saddam's threat to the region) we stopped the fighting."[41] Moving on to Baghdad and removing Saddam Hussein would have amounted to "changing objectives in midstream," and "mission creep."[42]

Against this position, one can argue that it is important to end the war in a way that minimizes the risk of a new war. If the war ends with punitive peace terms, the seeds for a new conflict might have been sowed. If the war ends with the same dictator in place, the conflict has not really been resolved. Following this logic, the United States might have prevented the war in 2003 if it had removed Saddam Hussein in 1991, and the Second World War might have been prevented if the First World War had ended differently.[43] Walzer puts the point this way: a war can end too soon, and by not creating a more stable situation than the prewar state of affairs, the parties may "fix the conditions under which the fighting will be resumed, at a later time and with a new intensity."[44] There will be cases, in other words, in which the prewar *status quo* should not be the goal for the end of the war.

Another important postwar topic is the punishment of war-related crimes.[45] Brian Orend says that the question of postwar trials has so dominated *post bellum* discussions that it has been equated with postwar justice altogether.[46] While that might be an exaggeration, it is true that this topic has received much attention, also by earlier just war scholars.[47] And it is an issue that clearly reflects the way just war scholars think more generally about war. When war is not fought out of necessity alone, but from choice, then it is both possible and necessary to hold statesmen and soldiers accountable for those choices. As Walzer puts it, if there is something called "aggression," then there are aggressors, and if there something called "war crimes," then there will be war criminals.[48] The connection between this postwar topic and the other two just war categories is also clear: war crimes can be defined as violations of *ad bellum* norms (crimes of aggression) and *in bello* norms (indiscriminate and disproportionate warfare, including war crimes and crimes against humanity.)

The Nuremberg proceedings after the Second World War were the first time political leaders were brought in front of an international tribunal for the crime of aggression. But this did not start a trend. International prosecutions of *in bello* violations like war crimes have become more widespread, as exemplified, for instance, by the International Criminal Tribunal for the former Yugoslavia (ICTY) in 1993 and the International Criminal Tribunal for Rwanda (ICTR) in 1994, as well as the establishment of the International Criminal Court (ICC) in 1998. But political leaders are rarely put on trial for the crime of aggression.[49] As Steven Ratner and Jason Abrams point out, "*Jus ad bellum* has remained far more immune to criminalization than *jus in bello*."[50]

In addition to providing a general justification for the punishment of war crimes, a theory of postwar retribution would include answers to questions like which crimes and which perpetrators should be punished; with whom the authority to punish rests; and how one should balance the desire to prosecute war criminals with other postwar values like those of peace and stability.[51] These are by no means easy questions to answer. Involved are philosophical issues about how punishment can be justified and how guilt should be distributed between the leaders and citizens of a democratic state who might have supported the war effort, and the extent to which a solider can blame his war crimes on "battle frenzy" or "superior orders."[52] Involved too are difficult considerations about whom to prosecute when the number of offenders is large and the legal system is slow. No country illustrates this problem better than Rwanda. In the year 2000, six years after the genocide, about 125,000 "lesser offenders" were still sitting in overcrowded jails under terrible conditions, and of these only about 2,500 had been tried.[53]

Should reparations be paid to nations that have fallen victim to the aggression of others? Should victims of war crimes be compensated for their losses? Perhaps the most well-known and hotly disputed case of reparations is the Versailles Treaty, which concluded the First World War. According to Sally Marks, the reparations clauses in this treaty are "among the least read, most written about, least understood, and most controversial sections of the Versailles Treaty."[54] The treaty firmly placed the responsibility for the war on the aggression of Germany and her allies, and demanded extensive reparations for damage and loss suffered by the Allied nations. The influential economist John Maynard Keynes argued that the reparations called for by the Allies reflected "imbecile greed" and concluded that,

> The policy of reducing Germany to servitude for a generation, of degrading the lives of millions of human beings, and of depriving a whole nation of happiness should be abhorrent and detestable,— abhorrent and detestable, even if it were possible, even if it enriched ourselves, even if it did not sow the decay of the whole civilized life of Europe.[55]

Thanks in part to Keynes's polemical critique, reparations have been associated with the vindictiveness of victorious nations. But the idea that victims of war as well as victims of gross and systematic human rights violations have the right to compensation is still widespread today.[56]

Reparation to victims of war is a form of corrective justice. That is, it tries to rectify or repair an injury or loss inflicted on one party by another. Reparation implies not only that the injurer transfers resources to the victim, but also that the injurer acknowledges the wrongdoing.[57] A full account of reparations should answer questions about what acts require reparations, to whom reparations are owed, how much money it is reasonable to ask for, and with whom the responsibility to pay rests.[58] Walzer and Gary Bass agree that a state that has become the victim of an aggressive war clearly has the right to reparations, but reparations might more generally also befall victims of war crimes.[59] Walzer continues this thought, saying that even if not all citizens in the aggressor state supported the aggression, they share the responsibility to pay reparations. The existence of unequal guilt does not necessarily result in an unequal distribution of cost.[60] Bass argues along the same lines that although the bill ideally should be paid by aggressive leaders, war supporters, and war profiteers, practicality will require some broader form of taxation.[61]

Just as a war will inevitably lead to material destruction and the need to rebuild infrastructure, it can also bring about the need for political reconstruction. The topic of political reconstruction is large, encompassing questions such as when a regime change should be the aim of a belligerent, and what defines a just occupation. While postwar reconstruction is by no means a new topic, it has become more prominent in the last several decades as international organizations have become involved in the administration and reconstruction of war-torn countries. A number of wars are now fought for humanitarian purposes, with the explicit aim of creating a more peaceful and just regime.[62] In some cases, like Iraq and Afghanistan, the need for reconstruction came in the wake of war led by a US coalition. In other cases, like East Timor and Bosnia, it arose after a secessionist conflict or the violent unraveling of a sovereign state.

When should a regime change be the goal of a war, and how should it be accomplished?[63] Walzer begins his answer by pointing out that international society consists of independent states that enjoy the rights of territorial integrity and political sovereignty. It is the citizens of these states who are entitled to determine their own affairs.[64] The right for communities to determine their own affairs means that the "burden of proof falls on any political leader who tries to shape the domestic arrangements or alter the conditions of life in a foreign country."[65] This was President George H. W. Bush's argument during the Gulf War. Alluding to the concept of self-determination, he held that "the fate of Saddam Hussein was up to the Iraqi people."[66] The responsibility to change the government inside Iraq did not belong to the United States.[67] Walzer expresses this point in the following way: "Even if Iraq 'needed' a new government, that need could only be met by the

Iraqi people themselves. A government imposed by foreign armies would never be accepted as the product of, or the future agent of, self-determination."[68] Making the point in a more general way, Walzer notes that while justice might require a new and better government in places like Cambodia, East Timor, and Rwanda, we have to ask who the agents of this justice are.[69]

Although there is a presumption against political reconstruction, both Walzer and Bass approve of it in some cases. Walzer argues that the rights of political reconstruction come into existence when the hostility is directed at entire groups of peoples, as was the case with Nazi Germany.[70] Bass holds that there is a *post bellum* duty to reconstruct genocidal states because "these regimes have sought to exterminate their citizens," and they therefore cannot enjoy any international standing.[71] Bass also argues that the desire to prevent another war can justify some reconstruction of the enemy's regime. As he notes, "Without some reconstruction, there would be another war, and that is an injustice in itself."[72]

Political reconstruction will usually require some kind of occupation or international statebuilding mission. The moral acceptability of an occupation will depend in part on who the occupying force is, what its goals are, how they are achieved, and how long the occupation lasts. Orend argues generally that in order to transform a defeated aggressor into a "stable, peaceful, pro-rights society," an occupier should, among other things, adhere to the laws of war; purge the top-level politicians and administrators of the old regime and prosecute war criminals; provide security for the whole country; rebuild the economy by forgoing reparations and encouraging investments; and leave as soon as the regime is viable to govern.[73] Walzer holds that what determines the overall justice of a military occupation is not so much how long it lasts, but its political direction and how well it distributes the benefits of the occupation. In an unveiled criticism of the US occupation of Iraq, he notes that by putting profiteering at the center, the Bush administration not only undermined the legitimacy of the occupation but also jeopardized its democratic goals.[74]

SHORTCOMINGS OF CONTEMPORARY
POST BELLUM DISCUSSIONS

It is somewhat surprising that current discussions of *jus post bellum* have not focused more specifically on what we should consider morally acceptable peace terms. To be fair, the outcome of a war has received some indirect attention in the discussions of when a war should end and in debates about whether regime change should be a goal of war. But other issues, such as territorial ones, have received very little attention. The usefulness of contemporary discussion of *jus post bellum* is also limited by two common underlying assumptions. First, these discussions generally look at just peace from the point of view of a state having fought and won a just war. Second, they assume that there is a close connection between the three just war categories and that postwar justice can be best defined by the *ad bellum* and *in bello* criteria.[75] Both assumptions are problematic.

Victory after a Just War

Most contemporary discussions of postwar justice approach the topic from the point of view of a state that has fought, and won, a just war. Scholars ask what a state with just cause for going to war should do at the end of the war. Orend, for instance, debates what goals a participant in a just war rightly can aim at with regard to its end, and builds much of the following discussion around the rights and duties of "aggressors" and "victims."[76] When not addressing questions surrounding occupations, Walzer confines his *post bellum* discussions to two situations, after defensive wars and after humanitarian interventions—both clear cases of just wars.[77] And Mark Evans asks what "just combatants" must be prepared to do to secure *post bellum* justice.[78]

Perhaps this focus on what a just belligerent ought to do can be explained by the fact that an unjust belligerent most likely will not care about postwar justice. Or maybe most discussions of *jus post bellum* are framed this way because it is hard to see how an unjust war can end justly. As Walzer argues, it is unlikely that a belligerent can "fight an unjust war and then produce a decent postwar political order."[79] Orend says that failure to satisfy the *ad bellum* criteria "results in automatic failure to meet *jus in bello* and *jus post bellum*."[80] If one sees the three categories of just war theory as intimately connected, postwar justice arises as a possibility only after a just war.

The assumption that the just war has ended in victory is also common. Orend defines *post bellum* as "what the *winners* of a war may and may not do to countries and regimes they have defeated."[81]

In Bass's article, *jus post bellum* concerns the rights and obligations that *victorious* states have with respect to the restoration of the sovereignty of a conquered country, and with respect to the political and economic reconstruction of a defeated power.[82] *Just post bellum*, that is to say, is often conceptualized "as a series of restraints on what it is permissible for victors to do once the war is over."[83] This premise for postwar justice is easy to explain. The question of when a war should justly be terminated, for instance, does not arise when the war was unjust to begin with. By all accounts, a state that starts an aggressive war should end it as soon as possible. A defeated nation or a fallen regime will not have the capacity to engage in postwar reconstruction. Thus, there is not much point in discussing its rights or duties. And as Alex Bellamy argues, many *post bellum* discussions are "predicated on the assumption that victors will seek to exploit the vanquished as far as possible for their own benefit, a not unreasonable assumption given warfare's long history of sacked cities, annexed territories and forcibly acquired riches."[84] For that reason, it is important to define the limits of victory.

The problem is that our theory will have limited relevance if we focus only on the rights and duties of a victorious state engaged in a just war. We cannot always identify a clear "victim" and a clear "aggressor." Moreover, due in part to the increased interventions by third parties, victory has become a less common way for wars to end.[85] A theory of *post bellum* justice, that is, must be able to encompass cases where it is unclear which party has justice on its side, and where the war ends in a stalemate or a negotiated settlement.[86]

The Interconnectedness of the Just War Categories

The three just war categories—*ad bellum, in bello,* and *post bellum*—are often assumed to be connected in important ways.[87] According to James Turner Johnson, for instance, "The way the war is fought and the purpose at which it aims, including the peace that is sought for the end of the conflict, are not unrelated, whether in practical or in moral terms."[88] That means, for one thing, that each of the three categories affects how we judge the war overall: the justice of the postwar phase helps determine whether the war as a whole was just. A war cannot be regarded as just unless it ended justly.[89]

But should our judgments about the postwar phase also be dependent upon *ad bellum* considerations? According to *post bellum* scholars like Orend, our evaluation of the postwar phase is clearly contingent upon *jus ad* bellum. He says,

> It is hard to imagine—logically, causally and historically—a war which X began unjustly yet, when X won and imposed its will, that justice was somehow ultimately served.[90]

By fighting an aggressive war, the belligerent's rights are lost. This means that, "When or *if an aggressor wins a war, the peace terms will necessarily be unjust.*"[91] Orend admits that one aggressor might impose peace terms that are better than others. But still, "We cannot call these terms just, since they remain the product of a war which, overall, was unjust."[92] Since the process leading up to the peace settlement was unjust, the settlement cannot be just either. But the following example illustrates why it is problematic to insist so strongly that the rights of an aggressor should not be taken into account at the war's end.

In 1990, the Rwandese Patriotic Front (RPF) launched an attack on the Hutu-dominated government inside Rwanda. While one might sympathize with RPF's aims—it wanted to secure the repatriation of the refugees from past conflicts and to change the Hutu-dominated political system—this was the first use of force, and by most accounts therefore also an aggressive war. One might especially be negative about RPF's use of force since there were positive signs of change inside Rwanda in the years before the war broke out.[93] The government had engaged in talks with Uganda to solve the refugee problem, and with growing international pressure for democratization, the president of Rwanda also announced that he would accept a multiparty system.[94]

Many wars, Rwanda being but one example, are started because the warring party has a grievance. Even if this grievance does not justify the war, and the party that started the war must be considered an aggressor, we should still ask that the war ends with a better distribution of rights. If we adhere strictly to Orend's idea that "all is lost to the aggressor," then we seem to have to conclude that the peace should somehow not bring about a more inclusive political system or that the refugees did not have a right to return. But that conclusion is wrong. The population that the RPF represented had legitimate political rights, and accordingly the war should end with a political system that accorded political rights to all segments of the Rwandan society. There will be cases, that is, where we would want to acknowledge an adversary's rights at the end of the war, even if we condemn the initial resort to force.

The view that the justice of the outcome of war depends on the just cause of the war, lands us in some other problems too. It seems to lead to the conclusion that the right end to a war is the *status quo ante bellum*. Walzer presents this argument, which he does not fully endorse, in the following way: "A just war (precisely because it is not a crusade) should end with the restoration of the status quo ante. The paradigm case is a war of aggression, which ends justly when the aggressor has been defeated, his attack repulsed, the old boundaries restored."[95] Orend explains the reasoning behind this view in this way: "The aggressor had an unjust gain and thus must lose that gain; whereas the victim had an unjust loss and thus must, where possible, be restored in that loss."[96] If a war is justly fought to vindicate violated rights, then it has justly been solved when those rights have been restored.

However, there are a number of situations in which the prewar state of affairs has ceased to exist as an option. A war might develop in such a way that some political solutions are effectively taken off the table. For instance, the restoration of the "old" Socialist Federal Republic of Yugoslavia could not have been an outcome to the Yugoslav wars after Slovenia and Croatia had secured independent statehood. It was simply impossible to go back, and so the prewar state of affairs could offer us little guidance in what was a just solution to this conflict. More importantly, the *status quo ante bellum* can be grossly undesirable. The situation that existed before the war started is, at least in part, the reason why the war began in the first place. Thus, it does not make much sense to insist on going back to the prewar state of affairs. Orend also acknowledges this point when he says that we "ought not to want the literal restoration of the *status quo ante bellum* because that situation was precisely what led to armed conflict in the first place."[97]

We should hope that the war ends with an improvement over the prewar situation. This is what Walzer has in mind when he refers to Liddell Hart's claim that "the object in war is a better state of peace."[98] "Better" can mean two things. It can mean more secure, which is what Walzer alludes to when he argues that a better peace is "more secure than the *status quo ante bellum*, less vulnerable to territorial expansion, safer for ordinary men and women and for their domestic self-determinations."[99] "Better" can also mean more just. In that sense, the war is an opportunity to right a previous wrong, even if the injustice perhaps did not justify going to war.

Take the following example of France during the First World War. France had not been prepared to go to war to regain Alsace-Lorraine. Yet, once the war was a fact, it became unthinkable to end it without taking back the territory it had had to give up in 1870. As the French foreign minister Stéphen Pichon explained, France aimed to liberate her territories and to recover what the earlier conflict had taken from France, including Alsace-Loraine.[100] The war provided an opportunity, a way to set the past right, even if the historic injustice could not by itself justify the initiation of the war. In the just war tradition it is common to say that the just cause is the one cause that justifies the initial resort to force. But this suggests, as Jeff McMahan has argued, that a war can have two or more just causes, one that justifies the resort to war (i.e., self-defense), and one that justifies the continuation of war (i.e., recovery of lost territory).[101]

When *post bellum* is linked closely to *ad bellum*, it results in a conservative idea of postwar justice. In this view, "wars can be fought only to defend or recover pre-existing rights."[102] But if we take the view that a war should result in a "better peace," we can argue for a reshuffling of rights in the postwar order. That is a much better point of departure. As Walzer has noted,

> We need criteria for *jus post bellum* that are distinct from (though not wholly independent of) those that we use to judge the war and its conduct. We have to be able to argue about aftermaths as if this were a new argument—because, though it often isn't, it might be.[103]

In what follows, I assume that postwar justice in important respects is a new argument. This does not mean that the existence of the war is unimportant, morally speaking. But the war's importance to the postwar phase must be carefully investigated, and not simply assumed.

OUTLINE OF THE BOOK

In the next chapter, I discuss in more depth three concepts that are essential to the argument in this book. I define the concept of an issue, or central problem of a war, and how it relates to the causes of war; I explain some core aspects of my account of justice; and I describe the concept of stability and some of the factors that help to create lasting peace. The remaining three chapters discuss what a just outcome to a war's issue more specifically can be said to be. In chapter 3, I ask when independent statehood should be the outcome to a secessionist war. In chapter 4, I discuss territorial wars, and what a concern about justice and stability might require at their end. In chapter 5, I discuss important institutional choices after wars that have been fought over government. In this last chapter, I also discuss why we might have to temporarily limit democratic rights in order to build a legitimate and stable democracy, and how this can be done in a way that does not undermine the legitimacy of the postwar order.

2

SOME THEORETICAL
CONSIDERATIONS

A war is a reflection of a disagreement between the contending parties—it is the expression of an incompatible position on an important issue. A central argument of this book is that if we want to assess how morally acceptable a peace is, we have to put the outcome of the war's issue at the core of our discussion. Any just peace must provide a just resolution to the issue the war was fought over.

This chapter lays out the theoretical foundation for the remaining book. I analyze, in turn, three concepts that are essential to my discussion. Since a just peace has to contain a just resolution to the issue the war was fought over, we need a clear sense of what the issues of the war are, and how they are related to the causes of the war and the possible motivations soldiers might have to fight. This is the topic of the first section. In the second section, I consider how to determine what justice requires at the end of war. Rather than relying on procedural or contractual notions of justice, I argue that contemporary political theories of secession, territorial rights, and democracy will provide the best resource for us. In the third and final section, I discuss questions of stability. I look at different explanations for why some cease-fires last, while others do not, and how this insight can be brought into our *jus post bellum* discussion.

THE ISSUES OVER WHICH
WARS ARE FOUGHT

Wars can be fought over a number of different issues—over rights to important resources like water or oil, over strategically important land or lost territory, over the desire to secure political rights or greater autonomy within an existing state, or over the desire to establish a new state. Wars can also be fought to improve the status and rights of refugees, to increase domestic or regional security, to come to the aid of a group threatened by genocide or ethnic cleansing, or to defend an ally. This book focuses on three main kinds of issues: wars fought over secession, wars fought over territory, and wars fought over government. I focus on these three issues partly because they are arguably the most important ones, and partly because other issues can be subsumed under them.

I follow the work by the Uppsala Conflict Data Program (UCDP) and put the war's issue at the very heart of the definition of armed conflict. According to the UCDP, a war can be described as "a contested incompatibility concerning government or territory over which the use of armed force between the military forces of two parties, of which at least one is the government of a state, has resulted in at least 1000 battle-related deaths in at least one calendar year."[1] A war is an expression of an important difference on questions of either territory or governance. In most cases the adversaries announce their position on the issue in a written or a verbal statement. The day after Argentina had invaded the Falkland Islands, for instance, Margaret Thatcher told the House of Commons, "I must tell the House that the Falkland Islands and their dependencies remain British territory. No aggression and no invasion can alter that simple fact. It is the Government's objective to see that the islands are freed from occupation and are returned to British administration at the earliest possible moment."[2] It is by looking for the reasons that the adversaries give for fighting that we can determine over which issue the war is fought.

Statehood, Territory, and Government

Often considered especially difficult and protracted, territorial conflicts are disputes over the status of a piece of land.[3] In interstate wars, territorial conflicts concern which state should have the right to exercise sovereignty over a particular piece of land. An intrastate war can also raise territorial issues. The war in Bosnia-Herzegovina is an example. Even after it became clear that Bosnia would be a sovereign state, there was considerable disagreement about which ethnic groups would control Sarajevo, Srebrenica, and a number of other towns and areas. Much like international arguments over territory, internal divisions can be both strongly contested and morally significant.

When wars are fought over government, the incompatibility concerns what type of government the state should have. In these wars there is often an explicit desire for regime change, for a better system of political rights, or for a more just allocation of political power.[4] Conflicts over government most commonly take place within a state, but other states can also get involved in these fights as the recent conflicts in Iraq and Libya show.

A third set of issues concerns the boundary of the political unit. Anticolonial struggles and secessionist conflicts fall into this category. According to the data compiled by Kalevi Holsti, more than half of the wars fought between 1945 and 1989 were expressions of the desire for independence or an effort of state-creation, no doubt largely a result of the wars of liberation in Africa, Asia, and Latin America.[5] But this issue has certainly been on top of the agenda in the post–Cold War world too, with, for instance, the breakup of the Soviet Union and of Yugoslavia.

Unlike UCDP, I consider conflicts over statehood a form of governance conflict.[6] The distinction between territorial and governmental conflicts may seem contrived as both are essentially disputes over who should get to govern a given piece of territory. One way to make sense of the difference is to look at how demands for territory or government are justified. In territorial disputes the parties try to establish a connection between the land and themselves. Such claims are often based on ideas about historical, religious, or cultural rights to the land. At the heart of the conflict are the opposing demands for the same piece of territory. In government conflicts, by contrast, the core demand is for a right to govern. Whether it is a demand for greater influence over national politics or a demand for a separate state, the conflict revolves around political rights. The primary concern is to be in a position to govern. The question of which territory these political rights are exercised over is therefore of subordinate (although not to say minor) importance. For this reason, I consider conflicts over political boundaries, such as secessionist conflicts, as a type of government conflict.

One might interject here that this typology of issues is not specific enough. Surely, wars are fought over issues other than secession, territory, and government.[7] What about economic issues, security concerns, political prestige, and resources such as water and oil? Although these issues can indeed be critical, conflicts over statehood, territory, and government are at the core of many of contemporary conflicts. So it is due to their importance that I will focus on them.

One might also interject that, rather than looking at conflicting interests, I should focus more directly on identity questions and psychological theories of conflict. An interest-based approach looks at the tangible resources that people fight over. These can be either material, such as oil, land, and water, or political, such as rights to govern or rights to statehood. But conflicts can also arise over values, emotions, and identity. Values, as Louis Kriesberg points out, "become matters in contention when one side insists on manifesting particular values that another party finds so objectionable that they try to forbid the manifestations."[8] The Cold War was fought over fundamentally different ideologies, and not merely material or political interests, although these also played a part in the conflict. There is also an important psychological dimension to most conflicts, such as animosity, fear, and stereotyping among the populations and leaders involved. These emotional factors can be vital to our understanding of some kinds of conflicts, especially those that have lasted a long time. As Robert Rothstein notes,

> Anyone who analyzes protracted conflicts quickly comes to understand that they are not merely conflicts about land, or resources, or sovereignty—that is, conflicts of interest. What is missing from interest-based analysis is the emotional depth of the conflict, the intensity of hatred, mistrust, and contempt that has developed and deepened over time. In some cases, the depth of these feelings may be so profound that some or many of the participants in the conflict may prefer to inflict pain on the other side than to gain something for themselves.[9]

If the Arab-Israeli conflict only revolved around a fair distribution of resources, for instance, it would be much easier to find a solution acceptable to both parties.[10] Conflicts in which identity plays an important part might be particularly difficult to find a solution to. As Timothy Sisk points out, when "the conflict is over identity, the positions at the table are not easily divisible or reconcilable."[11]

I seek in no way to underestimate the role of identity-related violence in contemporary conflicts, nor do I wish to suggest that an interest-based approach in itself can give complete account of these conflicts. But even when ethnic identity and longstanding animosity play a major role in the conflict, there will be other issues, relating usually to territory or government that the adversaries disagree about.[12] The adversaries demand political fairness, their own separate state, or the control over a particular piece of territory. Identity organizes the way these demands are voiced, but it is not in itself the issue. By extension, I do not wish to suggest that reconciliation and cooperation among former adversaries can come about merely by finding an outcome to the issues they fight over. As I will point out more fully below, focusing on material and political interests is not sufficient in order to create a stable peace—a complete conflict resolution has to include a transformation of the relationship between the contending parties.[13]

A War's Issues and Causes

One should not confuse the war's issue with the cause of the war. What the parties to a conflict state as the incompatibility is not necessarily the grounds for the war. Casual theories of war ask what the underlying and immediate factors that bring wars about are. More specifically, as Hidemi Suganami points out, when we ask what caused a war, we might in fact be referring to three different things.[14] A cause can refer to the conditions that are necessary for a war to occur, like the existence of anarchy in international relations or the nature of man. A cause of war can also refer to the sequence of events that brought a particular war about.[15] But a war's issue is not the same as the cause of the war in either of these senses. States and substate groups can disagree about an issue but never fight a war over it. As Kalevi Holsti points out, governments are faced with contentious issues on a daily basis, but these issues do not necessarily cause a war to begin. A territorial dispute might lay dormant for years before war erupts, or perhaps it will find its solution through arbitration or dialogue.[16]

A cause might also refer to the correlates of war, the circumstances that most frequently exist when wars take place.[17] Recent scholarship has shown, for instance, that although the size of a population is a risk factor for war, no clear statistical relationship exists between excessive population growth and the onset of civil war.[18] But factors that might make a country more prone to war, or motivate people to fight, are not necessarily the same as the issue the war is fought over. It is often assumed, for instance, that poor economic conditions are one of the most important underlying causes of internal armed conflict.[19] The quest for economic opportunities, if not outright greed, can be a motivation for war.[20] Countries with a large supply of primary commodities, such as diamonds and oil, are therefore particularly prone to conflict.[21]

The conflict in Angola is a good illustration. In 1991, after 30 years of extremely violent conflict, which initially started as a war of independence against Portugal and then developed into a civil war, a peace agreement was signed by the People's Movement for the Liberation of Angola (MPLA) and the National Union for the Total Independence of Angola (UNITA). The Bicesse Accords called for national elections and the creation of a multiparty democracy. After the first 1992 presidential elections, the votes were so closely split between MPLA's Eduardo dos Santos and UNITA's Jonas Savimbi that another round of elections was called for. But before the second election could be held, Savimbi rejected the result and resumed the fighting. Diamonds played a crucial role the war that followed.[22] Because it controlled between 60 percent and 70 percent of Angola's diamond production, UNITA could keep its war effort going. It has been estimated that between 1992 and 1998, UNITA earned about 3.72 billion dollars on the sale of diamonds—the diamond revenue enabled the rejection of the election results and supplied UNITA with munitions and other supplies. Control over gold, coffee, wildlife products, and timber were other sources of funds.[23] The MPLA, for their part, used Angola's substantial oil revenue to keep their war effort going. Yet, despite the centrality of natural resources in this conflict, it was not a war fought over either oil or diamonds. As Philippe Le Billon points out, "Oil and diamonds are neither the cause nor the only motivation for the Angolan conflict, but the availability, spatial distribution, and political economy of these resources have been crucial in the course of the conflict."[24] The control over resources had to be part of the solution to the conflict, but the war was not fought over resources. Instead, it was fought between MPLA and UNITA over access to government power.

Economic factors have also featured prominently as explanations for international wars. One suggestion is that leaders facing economic decline might go to war in order to stimulate the economy or attempt to expand their markets or take control of neighboring countries' resources.[25] Iraq's invasion of Kuwait in 1990, for instance, has partly been explained by Iraq's impoverishment and growing foreign debt following the war with Iran—Saddam Hussein needed a rapid injection of capital.[26] But although economic factors might help explain why the war came about, they cannot be defined as the issue of the war. Rather, in the case of the Gulf War, territory was the issue at stake. That was irrefutably made clear a few days after the invasion, when Iraq declared the "comprehensive and eternal merger" of Kuwait into its own territory.[27]

It is sometimes suggested that political leaders facing dire economic conditions decide to go war in order to distract the population.[28] The Falklands War can serve as an example here. This war was fought between Great Britain and Argentina over the status of the Falkland Islands—or the Malvinas Islands, as the Argentineans call them. What was "really" going on in this war, it has been argued, was the attempt by the governing Argentine junta to rally around the flag in order to divert attention away from the dire economic conditions inside Argentina.[29] But although economic factors might have played a role in causing the war, it was not a war fought over economic issues. In wars where economic factors are a background cause, the stated incompatibility might be cast in terms of control of the central government or, as in this case, territorial rights.[30]

Great Britain had few economic reasons for defending the Falkland Islands, but also for this country there was more to the war than the territorial issue. Margaret Thatcher writes in her memoirs that much was at stake for Britain: "We were defending our honour as a nation, and principles of fundamental importance to the whole world—above all, that aggressors should never succeed and that international law should prevail over the use of force."[31] At stake in the war was not only the status of the Falklands, but also the reputation of the British nation, the desire to "stand firm" in the face of aggression and to protect important international principles. But while honor and law might have played an important role in the British decision to defend the islands, those were not the stated incompatibility. Rather, the Argentine government claimed publicly that Britain was an illegitimate occupier of the islands, while Britain claimed that the islands belonged to it, both because it had ruled the Falklands peacefully and legitimately for almost 150 years and because the population of the islands desired to remain British. The territorial issue was the stated incompatibility, not the survival of the junta, economic difficulties, prestige, or international law.

By focusing on a war's issue, I highlight what people aim for and what they would like to achieve in a war. This approach says less about wars' underlying or immediate causes or what is at stake for the people involved in the conflict. My focus directs attention toward what the adversaries disagree about, to the subject of the conflict.[32] It reflects the assumption that, as Michael Howard notes, "statesmen in fact go to war to achieve very specific ends."[33] It is these ends, and their moral acceptability, with which this book is concerned.

POSTWAR JUSTICE

A number of things can be said to be just or unjust: a person's attitudes, decisions, or actions; a country's laws or the way they are being carried out in the legal system; a state's political system, its policies, and the way the policies have been arrived at.[34] When we seek to judge the justice of an outcome, we must assess how it distributes benefits and burdens, rights and obligations. An outcome is unjust when it gives some people more than their share or denies others their share. Before I go into more detail about how I think justice should be understood, I will address two general concerns one might have about analyzing the outcome of a war.

Moral Disagreement

One could argue that it is impossible to try to define postwar justice, since what justice requires, is exactly what people argue about during the war. The conflict over Kosovo is one of many examples. While Yugoslavia was still intact, it consisted of six republics (Bosnia-Herzegovina, Croatia, Macedonia, Montenegro, Slovenia, and Serbia), and two autonomous provinces (Kosovo and Vojvodina).[35] The conflict that started in the early 1990s involved, at least on one level, the status of these republics and provinces—should they remain in a joint federation, or should they receive more autonomy or full independence? In 1995, after a gruesome war that took place primarily in Croatia and Bosnia, the status of all Yugoslav subunits except Kosovo had been resolved.[36] Macedonia, Slovenia, Croatia, and Bosnia were independent sovereign states, and Montenegro and Serbia was joined in a loose federation, called the Federal Republic of Yugoslavia.

The dispute over Kosovo's status was couched in the language of justice. The large Albanian majority argued for independence, while Serbs both inside and outside of Kosovo claimed that justice required that Kosovo remain attached to Serbia. The Albanians supported their claim by referring to the past—centuries ago they had been the first to inhabit the land that was now Kosovo, and they had for that reason a strong entitlement. It was also argued that their majority status implied that their preference should have stronger weight. The Serbs also held that historical events gave them a right to the area. Kosovo was their ancestral home, the cradle of their identity as a people, the site of a medieval Serbian kingdom, and the location of important religious structures and symbolic battlefields. Both Albanians and Serbs pointed to the oppression they had suffered at each other's hands as further support for their claim.[37]

Individuals and societies disagree about what is right and wrong, just and unjust. What some people say morality requires is at odds with what others say it requires. This is what is referred to as *descriptive moral relativism*, or cultural relativism.[38] The question is what kinds of conclusions we should draw from the existence of moral disagreement. More specifically, should the existence of moral disagreement lead us to think that a discussion of justice cannot bring about a persuasive conclusion? That is the position suggested by J. L. Mackie. According to Mackie, "Radical differences between first order moral judgments makes it difficult to treat those judgments as apprehensions of objective truths."[39] In its most extreme form this is an argument for *metaethical relativism*. In this view, "Moral judgments are not objectively true or false and...different individuals or societies can hold conflicting moral judgments without any of them being mistaken."[40] Unlike judgments about facts, the truth of moral judgments simply cannot be objectively established.

I cannot here fully address the metaphysical status of moral judgments or whether moral beliefs can be true in any ordinary sense of that word. Suffice it to say that I believe that neither relativism nor its polar opposite, absolutism, paints a convincing picture of morality and moral judgments.[41] I think it is possible to arrive at moral truths or, at least, moral judgments that are valid with reference to intersubjective standards. But morality is complex, and we owe our allegiance to more than one moral principle and value. Morality, one might say, consists of a plurality of principles and values. One consequence of this pluralist position is that moral disagreement might be a reflection of a moral dilemma—a situation of irreconcilable obligations. Conflicting values cannot always be brought into harmony. This means, as Susan Wolf has pointed out, that "though there may be a moral truth, the truth will be more complicated than one might have wished—complicated, specifically, in such a way as to make the answers to certain questions indeterminate."[42] There will be situations where we can determine the right answer to a moral issue, but there will also be situations where no such answer can be found.[43]

It is worth pointing out that moral disagreement is often not really disagreement about morality, but about facts. Any moral judgment consists of several elements, each of which must be assessed and examined. The Albanian claim to Kosovo, for instance, was built on the view that a right to land can be derived from being the first group to occupy the land, and on the factual claim that the Albanians had in fact been the first to inhabit the area. To justify their claim, the Kosovo Albanians had to show not only why rights to land can be derived from first occupancy, but also establish the historical correctness of their empirical claim. In many cases, different views of what morality requires is simply the result of a disagreement about historical events or scientific facts. The existence of moral disagreement should not lead us to dismiss the usefulness of moral discussions, but rather prompt us to explore what the disagreement stems from.

The Moral Status of a Peace Agreement

It can be argued that that instead of analyzing the terms of the peace, we should care about the way they were arrived at. If the warring parties come together and negotiate an agreement they all consent to, should we not accept it as valid? Several scholars have argued that rather than analyzing the outcome of the war isolated from how it came about, we should focus instead on the process of negotiation and the joint agreement reached by adversaries.

Pierre Allan and Alexis Keller, for instance, hold that the process of arriving at an agreement is essential to a concept of *jus post bellum*. In this view, justice is "what parties decree it is, by having found an agreement among them."[44] A just peace cannot be defined by abstract moral principles, but exists when the adversaries have settled the conflict in common.[45] According to Allan and Keller, the process of coming to an agreement must meet certain criteria. The parties must recognize and accept each other as negotiating partners and fully acknowledge the humanity of each other.[46] Through compromise they must develop common rules that are officially announced. These norms define the rights and duties of the adversaries and the principles for acceptable behavior.[47] A just peace "describes a process whereby peace and justice are reached together by two or more parties recognizing each others' identities, each renouncing some central demands, and each accepting to abide by common rules jointly developed."[48]

An anonymous writer has made a similar point with reference to Bosnia. Instead of debating whether a given peace plan meets ideal principles of justice, we must accept the solutions that adversaries arrive at through negotiations.[49] It is the existence of consensus that gives the agreement its validity. In order to fully appreciate this argument, a bit of background is necessary: Bosnia consisted of three nationalities with very different views of Bosnia's future: Bosniaks, Bosnian Croats, and Bosnian Serbs. For the most part, Bosniaks wanted Bosnia to be a democratic and centralized state, which they would be able to dominate because their group was the largest.[50] Bosnian Serb politicians did not want an independent Bosnia, but wished either to join Serbia or establish their own independent state. On January 9, 1992, they announced the establishment of the Serbian Republic of Bosnia-Herzegovina (later called Republika Srpska), and declared it part of the still existing Yugoslav federation.[51] Bosnian Croats were largely against an independent Bosnia, too, and established their own parastate called Herzeg-Bosnia. It seemed that unless Bosnia gained independence, the Bosniaks would be left with a small, unviable state, or come under Serbian control in what remained of Yugoslavia.[52] A referendum on the future status of Bosnia was held on February 29 and March 1, 1992.[53] The result was almost unanimously in favor of independence, but most of the Serb population did not participate in the vote.[54] The war over Bosnia started shortly after.

During the war, the adversaries, with varying degrees of involvement from external mediators, took part in negotiating several peace plans: the Vance-Owen plan in late 1992 and early 1993; the Owen-Stoltenberg plan in the summer of 1993, and the amended version of it negotiated on the British aircraft carrier HMS *Invincible* in September 1993; the Contact group plan in 1994; and then finally, the Dayton Peace Accords in November 1995.

Anonymous argues that the HMS *Invincible* plan was negotiated largely without the help of outside negotiators. After the Vance-Owen plan had failed in May 1993, the mediators simply oversaw a process in which the parties negotiated among themselves "with complete freedom to make up their own minds."[55] This process led eventually to an agreement on the HMS *Invincible*. The peace plan called for a decentralized Bosnia, consisting of a union of three republics, one for each of the constituent people. The plan was not well received among some Western governments, who felt it gave too much to the Serbs.

> Again the howls went up from the pundits and the penwarriors: Bosnia is being ethnically divided; aggression and ethnic cleansing are being condoned; Munich has returned and Chamberlains are once more at work. A week later the Bosnian government, which had freely negotiated and accepted the deal, chose to repudiate it. It chose war over peace. And the dying continued.[56]

In this case, Anonymous argues, there was a clear conflict between justice in an ideal sense, and what the parties could agree to among themselves.[57]

Anonymous suggests that we should accept the validity of the HMS *Invincible* plan not only because it could have created peace, but because it was the result of a process in which the three parties had full freedom to come to an agreement on their own terms.[58] Anonymous is not saying that the HMS *Invincible* plan was just merely because it was negotiated, but he or she is suggesting that the plan had moral weight because it was a result of an agreement.

It is important to ask, therefore, what moral force we should accord a deal negotiated by the parties themselves.

Should we embrace a kind of contractual view of just peace, where the right outcome to the war is the outcome of a bargaining process among the belligerents? I think not. A number of loosely related theories can be classified as contractarian. What unites them is the belief that "moral norms or political institutions find legitimacy...in their ability to secure (under the appropriate conditions) the agreement of those to whom they apply."[59] The notion of agreement is essential, and can be brought about by an actual or a hypothetical process. A number of approaches, including game theory and various negotiation theories, discuss the *actual* process by which conflicting parties reach agreement. The most permissive of these theories, describe any outcome as just simply "by virtue of it having been agreed, with no constraints imposed on the standards applied or methods used."[60] But this position is clearly not convincing. If a person agrees to something with a gun to her head, we would not accept the agreement as morally binding. Nor would we accept as morally binding an agreement in which the people involved allocated resources that were not theirs to begin with. To accept the outcome of a negotiated agreement, we have to posit some minimum standards against which the negotiation process is measured.

Common sense considerations point to at least two such conditions. One is that there is some minimal equality between the negotiating parties. The parties to a negotiation process should not be of very unequal power, because if they are, the party with more power will have an undue advantage. That is why negotiations between a child and a parent, or between a beggar and a rich person cannot be considered examples of a fair bargaining situation. The playing fields in these cases are not level. One might discuss the specifics here, like how equality is to be understood and what exactly it takes for a playing field to be level enough, but some approximate equality is necessary.

In order to give an agreement moral weight, we might also demand that the negotiators have basic respect for the people they are negotiating with and on behalf of. This means that they should have the interests of the people they represent at heart. They are, after all, not negotiating on their own behalf, but on behalf of the people they represent.[61] They should also show a minimal respect for their adversaries. This is what Allan and Keller call "thin recognition." It implies that the parties accept each other as human beings and as "having the right to exist and continuing to exist as...autonomous agent[s]."[62] Why is this a necessary criterion? Because without it, it is impossible to say that the negotiators are acting in good faith or to hope that they will stand by the agreement they have come to.

Neither one of these conditions were met in the negotiations that took place in the summer of 1993 in Bosnia, and that culminated with the agreement on board the HMS *Invincible*. During that summer, the Bosnian Serbs, who made up about one-third of the population, were in control of about 70 percent of Bosnian territory.[63] Bosnian Serb military strength was amplified by the help from the Yugoslav National Army (JNA) and the Serbian government. The Bosniaks, for their part, were at a disadvantage. The United Nations Security Council had imposed an arms embargo against Yugoslavia in September 1991, with the hope that it would limit the conflict. Instead it benefited the Serbs and cemented the advantage that they had at the beginning of the war.[64] In June 1993, for instance, the Bosnian army had a large number of soldiers—more, in fact, than the Serbs—but they only had 40 tanks and 1 aircraft. The Bosnian Serb army, by contrast, had 350 tanks and 35 aircrafts.[65] The relationship between the parties to the Bosnian conflict during this time was therefore clearly not one of equality, but simply one of deep inequality.

More problematic perhaps, was the fact that the military and political leaders involved in this war did not show much respect each other. They were ultranationalists with no regard for the destruction and misery their warfare caused. The American diplomat Peter Galbraith, who had extensive contact with all the leaders involved in this conflict, has said that people like Serbian president Slobodan Milosevic and President Tudjman were indifferent to the human suffering their political ambitions led to. He has characterized Mate Boban, the president of the self-proclaimed Herzeg-Bosnia, and the Bosnian Serb general Radko Mladic, as flat-out sadistic.[66] Speaking of Radovan Karadzic, the Bosnian Serb leader, David Owen has said he hoped that he could find some "respect within the inner man for human life and dignity, but I was doomed to disillusion."[67] These were people who deliberately targeted the civilian populations through rape and torture, and who were responsible for massacres of civilians. It is fair to say, too, that the Bosnian Croat and Bosnian Serb leadership had no wish to coexist with the Bosniaks. As one of the members of the Serb delegation had put it a bit earlier that summer, "the Turks (derogatory reference to Muslims) are going to be like walnuts in a Serbo-Croat nutcracker."[68] We cannot give much moral weight to the agreement that the adversaries came up with on board the HSM *Invincible*. It was an agreement between wartime leaders who for the most part had no respect for their opponents or for the populations affected by war. As the indictments of the International Criminal Tribunal for the former Yugoslavia (ICTY) later confirmed, a number of the people on board that ship were indeed criminals.[69]

Unfortunately, the case of Bosnia is probably not unique. Many post–Cold War conflicts can be described as conflicts in which there is a clear asymmetry of power between the parties. They differ from more traditional, Clausewitzian, interstate conflicts by involving adversaries other than established governments. They frequently revolve around a national group's claim to independence or statehood.[70] By contrast, in regular, international wars the parties are recognized governments. They might be of unequal size, and have different bargaining power, but at least structurally speaking, they are equals. In situations of severe asymmetry of power, the bargaining situation is inevitably unfair. It also seems flawed to assume that peace negotiators will necessarily have the interests of their populations in mind. Both governments' representatives and insurgency groups might be more concerned with their own power and influence than with protecting the welfare of their populations. In a number of recent wars, politicians and military leaders have not only aimed to manipulate and radicalize the civilian population, but also make it a direct target for its warfare.[71] That in itself is a reason for questioning their ability to negotiate for the common good. As Jan Egeland, a Norwegian diplomat who has been involved in the mediation efforts of a number of post–Cold War conflicts, says,

> Academics sitting in universities or elsewhere often presuppose that we are dealing with rational actors in a rational context with an understandable interest of negotiating for the common good of their people. My experience and that of many of my colleagues here

is that we deal with completely irrational, very nasty people. They have hidden agendas that are very personalized.[72]

There are good reasons, then, to reject the view that a just peace is one to which the parties have agreed. Common-sense principles such as a minimum of equality between the parties and respect for others seem too often to be lacking. I do not mean to suggest that warlords and paramilitary groups should not be made part of a negotiation process. As a general rule, I think mediators have to negotiate with the people who are responsible for the fighting and who control the weapons. Nor do I mean to suggest that the HMS *Invincible* plan should have been rejected. Clearly, it was not a good plan for Bosnia, as it left the Bosniaks with a very small and unviable state. But if the plan had actually managed to keep peace in Bosnia, and that is a big "if," much suffering would no doubt have been avoided.[73] Finally, I am not suggesting that the way in which an agreement is arrived at is unimportant to the moral acceptability of the peace it hopefully creates. My point is merely that we cannot assume that an agreement is enough to specify what just peace terms are. It is important to assess the moral acceptability of the outcome independently of the process that lead to it.

Formal and Substantive Principles of Justice

It is useful to distinguish between formal principles of justice and substantive (or material) principles of justice.[74] The basic principle of formal justice is usually attributed to Aristotle and can be stated in the following way: "Equals should be treated equally and unequals unequally—but in proportion to their relevant similarities and differences."[75] Difference in treatment is not in itself unjust, but different treatment for irrelevant reasons is.[76] The lack of arbitrariness is therefore an important aspect of justice. John Rawls makes the point this way: "Institutions are just when no arbitrary distinctions are made between persons in the assigning of basic rights and duties and when the rules determine a proper balance between competing claims to the advantages of social life."[77] This is an appeal to impartiality—a political system should not give political rights to one group of people and not to another, unless there is some morally relevant difference between these two groups.

Proportionality is another formal element of justice. According to Aristotle, "This, then, is what the just is—the proportional;

the unjust is what violates the proportion.... for the man who acts unjustly has too much, and the man who is unjustly treated too little, of what is good."[78] It is not enough that we treat equal people equally. We have to treat them equally relatively speaking. If we were to distribute goods based on need, it would be unjust if a person with a small need received more than a person with a large need. Similarly, it is unjust if a judge metes out widely different jail time for offenses of similar kind and circumstance.

Consistency is the third element of the formal principle of justice. As Allen Buchanan and Deborah Mathieu point out, the appeal to consistency can be made on two levels.[79] The first is on the choice of distributive principles. If we decide that the right to vote in Burundi should be given to all adults, irrespective of gender or ethnic affiliation, it would be inconsistent, and therefore unjust, to say that in the case of Rwanda, only those identified as Hutu should have the right to vote. The way the principle of justice is applied also has to be consistent. If we agree that all adults in Rwanda should have the right to vote, it would be inconsistent to turn women away at the voting stations.

The formal principle of justice is but one aspect of justice—it has to be supplemented with substantive principles. If we are to treat equals equally and unequals unequally, then we need to know what properties are relevant for determining what makes someone equal or different. Substantive principles of justice "identify the benefits and burdens to be distributed, the relevant properties on the bases of which they are to be distributed, and the relative weights these properties have."[80] They help us come up with a justified distribution of rights and privileges in a postwar order. In the next three chapters, I seek to develop such substantive principles, based on contemporary political theories, and thereby develop a foundation from which we can judge postwar outcomes.

What Is Special about Postwar Justice?

Many conflicts over territory and government never lead to war. The dispute over the Spratly Islands, which have been claimed in whole or in part by China, Taiwan, Vietnam, Malaysia, and the Philippines, never led to more than minor skirmishes. Other territorial conflicts, like the dispute between Argentina and Great Britain over the Falkland Islands, have escalated into a full-blown military conflict. The question is, should we judge these cases differently? Are there any morally relevant differences between how we should judge the outcome of a territorial dispute that has become violent and one that has not?

One answer to that question is simply "no"—postwar justice is unexceptional. There is no relevant difference between an evaluation of an outcome of a territorial distribution that came about through dialogue and negotiation and one that was the result of war. Another answer, as I suggested in the introduction, is "yes"—we have to assume that postwar justice is a different class of moral inquiry, undeniably tied to the preceding war. Brian Orend argues for this position when he claims that the moral acceptability of the war's beginning is decisive for the rights and duties to be distributed at the end of war.

In my view, the right answer is somewhere in between these two positions. Justice after violent conflict is different from justice after nonviolent conflict, but it is not a mere extension of *ad bellum* justice either. One of the major purposes in this book is to explore this connection between the war itself and the resolution of it. I assume that there are two main categories of considerations that make postwar justice exceptional. First, there may be backward-looking reasons to conceptualize the outcomes of violent and nonviolent disputes differently. Such reasons include how the war was started and how it was fought. Second, there might forward-looking reasons for distinguishing between violent and nonviolent conflicts. Societies that have been through a war are in special circumstances. They are marked by strife, conflict, and the breakdown of normal structures. Some solutions might by all accounts be just, but they are very unlikely to create stability.

PEACE AND POSTWAR STABILITY

Peace is commonly defined narrowly as the absence of war. Some argue that this "negative" peace is not enough, and that peace must be understood in positive terms. Johan Galtung, for instance, rejects the negative conception because very "unacceptable social orders would still be compatible with peace."[81] Martin Luther King Jr. voiced a similar criticism, arguing that while there was no overt war in the American South, what existed was merely an "obnoxious negative peace." He wished for the transition to "a substantive and positive peace, in which all men will respect the dignity and worth of human personality."[82] This understanding of peace has inspired others as well. Former United Nations Secretary-General Boutros Boutros-Ghali argues that challenges to peace are not confined to military threats, but also include unchecked population growth, debt, barriers to trade, drugs, the widening gap between rich and poor, poverty, famine, oppression, and global warming.[83]

Although these commentators are right to point out that the mere absence of war is compatible with injustice, we should not underestimate the value of even a negative peace. War, even when we believe it is just, is accompanied by deep suffering and pain, and entails a difficult interruption of normal life. For these reasons alone, even a negative peace is of tremendous value.[84] And a negative peace—seen as only the cessation of fighting—may be an essential condition for a more fully just peace. It is therefore analytically problematic to build a concept of justice into our concept of peace. If we equate peace with justice, we cannot analyze when these two values support each other and when they are in conflict with each other. Peace might or might not be accompanied by a just political system, and war, as philosophers in the just war tradition have successfully argued, might or might not be undertaken with just cause and with just means.

The basic concept of negative peace can be developed in another direction, with respect to how stable it is. According to Kenneth Boulding, a stable peace exists when "the probability of war is so small that it does not really enter into the calculations of the peoples involved."[85] There is a cognitive and a temporal dimension to this definition. The cognitive dimension refers to how conceivable it is that the parties to a conflict use violent means to solve it. The temporal dimension refers to the amount of time stability has existed—to the maintenance, consolidation, and institutionalization of peace over time.[86]

Stability is not a question of either/or, but of degrees. Some scholars prefer to define peace as a continuum from merely the absence of war to solid and consolidated peace.[87] Others create categories of stability. Talking specifically about the relationship between nations, Alexander George distinguishes among precarious, conditional, and stable peace. His distinction is based on the extent to which the peace depends on threats. A precarious peace, in this view, is "a relationship of acute conflict between two states that may have already engaged in warfare in the past and/or have been and still are on the verge of major war. At least one state is dissatisfied with the status quo, and one or both see the use of military force as legitimate for either defending or changing the status quo."[88] This a very fragile peace. A conditional peace is less precarious and can be maintained by general deterrence. And a stable peace is a situation where the parties do not consider the use of force, and where the threat of force is not included as an instrument of foreign policy.[89] With respect to internal wars, it is common to talk about a self-enforcing peace, a situation in which "when the outsiders leave, the former warring parties refrain from returning to war."[90]

How, then, can a stable peace be created? How can the parties to conflict move from a fragile peace to a situation in which the use of force is unthinkable? Both with respect to international and internal wars, scholars point to three factors that help determine the stabilization of the peace: the outcome of the war, the conflict environment, and the way in which the challenges of the postwar phase are dealt with.

What Makes Peace Last? The Outcome of the War

The scholarship on the durability of peace is important to the discussion in this book for the following reason: a proposed outcome to a war, whether it was fought over statehood, territory, or government, must, as far as possible, be compatible with a durable peace. That is to say, it would be difficult to accept as desirable a territorial allocation that, although just, is likely to sow the seeds of new conflict. In my definition, a war will have an outcome even if that outcome is brought about by military victory. So when I talk here about the terms of the peace, I do not wish to suggest that my argument is only related to negotiated settlements. But what the terms of a just settlement are will, of course, be of particular interest to those who try to create a negotiated settlement to a war. As Caroline Hartzell and her coauthors have said, the "architects of a negotiated settlement, responsible as they are for providing for the safety of their followers, will want to know not only whether conditions favor an enduring peace but also whether measures can be devised to make such an outcome more likely."[91]

I will return repeatedly to what types of outcomes are most likely to promote stability later in the book, but a few general points can be made here. First, what is the relationship between the existence of a peace agreement and the durability of peace? According to Monica Duffy Toft, civil wars that end in military victory will provide a more stable outcome than negotiated settlements.[92] The assumed stability might come at a high price, however, because, as Roy Licklider notes, "while military victories may be less likely to break down than negotiated settlements of identity wars, they are also more likely to be followed by acts of genocide."[93] In international wars, scholarship suggests that the existence of a peace treaty is positively associated with a successful transition to a stable peace. If a country has signed an agreement, there is a greater chance that postwar stability will result.[94] As Virginia Page Fortna notes, if we assume that wars are fought to achieve political goals, a political settlement is a way to deal with the more underlying causes of the conflict and alter the relationship between the parties. If successful, a political settlement removes the reasons the parties have to fight.[95] Fortna therefore argues that an explicit agreement about the war's issues leads to a very durable peace. In fact, she contends, "in the last 50 years at least, war has not resumed between any states that reached an explicit peace agreement settling the political issues over which they fought."[96]

It has also been argued that both the clarity and comprehensiveness of a settlement will affect its durability. According to Stephen John Stedman, an "implementer who must work with an agreement in which every provision is contested will have a much more difficult challenge than one who must implement an agreement that is the culmination of years of problem solving, relationship building, and inclusion."[97] Of course, that begs the question why some agreements are vague and consist of contradictory provisions. Stedman offer different suggestions, including the possibility that it was simply too difficult to reach an agreement on some issues, and that the desire to find an agreement that would quickly end the war was more pressing than the desire to negotiate a comprehensive agreement.[98]

Scholars have also discussed whether peace settlements that include human rights provisions and some measure of transitional justice is more likely to promote stability than those who do not. Licklider notes that few conclusive studies have been done on this topic.[99] But according to one study, conducted by Jack Snyder and Leslie Vinjamuri, there is a link between stability and the way in which past human rights violations have been dealt with. While they find that "post-war trials do little to deter future violence and are not highly correlated with the consolidation of peaceful democracies.... Amnesties or other minimal efforts to address the problem of past abuses have often been the basis for durable peaceful settlements."[100] Licklider, however, doubts that transitional justice measures provide long-term stability and argues that the relationship between human rights and the durability of peace in no way is "simple and straightforward."[101]

A study by Daniel Druckman and Cecilia Albin has tried to directly test the relationship between justice and peace. They make a distinction between four principles of justice: equality, proportionality, compensation, and need. The conclusions reached by any quantitative study will naturally depend on how key variables have been operationalized and measured, and principles of justice seem especially difficult to quantify. But Druckman and Albin do conclude that there is a positive relationship between justice principles and a durable peace. The principle of equality has most explanatory power in their account. "Justice matters," according to Druckman and Albin, especially when the conflict environment is difficult.[102]

It is also important to look at the adversaries' views of the settlement—the settlement's legitimacy. Legitimacy refers to the perception that a political system or an agreement is fair and morally acceptable. An agreement is legitimate when it is widely supported. A just peace agreement might have a better chance of being legitimate than an unjust one, but I suspect also that a morally weak agreement can be legitimate too. Legitimacy depends in part on how effective political leaders are at selling the deal to groups that might sabotage it. And legitimacy, more than justice, might be more directly related to stability. As Stanley Hoffman has pointed out, "because there is no all-powerful Olympian judge able to define 'objectively' what constitutes justice, it falls to the leaders of nations to concern themselves with the feelings of injustice created by their decisions, rather than focusing solely on objective justice.... Peace which feeds resentment is bad peace."[103] Arie Kacowicz and Yaacov Bar-Siman-Tov have made a similar point. They claim that mutual satisfaction with the terms of the agreement is a necessary condition for the stabilization of peace. When the parties to the conflict are content with the agreement, the desire to revise the outcome of the war is also reduced.[104]

Stability, the Conflict Environment, and the Implementation Phase

In what ways are the conflict environment and the implementation phase related to the durability of peace? Michael Doyle and Nicholas Sambanis argue that some conflicts are more difficult to stabilize than others. It is, for instance, particularly difficult to create stable political institutions in conflicts marked by ethnic or religious differences, because the level of hostility is especially high and pervasive in such conflicts.[105] Other scholars have disputed this claim. Hartzell et al. assert that there is no significant relationship between the type of conflict and stability. In their view, while "the stakes in politico-economic conflicts may be more easily divisible than in identity conflicts, groups that fought and died in bloody conflicts over the former type are likely to consider the stakes just as high as in identity wars."[106] They explain their findings with a concern that people in all war-torn societies face: security. As the authors point out, "Antagonists in both types of conflicts face the same set of security concerns regarding questions of how and by whom and to what end central state authority is to be exercised after the war's end."[107]

Doyle and Sambanis also find that the human cost of the war (measured in terms of numbers of deaths and numbers of displaced people) negatively affects the likelihood that the peace will last. This might be because high-intensity wars create a more hostile postwar environment.[108] This finding is supported by Hartzell et al.[109] These studies also suggest that the more parties to the conflict, the less likely it is that it will come to a successful conclusion, which might be because the peace process is less coherent when more parties are involved.[110] The existence of spoilers—that is, individuals and groups who seek to undermine the peace process—and neighbors opposed to the agreement, also pose a threat to stability.[111]

A difficult conflict environment also explains why some international conflicts become protracted. The most comprehensive and recent treatment of this question is provided in Fortna's book on the durability of peace, and her argument runs in many ways parallel to the arguments on intrastate postwar stability. A number of situational factors of international wars affect the likelihood that a fragile peace will develop into a stable one. If the conflict has lasted a long time and been costly, there is a greater chance that the peace will be durable. Stability is also likelier to ensue if the war has clearly been won by one belligerent—conversely, a military stalemate is not as conductive to stability. If the conflict has taken place between neighbors, or been fought over territory, chances are that the peace will be less durable.[112] Fortna also found that the settlement of the underlying issue is not as vital for stability after an international war as it is after a civil war. Unlike belligerents who share a country, sovereign states can retreat to their respective territories even if their territorial or policy issues remain unsettled.[113]

Whether a peace settlement will develop into a stable peace also depends on how the postconflict phase is handled. In the aftermath of an internal war, a state can find itself in dire straits, perhaps without a functioning political system, judicial system, or police, and without the ability to provide basic services to its population. Postwar states often have high unemployment and crime rates and a large number of refugees and internally displaced people. In order to stabilize the state, order has to be enforced, and the political system must be reformed. In the longer term, there has to be economic reconstruction and some process of reconciliation between hostile groups.[114]

What happens immediately after the war is over is clearly critical. Scholars are united in pointing to the importance of creating security for populations affected by the war, and to the key role that outside enforcers can play in that respect. The likelihood that a country will stabilize will increase substantially if, for instance, a major power sees continued peace in its interest and work for that end. According to George Downs and Stephen John Stedman, only "when such interest is present has peace implementation succeeded against the opposing efforts of spoilers and hostile neighbors."[115]

Another way of looking at this is to say that stabilization depends on reducing the incentives to resume conflict. Peace will not last if spoilers find it in their interest to take up arms and restart the war. Both defensive and offensive incentives can prompt a group to renew the conflict. Defensive incentives are a consequence of the security dilemma. When groups cannot trust the central authority to protect their security, they might seek their own protection. But groups might also conclude that restarting the war is more beneficial for them than continuing the peace process, and that by taking up arms, they will get a better deal than the settlement offered them.[116] Again, the role of third parties is important: spoilers have a much harder time succeeding if international actors can help protect the peace. In cases where "international custodians have created and implemented coherent, effective strategies for protecting peace and managing spoilers, damage has been limited and peace has triumphed."[117]

Security concerns are also important in international wars, and both belligerents and third parties can take a number of steps to enhance a sense of security and reduce the incentives to resume the fighting. The creation of buffer zones can make it more costly for a belligerent to attack its opponent. Security guarantees from third parties can also make the resumption of war a less desirable option, and international monitors and peacekeepers can help the parties clear up misunderstandings and control the effects of accidents.[118] In Fortna's words, "Demilitarized zones, dispute resolution commissions, peacekeeping, and external guarantees help combatants alter the incentives to break the cease-fire, reduce uncertainty about each other's actions and intentions, and help prevent or manage accidents that could lead back to war."[119]

There are, to sum up, a number of factors that make the attainment of a stable peace more likely. Many of these have little to do with how the war ends, but rather with how difficult the conflict environment is, or how involved outside states are in trying to stabilize the situation. But the outcome of the war's issue is clearly important too. Whether the result of the war is established by a peace agreement, or by a military victory, it can sow the seeds for future conflict. The degree to which an outcome is regarded as morally acceptable can be more important to stability than whether it conforms to an "objective" moral standard. But moral philosophical discussions of justice do not have to be removed from people's views of what justice requires. By directly addressing the disagreements at the center of contemporary conflicts, it is possible to say something about what people have good reasons to regard as an acceptable outcome to a war.

3

OUTCOMES OF
SECESSIONIST WARS

In May 2009, the Sri Lankan government crushed the separatist movement led by the Liberation Tigers of Tamil Eelam (LTTE). For the first time in decades the government could take control of the northern and eastern parts of the island, the land on which the Tigers had aimed to create their separate state. The conflict between the Tamils, comprising about 13 percent of the population, and the ruling Sinhalese majority had started to simmer in the 1950s, and escalated to full war by 1983. Faced with increasing discrimination and repression, the Tamils had first sought autonomy and later full independence, a goal that was resisted by successive Sri Lankan governments. Mahinda Rajapaksa, the Sri Lankan president who oversaw the final military campaign against the Tigers, was not alone in seeking a Sri Lanka consisting of "one nation, one people."[1] And with the brutal end to the war—the Tamil Tiger leadership and many civilians were killed—he might very well have succeeded in crushing the hope of a separate Tamil state.

The Tamils are only one of many national groups who have fought for their own state.[2] It is not the only national group who has failed either: In the early 1960s, Katanga unsuccessfully tried to break away from Congo. A few years later, Biafra tried to break way from Nigeria with no more luck. And more recently, Chechnya tried unsuccessfully to break away from Russia. Other secessionist movements have fared better: After only a short war, Slovenia secured independence from Yugoslavia in 1991. Croatia broke away from Yugoslavia at the same time, but its territory was contested until 1995. East Timor formally received independence from Indonesia in 2002 after a long and bloody occupation. And in January 2011, after decades of conflict, the South Sudanese went to the polls to vote on independence. Ninety-nine percent wanted to secede from Sudan, and six months later the South Sudanese flag was raised in Juba, the new capital.

Secessionist wars are fought not between established states, but between a state and a group within it who desires to become a state. While such wars are fought over territory, they are motivated by a politically grounded demand by one group to have a state of its own. It is the boundaries of the political unit itself that are in question. How, then, should such wars end? When should a secessionist conflict end in sovereign statehood, and when should it not?

One way to approach the answer to this question is, to put it somewhat crudely, to say that the rightful end of war can be deduced from the way the war started and the way it was fought. If the secessionist group has fought a just war, then the war should end in secession. If the group did not, then secession should not be the outcome. I call this *the strict correspondence argument*. I should point out that this argument does not consist of a substantive judgment of what a just war is. It only says that the war has to be just in order for the peace that follows to be just. Just war scholars will often disagree on questions of substance, and for that reason the demand that a war be considered just does not by itself provide a solid benchmark against which to judge war outcomes.

While there is an undeniable elegance to the strict correspondence argument, it is not very helpful. It greatly overstates the degree to which we can deduce postwar justice from *ad bellum* justice. The main problem is that it fails to see that our judgment of when a war should be initiated is a different kind of judgment than our judgment of how it should end. We want to set the bar against going to war high because wars always lead to immense human suffering, but once war is fought we want an outcome that is just and stable. That might mean that we judge it wrong for a secessionist group to go to war, but once the war has been fought (and even if the group was in part to blame for the initiation of the war), the war should end in secession. By the same token, the insurgency that is fighting the war on the secessionists' behalf might not be fighting it justly, yet their unjust fighting does not invalidate the claim to secession. Disconnecting our *post bellum* judgments from our *ad bellum* judgments can also mean that even if the secessionist group had a clear just cause, the war should not end in secession, because such an outcome would be unstable. I am not arguing that *ad bellum* and *in bello* justice have no relevance for postwar justice, or that our judgment of how the war should end does not sometimes correspond to our judgment of the justice of the war itself. But the correlation between these judgments must be explored, not simply assumed.

My point of departure is that a war should end in a "better state of peace," a peace that is more just and more stable than the situation that led to the war in the first place. In order to determine what such a peace looks like, we have to begin with a discussion of the circumstances under which a nonstate group develops a moral claim to its own separate state. Do substate groups have a general right to their own state, based for instance on democracy, or is secession morally acceptable only under exceptional circumstances, such as when a group has become victims of genocide? Our answer to this question will provide a baseline position on the morality of secession. Second, we must look back to the war that just took place, and ask how, if at all, it should affect our baseline. Should the way the war started and the way it was fought impact our view of its outcome? Can a claim to statehood be lost if the would-be state fights an unjust war? Or can it be gained by fighting justly? Third, we must ask what would provide a stable outcome to the war. Are some outcomes, which we otherwise might consider just, unable to promote long-term stability? If so, how should considerations about future stability be weighted against our initial moral judgment? By separating these three steps of the argument, it is possible to be clearer about the different considerations that any evaluation of a war's outcome has to take into account.

My discussion is based on an important assumption about the nature of rights to statehood: such rights are not absolute or inalienable. In fact, because the word "right" suggests something that cannot be outweighed by other considerations, it can be misleading. A group that initially has a weak claim to statehood might over the course of a war gain a stronger claim. And conversely, a group that initially has a relatively strong claim to separate statehood might through time weaken it. That is why the term "claims to statehood" is more appropriate than the term "rights to statehood."[3]

I should also point out that a complete assessment of secessionist war outcomes has to take into consideration the alternatives to
outright secession. There will be cases where we might not want
to accord a group full sovereign rights, perhaps because we doubt
that the group will be able to set up a legitimate state or because
we worry about the stability of such an outcome. In such cases
we might want to acknowledge the secessionist group's right to
self-determination in other ways, for instance, through autonomy
agreements or minority-right protections. Arguing against secession does not mean that we argue against the secessionists' desire
to be more in charge of their own affairs.

The outline of this chapter is straightforward. In the first part,
I develop a baseline position on the morality of secession. While
I recognize a number of problems with the attempt to establish
a primary right to statehood based on democratic theory, I also
believe that there are good reasons to take people's preferences
into account on this issue. Remedial right theories, which limits
justified secession to cases where there have been massive and sustained violations of human rights, are too restrictive. But a claim to
statehood based on democratically expressed preferences is qualified in important respects: the secessionist group must display the
capacity to establish a viable and minimally just state and show a
clear commitment to the protection of fundamental human rights.
In the second part of the chapter, I ask to what extent the war
should influence how we judge its outcome. I discuss, in particular, the strict correspondence argument, the view that if we are
to acknowledge a right to statehood, the secessionist group must
have fought a just war. In the final part of the chapter, I discuss
secession based on stability considerations. I argue that there are
some cases where secession might provide a stable outcome, but
that more often, secession results in more conflict. In order to
make a considered judgment about when secession is the best outcome to a particular conflict, then, we have to take into account
the specific circumstances of that case.

Secession, Territory, and Government

I make in this book a distinction between conflicts over statehood, conflicts over territory, and conflicts over government.
This distinction is not as unambiguous as it seems. Conflicts over

statehood are clearly related to conflicts over territory. A secessionist movement poses an overt political challenge to the existing government. It is a "form of refusal to acknowledge the state's claim to political authority."[4] But because a secessionist group aims to govern a particular piece of territory, it also poses a territorial challenge to the existing state. A secessionist claim is implicitly a territorial claim. And, conversely, when a national group or a state makes a claim to territory, it actually makes a claim to *govern* that particular piece of territory. Thus, territorial demands reflect a desire to exercise political control over a piece of land as well as the people inhabiting it.

Yet, while claims to statehood and territory seem to be two sides of the same coin, they are justified differently. When a national group or a state makes a territorial claim, it tries to establish a bond between itself and the land. It might argue that it has the right to the land because of its historical past, or because of its religious or cultural significance. Claims to statehood are different. They are justified by reference to the right to political power or self-government in one form or another. The primary concern here is not to govern a particular piece of territory, but to be in a position to govern.

Lea Brilmayer would disagree with this typology. She believes the territorial challenge involved in secessionist conflicts is more fundamental than the challenge to the political authority of the state. In her view, separatist "movements cannot be understood or evaluated without reference to claims to territory." Secessionist demands "involve, first and foremost, disputed claims to territory."[5] According to this view, the normative force of a secessionist claim depends on the strength of the relationship between the group and the land they live on.

Empirically speaking, it is likely that a clear and undisputed territorial claim will make it easier for a secessionist movement to secede.[6] This holds true especially if the group can claim that its territory was previously unjustly taken. When the Baltic States tore away from the unraveling Soviet Union, for instance, they could argue that their territory had been both unjustly and illegally annexed, and that all they were doing was taking it back. However, though secession is intimately linked to territory, the territorial claim is not the most important. Whether founded on nationalism, injustice, or democratic rights to self-determination, secessionist groups demand control over their own affairs—they express a desire to be "masters in their own house." Thus, it is the challenge to the political authority of the existing state that is at the core of the demand: not simply control of territory, but whether political control is to be of or by the people living in that territory.

Part I: Moral Claims to Statehood

In his influential book from 1991, Allen Buchanan noted that the subject of secession had been accorded little scholarly attention.[7] That description no longer holds true. There is a large body of literature that now examines the normative and the empirical aspects of this topic. A recurring question in the normative debate about secession is whether it should be construed as a relatively selective right, accorded only to groups as a remedy for an injustice (*remedial right theories*), or whether it should be construed as a more encompassing, primary right (*primary right theories*). Two types of justifications have been offered for a primary right to secession—either secession is a right granted to groups defined by ascriptive characteristics, such as a shared nationality (*ascriptive right theory*), or it is a right based on democratic principles (*associative right theories*).[8]

Of these two perspectives, the remedial right theory is the least controversial. That is to say, there is a general consensus that groups that have been victims of severe and sustained injustice should have a right to secede. And it is perfectly possible to argue that groups should have both a remedial right to secede and a primary right to secede. But the reverse is not true: proponents of the remedial right-only approach strongly oppose extending the right to groups that are not the victims of injustice.

SECESSION AS A REMEDIAL RIGHT

According to the remedial right theory, secession is justified only when the members of a nonstate group have become victims of grave injustices. Most scholars would agree that a state breakup is justified if the very survival of the group is threatened, or if the human rights of its members are being systematically and seriously breached. According to Buchanan, a leading proponent of the remedial right-only theory, secession is justified if a group's fundamental rights have been severely and systematically violated, if it has become the victim of discriminatory redistribution, or if the group's previous sovereign territory has unjustly been taken from it.[9] In a later book, Buchanan discusses when there should be an international legal right to secession. He mentions three injustices that are grave enough to warrant such a right: large-scale and persistent violations of human rights, unjust annexation of territory, and a "state's persistent, serious, and unprovoked violations of intrastate autonomy agreements."[10] Another proponent of the remedial right theory, Wayne Norman, lists five types of injustices: systematic discrimination or exploitation, illegal annexation, valid territorial claims, cultural survival, and severe violations of constitutional rights.[11]

The question of when secession can be justified is intimately connected to the question of how the state itself can be justified. If we are to describe what can warrant the breakup of a state, we have to be able to explain why the state has moral value in the first place and why it deserves to remain intact.[12] I will return more fully to this question below, but one short answer is that a state deserves protection if it functions as a legitimate trustee of the people within it. It is important to note that this is an inquiry into the legitimacy of the state, and not the legitimacy of any given government. A state, Buchanan says, is "an enduring structure of basic institutions for wielding political power, where this structure includes roles to be filled by members of the government."[13] A government is the agent of the state. This means that a state might be legitimate even if its government is not. But the reverse is not possible: if a state is illegitimate, the government is by extension also illegitimate.[14]

This reasoning implies that secession is justified if the state never acquired the right to be a trustee, or if the state has forfeited that right. If a state has unjustly incorporated another state, for instance, it never became a legitimate trustee of the people. In that case, secession is "simply the reappropriation, by the legitimate owner, of stolen property."[15] The Baltic Republics is an example. They had the right to secede because the Soviet Union had unjustly incorporated them into its territory. The Soviet Union could therefore never claim legitimate authority over their territory.[16] Secessions can also be justified if the government behaves unjustly toward part of the population, for instance, by persistently violating their fundamental rights. In such a case, the group has a right to secede from the larger state as a last resort. Buchanan emphasized that "this does not mean that the government's unjust behavior voids the state's (more accurately the people's) claim to the *rest* of its territory."[17] The negative actions of a particular government cannot necessarily undercut the legitimacy of the state itself.[18]

There are strong moral reasons to allow for a remedial right to secede. If a government persistently violates the essential rights of a group, it has the right to establish its own state. But an evaluation of a secessionist conflict cannot *only* take into consideration whether the group has been the victims of injustice. There are several reasons for this. First, a remedial right theory is restrictive and *status quo*-oriented. It puts the burden of proof on the secessionist group, who has to show that the state should not be regarded as a legitimate trustee. As Buchanan himself points out, his theory "does not present a direct challenge to the territorial integrity of existing states."[19] While there are multiple examples of substate groups being victims of severe and persistent human rights abuses, the category of "unjust states" is very small.[20] One might argue that considerations of national and international stability argue against the adoption of a moral principle that poses a more serious challenge to established boundaries. However, it is worth considering a theory that more directly attempts to justify the boundaries around a political community.

Secondly, it is also worth considering a principle for secession that incorporates identity claims in one form or another. If one holds that secession is only warranted when it is based on a remedial right, one simultaneously rejects national-based claims for self-determination. A national group is a group that defines itself as a distinct community by virtue of a shared history, an attachment to a certain piece of territory, and a common culture. It is such national groups who usually voice secessionist claims. It is a problem that the remedial right theory does not engage directly with the reasons these groups have for wanting to become a sovereign state.[21]

Finally, while severe injustice should be one of the principles upon which we base an assessment of secessionist conflicts, it does not seem to cover all possible legitimate secessions. Take the following example: In December 1990, the citizens of Slovenia, one of the six republics of Yugoslavia, went to the polls to vote on Slovenian independence. The outcome was overwhelming: 88.2 percent of the population favored independence.[22] Different factors explain this result. Many saw the vote as an affirmation of their Slovene identity.[23] While the Yugoslav constitution secured linguistic and cultural rights, a number of people felt that Slovenian was a second-class language in a federation dominated by Serbo-Croatian.[24] Moreover, Slovenia had moved toward political liberalization and democracy, with multiparty elections and the adoption of new laws on political association.[25] The other republics were also moving in that direction, but many in Slovenia felt that their progress was too slow.[26] There were economic motives for the desire to become a separate state as well. Slovenia accounted for about 8.4 percent of the population in Yugoslavia, but produced 16.8 percent of the national domestic product. Many Slovenians wanted to decrease what they saw as subsidies to the less-developed regions of the country and to central institutions such as the federal army. People in Slovenia also wanted to move more rapidly toward a market economy than the other republics seemed to be interested in.[27]

The Slovenians had not been the victims of grave injustice. While they felt that their language was not given an appropriate position, they were not culturally oppressed. They questioned the political direction of the federation, but at the time of the referendum, they were not denied any political rights.[28] And economically speaking, they were better off than the other republics. According to remedial right theory, therefore, the Slovenians did not have a right to independent statehood. However, if we are committed to democratic principles, should we not acknowledge the desire of a majority of Slovenians to have their own state? According to primary right theories, we should. These theories justify secession on the basis of a group's fundamental right to form its own political community.

Secession and National Self-Determination

Most secessionist movements reflect a nation's desire for self-determination.[29] As Margaret Moore points out,

> In almost every case of secession, and every secessionist movement, the people who seek to secede are culturally and/or linguistically distinct from the majority population, with a somewhat different

history and different relationship to the majority group and the state, and who are situated on their ancestral territory—not recent immigrants. Secession is not simply an issue of political legitimacy or fulfilling the functions of a state but is closely tied up with sub-state nationalism, and the interplay between the state and the community's culture, symbols, and identity.[30]

A nation is a group of people who share a common culture and a historical past, or at least a belief in a historical past. In many cases the nation also shares a distinct language. Furthermore, a nation, unlike other minority groups, is defined by an attachment to a geographical area—it has a homeland.[31]

According to David Miller, "National communities have a good claim to be politically self-determining."[32] There are two parts to this argument. First, Miller believes that the nation is a valuable source of personal identity. Miller acknowledges that nationalism can be xenophobic and oppressive, but like other liberal nationalists he believes that a shared culture is fully compatible with liberal principles such as individual freedom and choice. More to the point, Miller believes a shared culture is a precondition for individual autonomy and freedom.[33] A common culture, Miller claims, gives individuals "a sense of where they belong" and "provides them with a background against which more individual choices about how to live can be made."[34] Conationals also have special obligations toward each other—nations are not only cultural communities but also moral communities.[35]

Second, Miller holds that a state is best able to develop the institutional structures that protect a national community, and allocate the duties and responsibilities that conationals feel they owe each other. National cultures can deteriorate if they are not protected, but the safeguards provided by a state can prevent this from happening.[36] A right to national self-determination, that is, "highlights the importance of provisions aimed at protecting the cultural, religious, and linguistic identity of minorities."[37] Such provisions include different sets of minority rights and various forms of self-determination, of which statehood is the most encompassing one. Miller, I should point out, does not suggest that every nation has the right to secede if it wants to. Given the number of nations in the world, that would quickly lead to chaotic political fragmentation. In addition to taking into account the strength of the national claim, we also have to assess the strength of the national group's territorial claim, and to what extent the new state will protect the rights of its minorities.[38] That said, he does believe that an independent state is the best way to accommodate national self-determination institutionally.

There are some obvious problems connected to this type of national self-determination argument. Not all cultures value the autonomy and individual choice on which liberals place so much emphasis.[39] In fact, a number of cultures seem to deprive the individual of the freedom to make choices on his or her behalf. And why is it that conationals are appropriate objects of identification, when most of us do not know very many of the people in our nation? National feelings seem somewhat irrational, resting on an imagined community, so why should the nation be a repository of moral values?[40] Furthermore, why it is that we have special obligations toward people with whom we have not voluntarily entered into a relationship?[41] That said, I think liberal nationalists are right in pointing to the importance a shared national culture can have for individuals. Culture can be a source of meaning and value. The negative effects from being deprived of one's ability to speak one's native language or live in accordance with one's cultural traditions are a testimony to that. There are good reasons, then, to protect national cultures. But the protection of a national culture cannot in itself justify statehood. As Daryl Glaser suggests, while secessionists often consider themselves a nation, that might not be why we should accept their claim.[42] It might instead be because they strongly desire to be a state.

SECESSION AND DEMOCRACY

According to Diane Orentlicher, "Political theorists generally have failed to consider the implications of democratic theories for the unit within which self-government should be exercised."[43] A primary right theory, however, makes an explicit connection between democracy and statehood. According to this theory, the right of a person to participate in politics includes a democratic right to make decisions about the institutional structure of the state.[44] Thus, in the view of Daniel Philpott, for instance, self-determination and secession are "inextricable from democracy; our ideals commit us to it."[45]

Harry Beran, Christopher Wellmann, and Philpott are all prominent proponents of the primary right theory.[46] Each of these scholars acknowledges a plebiscitary right to secession—the right a majority has, under certain conditions, "to form its own independent state if it so chooses, even if the majority of the state as a whole opposes its bid for independence," but the way they justify this right differs somewhat.[47] One common argument, of which Philpott is a exponent, is that democracy, and consequently self-determination, is grounded in individual autonomy. Because people have the right to make decisions about their own lives, they also have the right to participate in making collective, political decisions. This democratic right also means that they should have a say in where the boundaries around the state are drawn.[48] Primary right theories are not based on the value of membership in a national group, but a democratic right to secession is perfectly compatible with national claims to self-determination.

Democracy and Political Boundaries

Few would argue that we should disrespect people's democratically expressed preferences. The question is whether we should respect democratically expressed preferences concerning the question of statehood. One could say that while we must in general respect people's opinions, we should not do so when these opinions concern the boundaries of the state. According to this argument, there are certain questions that should never be made the subject of democratic decision making. For instance, one could plausibly argue that the question of basic rights should not be made subject to democratic decision-making procedures because their moral status is absolute—they cannot be negotiated. Buchanan makes a similar argument with respect to boundaries. There is, he argues, "something very odd about a view that makes the determination of state boundaries procedurally indistinguishable from decisions made within states."[49]

Recognizing a right to alter boundaries through democratic procedures might have unfortunate consequences: states could be repeatedly dismembered, and political conflict would not be solved by "principled, rational dialogue" but simply by altering the boundary of the political unit itself.[50] The point of a democracy is, as Buchanan argues, to resolve political disagreement through a legitimate procedure, and not to redefine the demos if such disagreement occurs. Buchanan's argument points to the possible consequences of recognizing a democratic right to alter political boundaries. That is undoubtedly an important consideration, but it is not an argument that explains why the question of boundaries *as a matter of principle* should not be on the democratic agenda.

I am not sure what a principled argument against making political boundaries the subject of democratic decision making would look like. The fact that political boundaries are important to people, as they clearly were to the majority in Slovenia for instance, seems to argue in favor of putting statehood on the democratic agenda, not for taking the issue off it. And the widespread acceptance of consensual secession is an indication that many liberals, Buchanan included, believe that the question of statehood can, in some instances, be determined by people's preferences.[51] The reason why Norway's secession from Sweden and the breakup of Czechoslovakia have been viewed as relatively unproblematic, morally speaking, is because the involved parties largely agreed.

If we agree that it is important to take people's preferences into account, we run into another problem. Whose preferences should we consider? How do we determine the group that gets to vote in a referendum on secession? This is what Robert E. Goodin has called the problem of "constituting the demos."[52]

Philpott and other primary rights theorists believe that only the secessionist group should be allowed to vote on the proposed secession. Philpott holds that "the members of the larger state may not deny the separatists their pure, essential, unalloyed right to govern themselves or even claim the right to vote upon the separatists' exit."[53] But this argument misses the point, because we might just as easily turn the question around and ask why the separatists have the right to deny the larger state an opportunity to prevent the secession from happening. Brilmayer expresses the point this way:

> The fallacy of this argument is obvious; it assumes that the relevant individuals to consult are the members of the secessionist group. In consulting the population of the entire state, one might find that a majority overall wished to remain a single country. What has not been explained is why only the separatists need to be consulted.[54]

It is common in primary right theories to assume that only the secessionist group should vote on the secession. Beran has tried to spell out how the democratic principle should work. He says that we have to use the majority principle repeatedly to determine political boundaries. Based on this theory,

> A separatist movement can call for a referendum, within a territory specified by it, to determine...whether it should secede from its state. If there is a majority in the territory as a whole for secession, then the territory's people may exercise its right of self-determination and secede. But there may be people within this territory who do not wish to be part of the newly independent state. They could show, by majority vote within their territory, that this is so, and then become independent in turn, or remain within the state from which the others wish to secede.[55]

According to this argument, then, Slovenia could call a referendum on secession, in which only the people living on Slovenian territory could participate. But this does not solve the problem. If a separatist movement can determine the territory on which the referendum should be held, could not a larger state call a referendum on the same issue for the whole of the state's territory? Could not, for instance, the Yugoslavian state have called a referendum on Slovenian secession in which all the people in Yugoslavia could have participated? And if the majority of Yugoslavs had voted against Slovenian independence, would that not have been the right outcome to the issue?

One might try to define the demos by reference to shared territory (which is what Beran implicitly does), or to a common history or nationality. I think the best way out of this corner is what can be called the "all affected interests" principle, according to which, "the decision-making body should include all interests that are actually affected by the actual decision."[56] The principle seems intuitively correct—I should have a say in decisions that affect me, but not in decisions that do not affect me. But some problems with this principle immediately arise. We cannot know whether someone will be affected by a decision unless we know the outcome of the decision. Thus, it seems that we cannot know who should be allowed to vote on a decision until after the decision has been made.[57] Equally troubling are some of the consequences this principle seems to have. For instance, people living in developing countries are very much affected by how much money Norwegians send in foreign aid. Does that mean that they should get a vote in

Norwegian elections? As Robert Dahl points out, the "all affected interests" principle seem to unlock a Pandora's box of problems.[58]

Despite its problems, the "all affected interests" principle captures the intuition that those most affected by a decision should have the most say in it. Presumably, secession matters more to those who wish for their own state, than to those in the remaining state. But the preferences of groups in the larger state cannot be ignored. One should, therefore, give special weight to the preferences of the would-be secessionists, but also take into account the preferences of the larger state. A strong opposition to the secession cannot be ignored.

Conditions of a Primary Right to Secede

No one who supports a primary right to secession believes this is an unbridled right. It is quite possible to acknowledge the right to secession, but be antisecessionist in the sense that one wishes that the would-be secessionists would not exercise their right.[59] Scholars often point to the many negative effects that acknowledging a general right to secession will have. Since there are so many potential nations, the world would descend into chaos if each of them exercised their right. As Ronald S. Beiner points out, "Think of what a 'right' of national self-determination, rigorously applied, would do to states like India, China, and Russia (to say nothing of the various African states, with their colossal ethnic-tribal heterogeneity and arbitrary state boundaries)!"[60] If we value the stability that comes from respecting established borders, as I argue in the next chapter that we should, then we should also be very careful about accepting a principle that would lead to countless border revisions. Another problem is that acknowledging a general right to self-determination may have perverse incentives. It can be taken advantage of by manipulative political leaders who want power for their own sake. And in few cases will the seceding group live alone on the territory on which they wish to build their state. A new state creates new minorities, whose lives might be negatively affected by the secession. This is what Lee Buchheit calls the "trapped" minorities problem.[61] Because of these problems, most scholars see secession as a last resort, as a solution we should embrace only if other ways of providing the would-be secessionists with a larger degree of self-determination have failed. As Philpott concludes, "I doubt that there are many cases to which my own theory would give a green light, but to which Buchanan's would grant a red or yellow light."[62]

It is also common to demand that the secessionist group meet certain criteria before its claim to statehood is acknowledged. It is reasonable to ask that in order for a people to have the right to statehood, they must be able to establish a viable and minimally just state. That means, among other things, that both the new state and what remains of the old state must have the ability to perform political functions. Unless a community is able to function as an independent political entity, it cannot have the right to self-determination. A group must also have the organizational knowledge to govern itself, tax its citizens, and maintain order.[63] It must be able to meet the most fundamental economic needs of its members.[64] The potential secessionist state must also meet certain minimum requirements of justice. One might discuss how strict this demand should be. According to Philpott, for instance, a secessionist group has to be "at least as liberal and democratic as the state from which they are separating," and able to protect minority rights.[65] But this seems overly restrictive. I think it is more reasonable to insist that the would-be secessionist demonstrate a willingness and capacity to develop just political institutions, and a clear commitment to the protection of fundamental human rights, including minority rights.

A Baseline Position

What are the minimal requirements of justice with respect to secession? Clearly, we should accept the conclusions of the remedial right theory: If a group is subjected to sustained and serious human rights violations, it should have a right to secede. Secession should also be granted in cases where the state never acquired the right to govern the territory in the first place. However, my argument also implies that democratically expressed preferences on boundaries are significant from a moral point of view. It cannot be the case that borders, as a matter of principle, should never be on the democratic agenda. And because people's preferences are important, the outcome of a referendum on independence is also morally significant. The opinion of the larger state has to be taken into account, although it seems less important than the preference of the secessionist group. If a group has a strong desire for sovereign statehood and seems committed to the protection of minority rights, secession might be the right outcome of the conflict. That is to say, the burden of proof is no longer only on the secessionist—the objecting state has to show why the secession is wrong.

Part II: War-Related Considerations

It is common to assume that the just war tradition can help us make judgments about postwar justice. In particular, it is common to assume that a judgment about when a war should be initiated can help us clarify how it should end. An aggressive war for territory, one might argue, has ended justly when the territory has been restored to its prewar owner. Brian Orend holds that there is such a close connection between *ad bellum* and *post bellum* justice. A failure to satisfy the *ad bellum* criteria, he claims, "results in automatic failure to meet *jus in bello* and *jus post bellum*."[66] An aggressive belligerent looses its rights in the postwar order, according to Orend.[67]

If we take this general assumption and postulate that there is a close connection between the morality of the war and the morality of the war's outcome, the following claim seems plausible: only if a secessionist group has fought a just war should its wish for independent statehood be granted. I call this the strict correspondence argument. It implies that in order for secession to be the right outcome to a war, the secessionist group has to fight a war that meets the requirements of both *jus ad bellum* and *jus in bello*.[68]

What does it take for a war to be just? A just war must be fought with a just cause, by the right authority, and with the right intention. A just war is also one in which there is reasonable hope that the cause can be achieved. Just wars must be fought as a last resort, and do more good than harm (that is, be proportionate). For warfare to be just, it must discriminate between combatants and noncombatants, and be proportionate. Scholars writing within the just war framework agree that these criteria are important, but can disagree about their relative importance. They also disagree about how more specifically to understand some of these criteria. For instance, there are important differences in how scholars define the criterion of just cause.

The strict correspondence argument does not in itself entail a substantive judgment of what a just war is. It says that the war has to be just in order for the resulting peace to be just, but not what more specifically a just war is. In that sense, a requirement that a war is just is a moving target—it does not provide a solid benchmark against which to judge war outcomes. Much will depend on how the *jus ad bellum* criteria are understood, in particular the just cause criterion. That said, regardless of how we define a just war, the strict correspondence argument strongly overstates the extent to which the war's justice is related to our judgment of its outcome. For reasons I will explain below, it simply makes too much of the connection between the justice of the war and the justice of the peace terms. But, there are some connections. The way the war began and the way it was fought can in various ways strengthen a secessionist group's claim. This would happen, for instance, if the state tried to prevent the secession from happening by attacking the secessionist group. A war might weaken a secessionist group's claim to independence too. That would happen, for instance, if a secessionist group set aside common rules of war like non-combatant immunity. By disregarding commonly accepted rules of warfare, the group has shown that it is not fit to become a separate state.

The Tamil fight for independence from Sri Lanka illustrates some of the ways in which the strength of a secessionist claim is affected by the way the war started and the way it was fought. It also shows some of the problems connected to the requirement that the war must be just in order for us to accept the secessionist claim. And this case illustrates how a national group, which in many ways had a strong claim to its own state, weakened its claim during the course of the war, due to the way the war was fought on their side. Analyzing the way the war was fought says something about the kind of state a secessionist group is likely to establish and it helps us assess whether the group will be able to set up a state that respects basic human rights, including the rights of minorities.

The Tamil Claim to Independence

The war in Sri Lanka has been the longest-lasting conflict in South Asia, and resulted in at least 100,000 deaths and a million displaced people.[69] Sri Lanka consists of two main national groups. The majority, which comprised 74 percent of Sri Lanka's population in 1981, is Sinhalese, while the largest minority, the Sri Lankan Tamils, comprised about 13 percent of the population.[70] There are religious differences between the two groups: the Sinhalese are primarily Buddhist (the remaining 10 percent are Christian), while the Tamils are Hindu (about 80 percent) or Christian. There are language differences between the two groups too; the Sinhalese language belongs to the Indo-European family, while Tamil is a Dravidian language.[71] The Tamils dominate the northern and eastern part of Sri Lanka. But it is too simple to explain the division between these two groups as merely cultural, because, as Stanley Tambiah points out, these groups also share cultural characteristics like caste, rituals, and customs. Therefore, they were polarized less by unchanging, long-lasting ethnic differences, and more by postcolonial political processes that increased the salience of ethnicity."[72]

When Britain left after having ruled Sri Lanka from 1796 to 1948, they established a centralized, majoritarian political system.[73] In this type of democracy, also referred to as the Westminster model, the political party that receives the majority of votes forms the central government, while the losers are expected to form a loyal opposition.[74] The electoral system in most majoritarian democracies—which will give the parliamentary seat to the party with a majority of the vote in a particular district—have a tendency transform even a relatively small victory on the ballot box into a large victory in the parliament. While this can be a good model for relatively homogenous countries like Britain, it proved ill-fitting for a heterogeneous country like Sri Lanka. A culture of ethnic outbidding arose. The two main Sinhalese political parties attempted to win votes by discriminating against the Tamils.[75] The Sri Lanka Freedom Party (SLFP), for instance, won a landslide victory in 1956 with the slogan "Sinhalese Only!"—and began a process of marginalizing not only the Tamil language but also Tamils on the job market.[76] The result was what Sumantra Bose has called an "ethnic democracy," that is, the combination of "democratic institutions and procedures with the systematic, encompassing dominance of one ethnonational community."[77] To make matters worse, the main Sinhalese parties would compete for votes by appealing to anti-Tamil sentiments. In the years that followed, the Tamils were increasingly sidelined. The

Sinhalese-dominated parliament adopted a number of laws relating to employment, land, language, and education that worked to the strong disadvantage of the Tamils. Two constitutional amendments in the 1970s institutionalized the ethnic dominance by the Sinhalese.[78]

In the mid-1970s, Tamil political parties, who had until then called for more influence and autonomy, started advocating a separate state. In 1976, the first National Convention of the Tamil United Liberation Front, which consisted of all Tamil political parties, adopted the Vaddukoddai resolution, which declared,

> The Tamils [have become] a slave nation ruled by the new colonial master, the Sinhalese, who are using the power they have wrongly usurped to deprive the Tamil Nation of its territory, language, citizenship, economic life, opportunities of employment and education, thereby destroying all the attributes of nationhood of the Tamil people.... This convention resolves that restoration and reconstitution of the Free, Sovereign, Secular, Socialist State of Tamil Eelam, based on the right of self-determination inherent to every nation, has become inevitable in order to safeguard the very existence of the Tamil Nation in this country.[79]

The LTTE was formed in the same year, 1976. They too argued that the only way the Tamils could live with dignity was if they created their own state.[80]

When the war in Sri Lanka started, in 1983, the Tamils had a fairly strong claim to a separate state. They might not have been able to claim a remedial right to secession, but they clearly had a justified grievance against the Sinhalese-dominated state. There was also broad consensus among the Tamil political parties that secession was desirable, and thus the Tamil claim was backed up by a democratically expressed preference.

SECESSION AND THE RESORT TO WAR

Must a secessionist group always be fighting a just war in order for us to want the war to end in secession? In this section, I explore some of the reasons why I believe the answer to this question is "no" and why there cannot be a strict correlation between *ad bellum* and *post bellum* justice.

Just Cause

One of the core requirements for a just war is that it is fought with a just cause. The criterion of a just cause points our attention to the occasion for the war, to "those instances when we are permitted or required to use lethal force."[81] Under what circumstances, then, does secession provide a just cause for going to war? Classical and contemporary scholars have in different ways given substance to the criteria of just cause. I will here discuss two broad conceptions. The first, and most restrictive, view sees a just cause as a defensive war against aggression, which in turn is identified as the first use of force. In this view, a secessionist group would only have a just cause if they were attacked first. A second, more permissive view, sees just cause as a response to an injury. In my view, the latter is a better conception.

It is common to argue that self-defense provides the most clear-cut case of just cause. Self-defense is usually understood as the defense against an aggressor. Just as an individual has the right to defend himself against the aggression of a murderous intruder, so does a state have the right to defend itself against the aggression of another state.[82] Thus, Michael Walzer claims, "nothing but aggression can justify war."[83] And Jeff McMahan writes that "a war of defense against aggression is currently thought to be the paradigm of a just war, or indeed the *only* kind of just war."[84] Moreover, aggression is identified by some scholars as the first use of force. The first use of military force, as McMahan points out, is often thought "to be a necessary condition of aggression and is in general sufficient."[85] I should quickly point out, however, that both Walzer and McMahan hold that there are cases in which the first use of force might not be considered wrongful or unjustified. This can be the case when a state is faced with an imminent threat of attack and uses force as a preemptive measure or when force is used for the defense of others, as in the case of a humanitarian intervention.

There is another reason why equating the first use of force with aggression is not always helpful. Take again the case of Sri Lanka. After a steady decline in Sinhala-Tamil relations—in 1981, for instance, a library in Jaffna was set on fire by policemen and government supporters, destroying 100,000 rare Tamil manuscripts and leading the Tamils to feel that they were the victims of a cultural genocide—full-scale war broke out in 1983.[86] The watershed, it is often argued, was that the LTTE killed 13 Sinhalese soldiers in an ambush in the Northern Province in July. This sparked a round of anti-Tamil rioting: Tamil homes were looted, women were raped, and many were killed or left the country as refugees.[87] According to some estimates, between 2,000 and 3,000 Tamils were killed in what has been called the Black July massacre, and about 150,000 were made homeless.[88] But if the Sinhalese could blame the Tamils for the killing of 13 soldiers, the Tamils, as Tambiah points out, could blame the Sinhalese occupying army for "going on punitive expeditions killing innocent civilians and torturing several hundreds without cause."[89] Indeed, it would be possible to list a number of recriminations, accusations, and counter-accusations going back months and years. The identification of a clear aggressor is simply not always possible.

Perhaps we need to put the idea of first use of violence aside, and focus instead on who has a just cause otherwise conceived. That is Elizabeth Anscombe's argument:

> The present-day conception of "aggression," like so many strongly influential conceptions, is a bad one. Why *must* it be wrong to strike the first blow in a struggle? The only question is, who is in the right, if anyone is?[90]

Here self-defense can be coupled with a broader notion of unjust injury. In this interpretation, a defensive war is a war that defends rights that are either gravely threatened or have been violated. A just war is in that sense a response to an injury.[91] This conception corresponds to the way classic just war theorists saw just cause as well.

If a just war is a response to an injury, we have to ask what qualifies as an injury or injustice. Let me discuss three possibilities from my above discussion of secessionist theories: secession as a response to large-scale and persistent violations of human rights, secession in response to unjust annexation of territory, and secession as a primary right of self-determination. It seems reasonably uncontroversial to argue that a secessionist group should be allowed to go to war in response to large-scale and persistent violations of human rights. If the group, for instance, is the victim of attempted genocide, it has the right to defend itself. Indeed, in such cases other states should arguably step in and help it.

Going to war to undo an unjust annexation is more disputable. Buchanan, as shown above, holds that unjust annexations means that the state as a whole lacks legitimacy, but that does not mean that fighting a war to rectify the injustice is right. McMahan goes some way in accepting war to rectify this type of previous wrong. He asks us to consider the case in which a state is wrongfully attacked and the aggressive state occupies its territory or imposes a puppet government:

> In such cases it would be absurd to suppose that the victims lose their rights when they lose their war of defense. If it later becomes possible for them (or third parties acting on their behalf) to reassert through armed rebellion the rights that were violated by the earlier aggression, and thereby to recover the territory or political independence of which they were unjustly deprived, they will not wrong the aggressor if they do so. Successful aggressors remain liable to attack as long as they retain the spoils of their wrongful aggression.[92]

Since the state as a whole is illegitimate, the previously wronged group has the right to take back what they were wrongly deprived of. This would be the case even if it meant taking up arms first. McMahan qualifies this argument by adding a moral a statute of limitations. An occupying people may gain rights to the territory if much time has passed and they therefore cannot be blamed for the initial aggression.[93] I will have more to say about how territorial rights can be acquired and lost in the next chapter. The point here is that although the initial annexation was wrong, the consequences of this wrong might diminish over time. If the annexation has lasted several decades, for instance, it is more difficult to justify a military action to undo it. It is also important to consider how the annexed population has been treated. It is much easier to justify going to war to undo an annexation if the population has been continuously mistreated and systematically discriminated against, than if the annexing state has governed in a reasonably just way.

That said, if a previously annexed people go to war to reclaim their territory, the larger, and illegitimate, state does not necessarily have the right to defend itself either. This might be a situation, that is, where neither side has a just cause. As Walzer has noted, there are "wars that are just on neither side, because the idea of justice doesn't pertain to them or because the antagonists are both aggressors, fighting for territory or power where they have no right."[94] Secessionist conflicts sometimes fall into this category. This is because the state that the government is trying to defend is not a state that the secessionists want to be a part of. Why should the state claim a right to self-defense if it cannot be considered a legitimate agent of the communities within it? The group desiring statehood might not have the right to go to war to achieve secession, but the government trying to prevent it might not be justified in fighting the secessionists either.

Does a democratic desire to secede justify an armed struggle? In my view, it does not. In the just war tradition, the bar for justified resort to war is rightly set high. Given the destructiveness of war, a just cause for war should only be accepted for very severe injuries. This means that unless a secessionist group can show that they are, or are threatened to be, the victims of serious injuries or wrongs, they cannot claim to have a just cause for going to war.[95] So while I would argue that the Slovenian democratically expressed desire for statehood was not morally insignificant, it did not provide a just cause for war. It was only after the federal government threatened Slovenia with the use of force that Slovenia could claim going to war was a measure of justified preemptive self-defense. On the other hand, if we accord some moral weight to Slovenia's desire for independence, as I believe we should, we must question whether the federal government had the right to try to stop Slovenia with the use of force. If the "self" that the Yugoslav government was trying to defend was not one that the Slovenians wanted to be part of, it seems that it could not claim resorting to force based on a right of self-defense.

My argument is that in conflicts over secession, the claim to self-defense might be one that neither the secessionist group nor the larger state very comfortably can appeal to. These types of wars, as the Sri Lankan case shows, often come about through a process of escalation. It can be difficult to identify a clear aggressor or a clear victim. Moreover, given the muddled justice of the beginning of many such wars, we cannot ask that they only end in secession if the secessionist group had a clear initial just cause. When we judge the ends of these wars, we should to pay more attention to the strength of the secessionist claim than who can rightly be called the aggressor or the defender.

Other *Jus Ad Bellum* Requirements

In addition to the just cause criteria, a just war must also be fought by the right authority, and with a just intention. There must be a reasonable hope that the war succeeds in its cause, and the war must be proportionate, and fought as a last resort. Let me here point to some of the connections between these criteria and *jus post bellum* considerations.

Should we deem secession wrong if the secessionist war is fought without right authority? Right authority is a two-fold question concerning both who has the right to go to war and how that right can be justified. In a very narrow and increasingly outdated notion, right authority is defined in legal terms, as the right states had to determine their own affairs. For other states, this legal notion of sovereignty implies a duty of nonintervention. But neither current state practice nor contemporary moral conceptions of right authority supports this view. There is increasing consensus that there is a responsibility to protect people from mass atrocities like genocide and war crimes.[96] As James Turner Johnson points out, the legal notion of sovereignty "gives cover to individuals and parties who use the powers of rule to menace and oppress their own people and others while seeing to no higher end than their own aggrandizement. Something is very deeply flawed in a conception that casts the mantle of sovereign protection over demonstrably evil rulers as diverse as Mobutu, Milosevic, Saddam Hussein, and Kim Jong Il."[97]

In the moral notion, which is reflected in earlier just war thinking, the rights of sovereignty are linked to the obligations of sovereignty. Here "a person (or people) in sovereign authority is responsible for the good of his, her, or their political community, for the 'common weal.'"[98] If a sovereign did not fulfill his obligations, he could no longer claim the rights of sovereignty. In other words, much like the contemporary theories of secession, this idea of sovereignty assumes that right authority rests with the political community, and that rulers and governments are agents of that community.[99] A state cannot be said to have right authority if it is not acting on behalf of the political community. In some cases, it will be easy to make the judgment that a state has lost its authority. This would be the case if the state is tyrannical or if it is waging a war against its own people.[100] Thus, victims of genocide have the authority to take up arms to protect themselves, and outside states have the right to violate the norm of nonintervention in order to help them. But there are a number of cases where the situation is less clear-cut. Does a state lose its authority if it merely discriminates against a substate group? At what point has a government stopped fulfilling its obligations toward its citizens?

There is another complicating issue here.[101] In the moral notion of sovereignty, right authority rests with the agent of a community. Private individuals, as the early just war thinkers pointed out, do not have the authority to start a war. Thus, we have to assess the legitimacy of the agent that claims to represent the secessionist community. An insurgency or rebel group might not have the interests of its people at heart, nor does it necessarily represent the population for which it claims to speak. In fact, Bertrand Spector claims, for instance, that terrorist groups cannot be "legitimate representatives of a physical territory or population." Such groups "lack formal accountability to any constituency and thereby may not abide by international law, norms or principles."[102]

A secessionist struggle is often led by an insurgency that has not been formally elected, and we therefore have to question whether they are the "true" agents of the people they claim to fight for. But even in cases in which a community lacks a legitimate agent, the secessionist claim will still stand. The claim to statehood rests with the community, and not with the agent of that community. Or, to put it slightly differently, right authority rests with the agent of the community, but the right to independence rests with the community itself. While a community will have some influence over who represents them, it seems implausible to invalidate the secessionist claim because the insurgency group is not a legitimate representative. A war fought by an illegitimate insurgency group would fail the just authority criteria, but not necessarily the just cause criteria.

What relevance does the requirement of a right intention have for postwar justice? This criterion has both a negative and a positive part. It asks that certain motivations be absent among those who initiate the war. The war should not be fought for the sake of personal aggrandizement or because the rulers see violence as an end in itself. By ruling out ulterior motives and hidden agendas, the demand of a right intention is linked to the criteria of a just cause.[103] We should only accept as just a war fought for a morally acceptable aim. Right intention also carries with it a positive demand—a war must be fought for the sake of peace. As John Rawls notes, the "way a war is fought and the deeds done in ending it live on in the historical memory of societies and may or may not set the stage for future war."[104] It must be fought in such a manner as to make a durable and just peace possible. According to Johnson, this means that belligerents must explicitly work for peace. In his view, "for any use of force to be justified, it should not only respond to the disordering or absence of peace but should also include concrete plans for creating a peaceful society in the aftermath of conflict."[105]

In what way is the question of right intention relevant to the way the war ends? This criterion has some significance because it can help us gauge how interested the belligerents are in creating a stable postwar order for their own and for their adversary's community. The just war tradition accepts that a war is sometimes necessary in order to achieve an important goal. But if belligerents fight in a way that undermines the goal of peace, we can no longer trust that they are fighting for the good of their own community. This would indicate that the aim of the war is not secession, but something else, like personal power. On the other hand, as long as the claim to statehood rests with the community, the existence of ulterior motives among the leadership cannot invalidate a secessionist claim altogether.

Secession and the Way the War Was Fought

The just war tradition asks warfare to be conducted in accordance with two general norms. The first is *discrimination*. This principle distinguishes those who are legitimate targets in war from those who are not. It asks that weapons and warfare tactics protect noncombatants. There is some disagreement about who should be considered noncombatants, but civilians and wounded soldiers are uncontroversial examples. If we use a contemporary conception of rights, one might explain the duty not to harm noncombatants by the right that every person has to not be harmed or exposed to excessive risk of harm. This right can only be set aside if that person engages in an activity that removes its moral force. Engaging in combat operations would be one example of such an activity.[106] The other *in bello* principle is *proportionality*. This norm aims to limit the conduct of warfare by prescribing that the military advantage of an act of war outweighs its negative consequences. Put this way, it is a straightforward consequentialist norm, proscribing that the good a military action produces must exceed the harm it inflicts. Unnecessary or ineffective military actions are wrong.

What consequences should the way the war is fought have on the way it should end? One scenario clearly strengthens the secessionist group's claim to independence: if a government tries to stop it by engaging in unjust warfare, for instance, by initiating a genocidal campaign, the secessionist claim grows stronger. In such a case, the secessionist group will develop a remedial right to statehood. But how should we judge a case where the secessionist group fights unjustly? Can violations of *jus in bello* weaken a secessionist claim? My answer is a conditional yes. The reason is this: the way the war is fought will say something about the kind of state that the secessionist group will establish. If an insurgency uses unjust strategies like ethnic cleansing, repeatedly and over time, it shows lack of respect for fundamental humanitarian values. Immoral warfare is an indicator of the extent to which the rights of dissenters and new minorities will be respected in the new state. Granted, it is not the secessionist community that is carrying out the unjust warfare, but the insurgency group. Thus, *in bello* violations cannot invalidate a community's claim to statehood altogether. But it is a warning sign for future stability and justice if the community is unable to produce a better leadership.

Take again the case of Sri Lanka. I have argued that the Tamils had a relatively strong claim to statehood at the start of the war. However, the way the war was fought on their side served to cast doubts about what kind of state they would actually establish. One problem was that the LTTE did not seem to tolerate dissidents or other minorities. The organization murdered moderate Tamil citizens, and according to one account, killed more Tamils between 1983 and 2006 than Sri Lanka's military forces did.[107] The LTTE also contained or eliminated other rival Tamil secessionist groups and mistreated minorities living in the northern and eastern parts of the island.[108] In October 1990, for instance, about 75,000 Muslims were expelled on short notice from the Jaffna peninsula.[109] A few years later, Muslim leaders warned that unless the LTTE stopped its policy of ethnic cleansing, they would initiate a holy war.[110] The LTTE also sought to ethnically cleanse its areas of the Sinhalese population, by killing civilians or forcing them to leave their homes.[111] The LTTE's rule of the northern and eastern parts of Sri Lanka did not benefit Tamil civilians either. Jaffna, the Tamil capital on the northern tip of the island, became increasingly isolated, and trade with the rest of the country suffered. The property of its dissidents was frequently expropriated, and the civilian population suffered under taxes used to fund the war effort.[112] There were also reports that the LTTE forced children to serve in its armed forces.[113] Based on the way the LTTE ruled the northern and eastern provinces during the war, it seems unlikely that it would have established a Tamil state that would respect the rights of political dissidents and ethnic minorities.

CONCLUSION

The relationship between *jus ad bellum*, *jus in bello*, and *jus post bellum* is more complicated than the strict correspondence argument postulates. The beginnings of wars are often messy, and it is not always possible to identify a clear aggressor and a clear defender. In secessionist conflicts, neither adversary might be said to have an unquestionable just cause. While going to war to achieve independent statehood rarely will meet the requirements of just cause, the attempt to stop a secessionist movement is not necessarily just either. And even if spearheaded by an illegitimate insurgency group, the underlying grounds for independent statehood might still be valid.

One of the problems with the strict correspondence argument is that it depends too much on the past to determine the shape of the future. The past war, how it started and how it was fought, is not irrelevant to the postwar order, but its relevance has more to do with what it says about possible futures. While the unjust actions of an insurgency cannot invalidate a secessionist claim altogether, the way the war is fought will suggest something about the type of state the secessionists might create. It is important that the secessionist group can reassure us that it will be able to set up a legitimate state that respects basic human rights norms. A strong claim to statehood only exists if the community has shown that it is capable of governing itself in a reasonably good way.

Part III: Considerations Related to Stability

What unites almost every scholar who writes on the question of secession is the belief that stability is best served by strongly restricting the right to secede. This consensus is founded on the recognition of several facts. There is a great gap between the number of groups that might claim the right to self-determination and the number of viable states.[114] Woodrow Wilson, who so strongly is associated with the principle of national self-determination, admitted that, if pushed to its extreme, the principle would mean endless disruptions of existing governments.[115] Scholars also point to the fact that there are few historical examples of peaceful secessions but many examples of secession attempts that turn violent. Given the stakes involved, there is every reason to expect that a majority of secessionist movements will be met with military resistance. And, finally, scholars point out that secessions seem to worsen the conditions for ethnic minorities within the secessionist area. The problem, Donald Horowitz suggest, is that,

> By the time it is concluded that the majority in the undivided state is unalterably hostile to minority interests, thus in some formulations permitting the minority to secede, that group may have accumulated so many grudges that, in their turn, minorities in the secessionist region may be particularly vulnerable to the expression of violent hostility or the settlement of old scores. There are many examples: the fate of Serbs and Roma in Kosovo, of Biharis in Bangladesh, of Sikhs and Hindus in Pakistan at the time of partition, and of Muslims in India at the same time.[116]

These considerations, however, are most relevant if we are considering the establishment of a general right to secede. But my concern here is what the most stable outcome after a particular war is. What kind of outcome in any given case is most likely to promote stability? On this issue, there is no clear consensus.

The lack of consensus is in part due to divergent empirical studies and different views on how to interpret their results. It is also due to disagreement about how stable other, alternative, outcomes of secessionist conflicts are. There are two main alternatives to secession: full victory of one group, that is, either the secessionist or the government takes full control of the territory, or a democracy based on power-sharing. It is not an argument against secession that it is an unstable outcome, if all the alternative outcomes are even less stable. I will return to the question of how stable a power-sharing democracy can be in chapter 5. Here I will just discuss the main problems with secession from a stability point of view.

ARGUMENTS FOR AND AGAINST SECESSION

According to one line of argument, we can expect secession to be a much more stable solution to a secessionist conflict than any of the alternative outcomes. Chaim Kaufmann has famously made this point. It should be noted that his topic is internal wars between national or ethnic groups, and not secession as such, but much of his argument is relevant to secessionist conflicts as well. Kaufmann believes partition, that is, separating the warring parties into their own separate states, is the most stable solution to ethnic civil wars.[117] Other solutions, such as multiethnic democracy and power-sharing between national groups, he argues, are unlikely to prevent the resumption of the war.

There are two reasons why Kaufmann believes partition is the most stable solution. First, wars fought between national or ethnic groups increase the salience of national identities. The mobilization that takes place during the lead-up to the war and during the war itself increases the importance of ethnic identity and solidifies antagonisms.[118] Wars harden ethnic identities. The result is that individual loyalties become inflexible, and political appeals across ethnic boundaries become more or less impossible.[119] A solution that rests on ethnic cooperation, such as a power-sharing democracy, would therefore not work. The war, Kaufmann argues, simply "destroys the possibilities for ethnic cooperation."[120]

Second, partition is the solution that best handles what is often referred to as the security dilemma. This assumption draws on the neorealist theory of international relations. Neorealists explain conflict in international affairs by pointing to the absence of a sovereign power that can provide security. In this type of anarchy, a state has to provide for its own protection.[121] A similar security dilemma can exist if a state becomes deeply divided between antag-onistic national or ethnic communities. According to Kaufmann, as soon as the violence "reaches the point that ethnic communi-ties cannot rely on the state to protect them, each community must mobilize to take responsibility for its own security."[122] But the defensive steps that one group takes to protect itself can be interpreted as an offensive action by the other group. This prob-lem is exacerbated by the fact that the government is not a neutral middleman, but supports, or in fact, is, one of the parties to the conflict.

In order to promote stability, according to Kaufmann, an outcome must solve the security dilemma. Two possible options present themselves: military victory or partition. Victory is often not possible, but when it is, it can come at a very high cost.[123] Partition, on the other hand, reduces the incentives and oppor-tunities for future warfare because it physically separates hostile populations.[124] The security dilemma might also be alleviated if a third party intervenes, but this will only reduce conflict for as long as the intervention lasts.[125] The restoration of a multiethnic democracy, or any solution that requires power sharing among national elites will not work, because the parties feel that the best defense is to be offensive, and because they cannot cooperate on matters of security.[126]

In his second article on the subject, Kaufmann modifies his position somewhat, and argues that partition is the right solution only in some cases. Partition will not create stability and reduce conflict unless the hostile populations are actually separated into distinct territories. If the partition does not "unmix hostile popu-lations" it might actually exacerbate violence. For partition to pro-mote stability, it is also vital that there be defensible boundaries between the new and the old state. But in cases with large-scale violence and where there is an intense security dilemma, partition remains a good solution.[127]

Is Kaufmann's argument correct? Is partition, or secession, more likely to promote stability than the alternatives? Several scholars have tried to find an answer to this question by con-ducting quantitative empirical studies.[128] Some studies support Kaufmann's argument. Thomas Chapman and Philip Roeder, for instance, find that warfare resumes less often if the war ends in partition. They consider 72 nationalist civil wars between 1945

and 2002, and argue that "only 14% of the parties to de jure partition experienced a resumption of violence within 2 years, but this
frequency rose to 50% for the parties to a de facto separation, 63%
for the parties bound in a unitary state, and 67% for the parties
to an autonomy arrangement."[129] Others find little support for
Kaufmann's claims. An article by Nicholas Sambanis and Jonah
Schulhofer-Wohl suggest that quantitative studies run into various
methodological problems that undermine the reliability of their
conclusions. In addition to the difficulty of coding different cases,
it is also problematic that there few cases, and that many of them
are ambiguous.[130] Sambanis and Schulhofer-Wohl's main conclusion is that "there is no significant positive correlation between
partition and no war recurrence."[131]

In some cases, partition seems to increase the likelihood of
future violence. This can happen if there are lingering territorial
disputes, or if the regime in the new state is contested. War might
also return if new minorities are mistreated and start to rebel.[132]
That the creation of new minorities can incite violence is at the
heart of Donald Horowitz's argument. He points out that the
assumption that partition will create more ethnically homogenous
states is simply wrong. Rather, "the only thing secession and partition are unlikely to produce is ethnically homogeneous or harmo-
nious states."[133] While the war in Bosnia was raging, it was argued,
for instance, that one solution would be to separate Bosnia into
ethnic states. But partition along ethnic lines would actually have
exacerbated conflict in this case, Richard Holbrooke argued:

> Dividing the country along ethnic lines would create massive new
> refugee flows. Serbs, Croats, and Muslims who still lived as minor-
> ities in many parts of the country would be forced to flee their
> homes, and fighting would be certain to break out as the scramble
> for land and houses erupted again. Thus, contrary to the arguments
> of the partitionists, the chances of fighting would be increased, not
> decreased, by partition and the relocation that would follow.[134]

Partition can also destabilize surrounding states. That has been
one of the arguments against statehood for Kurds in Iraq. Given
the Kurdish populations in neighboring Turkey, Iran, and Syria,
the acceptance of a secessionist demand could spread and cause
regional unrest.[135] One simply cannot assume that partition solves
the problem of ethnic or nationalist violence.

That said, there do seem to be situations where partition is a good outcome from the point of view of stability. Sambanis and Schulhofer-Wohl suggest that partition might work in cases where it leaves none of the warring parties behind in the other's state (that is, where the partition creates homogenous states), where the partition does not create a distributional conflict, and where the partition does not have any destabilizing regional effects.[136]

It is difficult to draw general conclusions about the empirical relationship between secession and stability. This means that we can only judge the likelihood that a case of secession will promote stability by considering each case on its own merit. Chances are, stability will not ensue if the territory of the secessionist state is contested, if the new state will house new minorities, or if groups of the same nationality as the secessionist live in neighboring states. But if the secession can separate populations behind defensible borders and create relatively homogenous states, it might promote stability.

CONCLUSION

The war in Sri Lanka ended with the full victory of the government forces. The victory came at a high cost. In May 2009, most of the LTTE's leaders were killed in battle, and soldiers and sympathizers who did not surrender were mopped up by the Sri Lankan military.[137] The government also used "paramilitary squads to kidnap, torture, extort, and murder thousands of Tamils thought to be sympathetic to the LTTE; attacked and assassinated journalists reporting negatively on the war or war-related corruption; carried out bombing operations in Tamil areas without adequately differentiating between LTTE cadre and innocent civilians, and blackguarded those critical of human rights violations as 'anti-Sri Lankan' and 'traitors.'"[138] The Sri Lankan government's brutal actions ironically served to strengthen the Tamil claim to statehood. Tamils could now reasonably argue that the Sri Lankan state did not provide for their safety. Yet, if the government's actions strengthened their claim, the LTTE actions during the war weakened it. Its policies and actions repressed both Tamil dissenters and Sinhalese and Muslim groups. There were good reasons to worry that a Tamil state, at least if led by the LTTE, would have been oppressive. Since a Tamil state would not have been heterogeneous, we cannot object to the outcome based on stability considerations either. Yet, we can hardly call this outcome just, in particular because the Sinhalese government showed little interest in respecting justified Tamil demands for self-determination. And only time will show whether the outcome will, in fact, prove stable.

It is not possible to come up with a general rule that determines the occasions in which secession is the best outcome to a war. We cannot just apply the criteria of the just war tradition to a secessionist conflict or assume that secession is the right outcome only if the secessionists have fought a just war. It is simply not the case that a secessionist group's claim to statehood is invalidated by violating *ad bellum* or *in bello* requirements. Instead we have to make an all-things-considered judgment, which includes a consideration of the strength of the secessionist claim at the end of the war, the likelihood that the secessionist state will respect fundamental human rights norms, as well as considerations of domestic and regional stability.

There is no simple correlation between justified beginnings of secessionist wars and just ends to them. In fact, my argument has suggested that the category of just for wars over secession might very well be smaller than the category of wars that should end with secession. I do not see a way out of that inconsistency. If we take seriously the claim that wars should end in a better state of peace, one that is more just and more stable than the *status quo ante bellum*, this contradiction seems inevitable.

4

OUTCOMES OF
TERRITORIAL WARS

Conflicts over territory are common, war prone, and difficult to solve.[1] According to one statistic, more than half of the wars that took place between 1816 and 1997 were territorial.[2] According to another study, there were 129 cases of states arguing over a particular piece of territory between 1950 and 1990.[3] And 11 of the 30 wars that were being fought in 2010 were defined as territorial.[4]

The problem is not only that territorial conflicts are common, but also that they seem particularly war-prone—more than other issues, they lead to war. Summing up the results from a number of different studies on territory and conflict, John Vasquez says that adversaries are especially inclined to try to solve territorial issues with the use of military force.[5] This territorial explanation of war "maintains that there is something about territory that makes states more willing to go to war."[6] Territorial issues also seem especially intractable. That is, once a territorial issue has led to a militarized dispute, it tends to recur. Adversaries fighting a territorial war are less likely to start peace negotiations, and if such negotiations do start, they often fail.[7] What is more, once territorial disputes occur, they quickly escalate and tend to be more severe and more lethal than nonterritorial disputes.[8]

Scholars have offered several possible explanations for why territorial conflicts are so common and intractable. Political leaders, Barbara Walter reasons, might worry that if they give up on one territorial issue, there will be a slippery slope leading to losses in other territorial conflicts. Governments do not necessarily fight territorial wars because the territory has strategic or material value, but rather because they are concerned that if they make one territorial concession, they will have to make others as well. Governments want to be perceived as unrelenting.[9] Another explanation focuses on the moral and symbolic importance of territory. A given piece of territory is not just land. It is infused with cultural and historical significance, and can be thought of as the heart and soul of the national group. When symbolic and moral stakes are involved, political leaders tend to think in zero-sum terms: one adversary's loss is the other's gain.[10]

Given the frequency and intractability of territorial disputes, it is not surprising that people find it difficult to see a simple solution to them. It is especially difficult perhaps, to see how we should solve territorial conflicts where two national groups lay claim to the same piece of territory. David Miller has expressed his frustration with these types of conflicts this way:

> People of a liberal disposition . . . will throw up their hands in despair when asked to resolve the practical problems that arise when . . . two nationalities make claim to the same territory, as for instance in the case of the Jews and the Palestinians in Israel.[11]

While it might be difficult to identify the ideal solution in many cases of territorial conflicts, some outcomes will clearly be better, that is, more stable and more just than others. In order to determine what these are, several kinds of considerations have to be taken into account. Most fundamentally, we have to ask what justifies territorial rights. What explains a state's right to territorial sovereignty over a particular piece of land? I argue that a group of people develops a valid territorial claim when they live on a particular piece of land over a period of time, and establish both material and cultural bonds to it. This is the claim of settlement. If this group of people is governed by a minimally just state, that state has a prima facie right to territorial sovereignty. This implies that there are good reasons to assume that current borders are morally acceptable and that there consequently is a moral presumption against territorial change. There might, however, be other claims that can outweigh the settlement claim.

Are there situations in which a state has the right to take back territory that it has lost in a previous conflict? In the second part, I argue that the presumption against territorial change follows not only from a consideration of valid territorial claims but also from the norm of territorial integrity. But there will be situations in which a reshuffling of borders is preferable to a return the *status quo ante bellum*. That will be the case if the territorial change provides a better distribution of territorial rights and, at the same time, upholds the principle of territorial integrity.

In the third part, I discuss whether there is a right to take territory as a measure of preemptive self-defense. This argument suggests that a state should be allowed to instigate territorial change in order to make its boundaries more defensible. I discuss some theoretical and empirical problems with this argument, and argue that the relationship between territory and security is much less obvious than it perhaps once was.

The State, the People, and the Land

One might think of land rights as everything from the rights an individual has to her own property, via the rights a group has to enjoy or inhabit a land, and the rights a group has to use and extract resources from the land, to the right a state has to territorial sovereignty.[12] In some accounts these rights are intimately related. According to Hillel Steiner, for instance, a state's territorial right derives from the property rights of its inhabitants.[13] A more plausible view is that while the same mechanisms are involved in establishing different types of land rights, a state's right to territorial sovereignty is a fundamentally different type of right than other types of land rights.

I follow David Miller in distinguishing among three elements of the right to territorial sovereignty.[14] First, there is the right of jurisdiction, that is, the right to make, adjudicate, and enforce a system of laws within a particular piece of territory. Individuals who live or are present on the territory are subject to that system of law. Second, a territorial right also entails the right to use, control, and benefit from the resources on the territory, such as oil and minerals. And, third, a territorial right entails the right to control border crossings, that is, "the movement of goods and people across the borders of the territory."[15] A state's territorial right is therefore a more encompassing right than a property right, because it includes, among other things, the right to make laws regarding private property as well as to tax it. That means that a state may exercise territorial jurisdiction on one part of the earth, while at the same time own land in another state's jurisdiction.[16]

Any theory of territorial rights has to overcome two important challenges: First, it has to explain with whom the territorial right rests. While it is only a state that can exercise territorial rights, most scholars argue that the right does not rest with the state, but with the people whom the state represents. According to the liberal nationalist theory of territory, represented here by scholars like Miller and Tamar Meisels, the people should be understood as a cultural nation—a group who share particular cultural characteristics that set them apart from other groups.[17] When a state has a territorial right, according to this view, it is because it is a legitimate representative of the nation in question.[18]

Anna Stilz takes a different point of view. She agrees that territorial rights rest with states since states represent the people they govern, but the people, according to Stilz, should not be defined as a cultural nation. Rather, they are defined by the state itself. It is by being "subject to state institutions and by participating together in shaping these institutions" that the people are made into one collective body.[19] Whether or not this collective is united by a common culture is irrelevant. According to Stilz's theory, which she calls the legitimate state theory, "invoking nations is neither necessary nor sufficient to explain territorial rights."[20]

I agree with Stilz that a group does not have to be a *national* group in order to qualify as a people. I think it makes sense, for instance, to say that the people who live in the United States have a collective right to the territory defined by US borders, although there is more than one cultural nation within those borders. However, it is not only by being part of a state that a group is made into a people with territorial rights. Take, for instance, the conflict between Israel and the Palestinians. The Palestinians do not yet have their own state—at least not in the sense of having the status of member-state in the United Nations—but I think most would agree that they have a claim to the land they have lived on for centuries. Or, take secessionist conflicts. When states break apart, groups defined by their shared nationality will lay claim to the territory they inhabit. These groups can no longer be defined by the state, yet we should still acknowledge that they can have a valid territorial claim. Since nonstate groups are involved in many of the territorial conflicts that dominate the world, it seems more appropriate to take such groups as the point of departure for our analysis.

The second challenge for theories of territorial rights is to explain why it is that a state has the right to exercise its territorial sovereignty over a particular piece of land.[21] It is not enough to explain why a group of people has a general right to live somewhere. One has to explain why the group has a right to live on land A, rather than on land B, C, or D. One might argue, for instance, that national groups have the right to territorial sovereignty based on a more general right to self-determination.[22] But that does not explain why the national group has a right to be located in a particular area. A theory of territorial rights has to explain why the relationship between the people and the land they lay claim to is morally significant.

It follows from the last chapter that there are certain requirements attached both to the state and to the people claiming statehood. In order for a state to have the right to territorial sovereignty, it is not enough that its people have a valid territorial claim. A state also has to be a legitimate representative of the people in question. As I argued in the last chapter, a substate group has the right to secede if its government is systematically and persistently violating its rights, or waging a war against it. That also means that the government can no longer claim territorial sovereignty over the territory on which that substate group lives. Moreover, in order for us to acknowledge its demand for territorial sovereignty over a particular area, a group must, as a minimum, demonstrate a capacity to establish a viable state that protects fundamental human rights.

There will be cases in which we might not want to accord a group full sovereign rights, perhaps because we doubt that the group will be able to set up a minimally just state. There are also cases in which two different groups want to exercise sovereignty over the same piece of territory, which might be practically impossible. In these cases, we may accord a group the right to reside in a territory, but not the full right to territorial sovereignty. The right to reside is a lesser right than the right to territorial sovereignty, but it is a type of territorial right. It is the right to live and continue to live in a particular place. It can also, as Cara Nine points out, include the right to vote and take part in other political processes, but it does not include the right to set up one's own sovereign government.[23] Thus, the right to reside is a second-best solution. Yet, it is not a trivial right. If we accord a group a right to reside on a particular piece of territory, we would also, for instance, have to support the right refugees have to return to their homes.

Part I: Moral Claims to Territory

I make in this section a distinction among three types of territorial claims. The first category refers to the cultural and historical bonds that exist between a people and the land. The second draws directly on John Locke's theory of territorial acquisitions. The last, which I refer to as the settlement argument, and which I find most convincing, draws more loosely on Lockean principles and emphasizes both the material and the cultural relationship between a nation and a piece of territory.

CULTURAL CLAIMS TO TERRITORY

Territory is often deemed important to a group because of the role it plays in the nation's history and culture.[24] Chaim Gans invokes an analogy to the ties that usually exist between individuals and their parents. Just as an individual has an interest in protecting the bond between herself and her parents, so does a nation have an interest in protecting the bond between itself and the land.[25] The territory is considered the nation's "homeland" because important events have taken place on it, and because it is central to the group's history and traditions.[26] This type of argument can be made both by a population that currently lives on the land and a population that has been forcefully dispossessed.

A particular piece of territory is often thought to be of "primary importance in forming the historical identity of the group."[27] The Serbs, for instance, have long maintained that Kosovo is their ancestral home. In medieval times they ruled an empire on this land and fought many important battles there. One in particular has taken on a significant meaning: On June 28, 1389, the Serbs fought and lost to the Ottomans on Kosovo Polje, "the field of blackbirds." The battle has come to signify Serb heroism and pride, and it has been a source of a number of epic stories and nationalistic paintings.[28] It was in part by tapping into this national story in a speech to Kosovo Serbs at Kosovo Polje in April 1987 that Slobodan Milosevic established himself as the leader of the Serb nationalist movement.[29]

Cultural attachments to territory do not always derive from specific events. More often the bond is created by the longstanding history between the group and the territory, and by what the land has come to mean for the people who live on it. The attachment is created by the importance that the landscape itself has to the people; by the role that ancient wars and the sites on which they were fought have for a sense of common national identity; by the cultural importance of religious monuments and burial grounds; and by the ways in which historic myths and stories related to the land have become part of a people's common identity.

The cultural argument for land can be challenged on several scores. One problem is that it so strongly relies on history. The Serbs claim Kosovo because it was the site of a Serb empire in the Middle Ages. But the Kosovo Albanians, who constitute about 90 percent of Kosovo, claim that they descend from the Illyrians who inhabited the Balkan Peninsula long before the Slavs came.[30] When cultural historical claims collide, as they often seem to do, how do we assess which is stronger? An assessment of competing cultural claims that are founded on historical factors, as Margaret Moore points out, depends on "where in history one starts and whose history one accepts."[31] When two groups both have historical claims to the same area, there is no straightforward way of working out which claim is stronger.

A similar problem has to do with the validity of such claims. Moore argues that historical and cultural claims are problematic because they are "based on a biased, internal understanding of the particular group's tradition or history or religion."[32] Historical facts are contested—they depend, often to a substantial degree, on who interprets historical evidence and writes about the past. These types of claims are also vulnerable to myth-making. One might hold that historical myths are not necessarily a problem in themselves—the problem is that political leaders can use them (and indeed create them) to further their own aggressive, nationalist politics, often with increased conflict as a result.

That said, it would be wrong to dismiss cultural claims to territory altogether. The cultural argument is, in essence, based on the groups' emotional attachment to a certain piece of land. The land has become part of the people's identity, of their emotional landscape. That in itself should be given some significance. The experience of losing an important part of one's cultural identity can create unhappiness even if this identity is built on myths and poorly documented past events. But the cultural argument does not justify full sovereign rights to territory and cannot necessarily outweigh or override similar claims held by other groups. A cultural claim can justify having the access to and use of a piece of territory, but not to the exclusion of other groups who might have similar attachments to the same piece of land.[33]

LOCKEAN THEORIES OF TERRITORIAL RIGHTS

Several contemporary theories of territorial rights draw on the British liberal philosopher Locke's theory of land rights. Locke sought to establish individual property rights to unused land. In order to acquire rights to land, a person has to "mix his labor" with it. In Locke's words:

> Though the earth, and all inferior creatures, be common to all men, yet every man has a *property* in his own *person*: this nobody has any right to but himself. The *labour* of his body and the *work* of his hands, we may say, are properly his. Whatsoever then he removes out of the state that nature hath provided, and left it in, he hath mixed his *labour* with it, and joined to it something that is his own, and thereby makes it his *property*.[34]

From the starting point that the earth belongs to all of mankind, and that each person owns his own body and labor, Locke argues that "mixing one's labor" with something makes it one's property. When a person labors on a piece of land to cultivate it, he adds his labor to it, and therefore gains a right to the fruits of that labor. Thus, "as much land as a man tills, plants, improves, cultivates, and can use the product of, so much is his *property*."[35] By mixing one's labor with barren land, one takes it out of that which is common to mankind, and acquires an original title to it.[36]

On most readings, Locke imposes two conditions on the labor mixing argument.[37] First, he says that there should be "enough, and as good, left in common for others."[38] If I drink from a river, to use Locke's example, I do no harm to others who are thirsty, for there is enough for them to satisfy their thirst as well.[39] Similarly, if I appropriate land and leave enough left for others to cultivate, my action is legitimate. Second, no one is allowed to appropriate more than he or she can make use of before it goes to waste. In the words of Locke, "Nothing was made by God for man to spoil or destroy."[40] Locke provides a further reason for the argument that agricultural development justifies land acquisition. According to him, "The provisions serving to the support of human life, produced by one acre of enclosed and cultivated land, are (to speak much within compass) ten times more than those which are yielded by an acre of land of an equal richness lying waste in common."[41] A cultivated piece of land is able to support more people with food than an uncultivated piece of land, and therefore the person who cultivates land does not take something away from others, but rather does a service to them.

Locke's argument raises some questions. For instance, what does it mean that there should be "enough, and as good, left in common for others"? Who are the "others"? Are they confined to the members of one's own society, or should we leave enough for people in other parts of the world as well? And are they confined to the current generation, or should we not also take future generations into account when we contemplate appropriation?[42] The idea that "labor mixing" is a way to acquire property rights or land rights is also controversial.[43] What exactly does "mixing one's labor" mean? In what sense do I "mix my labor" with a deer if I kill it, with an acorn if I pick it, or with a field if I plow it? Does it mean that I "infuse" something of myself into the object, that I "create" a new object through my working on it, or that I "enhance the value" of the object by working on it?[44] And what is it about mixing your labor with something that makes it yours? Why, as Robert Nozick asks, "isn't mixing what I own with what I don't own a way of losing what I own rather than a way of gaining what I don't?"[45]

It might be difficult to spell out exactly why it is that cultivation can be a source of land rights, yet many share the intuition that laboring on an object creates an entitlement to it. As Jeremy Waldron notes, "Surely the fact that a labourer has made such a difference to an object is of considerable importance in determining the just way to dispose of the product."[46] More important for this discussion, is to ask whether individual property rights can justify sovereign rights held by a state. Territorial rights, as I have pointed out above, are collective rights to territory. Thus, a link has to be made between the individual right to land and the collective state right to territory. Locke's own answer to this question was somewhat rudimentary. A state has a territorial right, he believed, if individual property owners consent to placing their property under the jurisdiction of a state.[47]

Contemporary philosophers have used Lockean ideas to base territorial rights in roughly two different ways. Some follow Locke closely and argue that a state's territorial right is based on the consent of individual property holders. Hillel Steiner is a proponent of this view. Others argue, more plausibly I believe, that collectives can gain land rights through the development and settlement of land. Meisels and Miller are representatives of this latter approach.

Steiner attempts to derive territorial rights directly from the property rights of individuals. Territorial claims, he argues, "must be reducible to the legitimate claims of individual persons."[48] He continues: "Since nations' territories are aggregations of their members' real estate holdings, the validity of their territorial claims rests on the validity of those land titles."[49] I will not explore Steiner's theory in any depth here. Rather, I wish only to discuss some of the problems that the move from individual property rights to a state's territorial rights run into. Allen Buchanan points to one important difficulty. Property rights and territorial rights, he notes, are two different types of rights. The right to territory entails the right jurisdiction, "the right to make, adjudicate, and enforce legal rules within a domain," but a property right does not.[50] Since these rights are of a different kind, how then can the aggregate of property rights ground a territorial right?

Another problem is this: assume that we understand these individual property rights as legally defined rights spelled out, for instance, by the laws of the United States. Such legal rights cannot ground territorial rights because the property rights are assumed to be chronologically prior to the territorial rights. The US territorial right is a right to jurisdiction, which encompasses the right to make and adjudicate property rights, so no property rights can exist before they have been defined by the state. Thus, the argument seems to put the cart before the horse.[51] It tries to establish a territorial right by referring to rights that are established when a state exercises its territorial right.

Perhaps then it is better to understand Locke's individual property right as a natural right. In this version, individual property owners join together to form a state. The state's territorial right is a result of "the individual's right of property and their right of contract."[52] But, as Nine points out, there are several problems with this account, too, relating to the nature of the individual property right. One problem arises if we argue that the territorial right includes what Nine calls metajurisdictional authority, that is, the right to make and change jurisdictions. If we accept that included in the property right is this kind of metajurisdictional authority, then individual property owners would have the right to exit the state, with their property, when they so decide.[53] But this seems to torpedo our view of territorial rights, where states have the right of jurisdiction over the geographical area defined by the state's borders.[54] Borders, as Nine argues, cannot be "subject to unilateral change initiated by individuals acting individually."[55]

THE SETTLEMENT ARGUMENT

It seems problematic to derive territorial rights directly from individual property rights.[56] Another approach, which is more promising, is to establish territorial rights by using Lockean principles more loosely. According this type of argument, presented for instance by Miller and Meisels, it is national settlement—the living and laboring on a land over time—that grounds territorial rights.[57]

The first part of the settlement argument suggests that a group of people can add value to the land on which they have lived for an extended period of time. By building roads, bridges, railroads, towns, and, cities, and by developing the land for material purposes, the people enhance the territory. The value is embodied in the land itself, through its fields, houses, and infrastructure. The nation as a whole has increased the value of the land, and as a whole they now have a legitimate claim to it.[58] Meisels puts the point this way:

> A nation seeing recognition of title to a settlement set up by its members is in a strong sense claiming ownership rights to an object which its members in effect brought into being. At the very least, its nature and current value are of their making. Having "mixed their labour" with a portion of the earth's surface, thereby forming it into something new which did not exist (in its current form) prior to their collective endeavour, they now possess a morally significant interest in the products of their labour. Properly speaking,

then, far from claiming the right to appropriate territory, they are
actually seeking recognition of their interest in something that, for
the most part, they themselves established.[59]

Meisels draws here on the Lockean idea that those who labor on a
piece of land have a claim to the products of their labor.

There are some problems with this argument. Stilz points to
two. First, why is it that the state as a whole can claim the right
over a territory, when it is not the state as a whole that has labored
on it? As Stilz observes, when value is added to land, it is by the
labor of private individuals or private companies, not by the people or the state as a collective unit. So why, then, should not the
people who actually do the laboring gain private ownership rights
to the objects?[60] One way to respond to this criticism would be to
say that when a private individual or company labors on a land, it
is often understood that they are not doing it only for their own
private gain. A company might get an assignment to build a road
by the local government, but because the company is paid to do
this job for the government (i.e., the people whom it represents), it
does not gain property rights to the road.

A second problem is this: if it is the case that laboring creates
the entitlement, how can a state claim the jurisdiction over all of
its territory? It seems that the settlement argument would justify
entitlement only to the houses, roads, and other land developments for which the group is responsible. But what about the land
that has not been labored on? What about national parks, large
forest areas, and lakes? If no laboring or value adding has been
involved, how can the state claim sovereignty over that undevel-
oped land?[61] To this, one might respond with a pragmatic argument. No people can (or should) develop every single inch of the
land under its jurisdiction. But it would be practically very difficult
to manage a territory if the jurisdiction only extended to the land
that actually had been transformed.

The second part of the national settlement argument is a cultural argument. When a nation has settled on a piece of land, it
shapes that land in a culturally meaningful way. According to
Miller, there is a mutual relationship between territory and culture. On the one hand, the land will set its mark on the people
who live there—they must adapt to the possibilities and limitations of sustenance that the land offers. But the people also shape
the land, by farming on it and building industrial plants, roads,

and railroads, and churches and memorials, and by building towns and cities.[62] As Miller argues,

> Living on and shaping a piece of land means not only increasing its value in an economic sense, but also (typically) endowing it with meaning by virtue of significant events that have occurred here, monuments that have been built, poems, novels and paintings that capture particular places or types of landscape. . . . The case for having rights over the relevant territory is then straightforward; it gives members of the nation continuing access to places that are especially significant to them, and it allows choices to be made over how these sites are to be protected and managed.[63]

Meisels similarly argues that national groups' decisions regarding land use reflect their culture. In that sense the nation "mixes" its culture with the land.[64]

This argument is in many ways similar to the cultural argument presented above. Both arguments hold that an important cultural relationship may exist between a territory and a group. The main difference between them is that in the national settlement version, the cultural group in question actually lives on the land. In the cultural version there is an assumption that the group has lived on the land in the past, but not necessarily that it does so now. The cultural argument has therefore more to prove—it has to explain not only why the group in question has a cultural attachment to the land, but also why its claim is more important than the claim the current occupants have.

A Moral Baseline

Settlement provides the strongest claim to territory. Miller summarizes the argument in the following way:

> The people who inhabit a certain territory form a political community. Through custom and practice as well as by explicit political decision they create laws, establish individual or collective property rights, engage in public works, shape the physical appearance of the territory. Over time this takes on symbolic significance as they bury their dead in certain places, establish shrines or secular monuments and so forth. All of these activities give them an attachment to the land that cannot be matched by any rival claimants.[65]

The claim of settlement has both material and cultural elements. The material aspects have to do with the fact that people have made their living on the land and developed it to meet their needs. Long-term settlement also takes on a cultural and emotional significance, because the identity of the people becomes connected to the territory they inhabit.

For the claim of settlement to have any moral weight, it has to have lasted for a sustained period so that the material and cultural bonds have had time to develop. But it is difficult to specify how long a settlement must last in order for a valid claim to arise. What we might say is that the group must have been there long enough to make its material and cultural life there. That will usually take more than a generation.

Settlement seems to justify most current borders and territorial divisions. In some ways this is a paradoxical conclusion, because the reality of most current territorial possessions is, of course, that they have been acquired in an unjust manner. Current boundaries and territorial divisions are more often than not the product of previous military struggles, dispossessions, and political fights. As Buchanan says, "Even the most cursory 'title search' would in most cases reveal that at least some parts of most of the areas over which territorial sovereignty is now claimed were unjustly acquired by conquest, genocide, or fraud."[66] The observation that current borders are immoral, or at best morally arbitrary, seems to push us, as Lea Brilmayer observes, into a position of anarchy.[67] If borders have been established in an immoral way, should they not be subject to revisions based on a more morally acceptable principle? If we give prominence to the principle of settlement, the answer to this question is "no." Occupation gives moral legitimacy to current territorial divisions because the populations in question have forged material and cultural bonds to the land they live on. This argument is especially convincing when the borders in question have lasted a long time and are stable.[68]

When a state is exercising territorial sovereignty over a particular piece of land, we should also grant it a prima facie right to do so. But we have to ask if there are considerations that might undermine or override this claim. Such "defeater claims" can be of several different types.[69] First, the state might not be legitimate. The claim to territorial sovereignty depends, I have argued, on a legitimate relationship between the people and the state. If a government systematically and severely violates the human rights of its citizens, as I argued in chapter 3, it cannot claim the right to territorial sovereignty. In such a case, the people who live on the land will still have a right to continue to live there. Second, another group might have a stronger claim to occupancy. This can happen if the group recently has been wrongfully displaced or wrongfully annexed. A group has been wrongfully displaced, for instance, if a military campaign has expelled it from its land. It has been annexed if another state has appropriated its territory.[70] In these cases, we may hold that territorial sovereignty should be restored to the people who were dispossessed or annexed.

Part II: Wars and Morally Acceptable Territorial Changes

Wars are often initiated by one state in order to take territory that it considers its own. Consider the following two cases: In 1982, Argentina went to war to take control of the Malvinas Islands, known in the English-speaking world as the Falkland Islands. According to the Argentinean military junta, this was not an act of aggression, because the British occupation of the islands was illegitimate. In a radio and television address on the day of the invasion, the Argentinean president, Leopoldo Galtieri, said that the country had merely recovered the Malvinas Islands, "which by legitimate right are part of the national patrimony."[71] Foreign Minister Costa Mendez expressed the same position a few months later to the United Nations Security Council. He argued that the Argentinean resort to force was an attempt to recover the Malvinas, which the British had illegally occupied for 149 years. "Those islands," according to Mendez, "belong, and have belonged from the time of independence, to the sovereign Argentine Republic."[72] The short war ended with Britain resuming control of the islands.

The desire to reclaim lost territory was also the reason for Operation Storm, the largest military campaign during the war in the former Yugoslavia. Launched on August 4, 1995, by the Croatian government, the goal of the campaign was to take back the Krajina, which had been under control of the Croatian Serbs since 1991.[73] The recovery of the Krajina had been an explicit goal of the Croatian government during this period. In a conversation with Richard Holbrooke in 1992, for instance, the Croatian foreign minister, Mate Granic, complained,

> Over twenty-five percent of our land is occupied by the Serbs
> ....Before the war there were two hundred and ninety-five thousand Croats in the Krajina. Now there are only three thousand five hundred. This is our land. This is our country. The Serbs have cut our country almost in half. This is wholly unacceptable to us.[74]

Operation Storm succeeded and Croatia regained control of the Krajina.

How should wars fought over territory end? If our moral baseline is that the state that is currently exercising sovereignty has a prima facie right to do so, under what circumstances should a war end in a different territorial arrangement? What types of considerations would justify a change of the *status quo ante bellum*, and to what degree should our judgment of the outcome be affected by considerations of *ad bellum* or *in bello* justice?

My point of departure is that there is a presumption against territorial change. That follows not only from the moral baseline I arrived at in the previous section, but from the so-called territorial integrity norm and its sister norm, *uti possidetis*, both of which I will discuss below. But there will be cases in which the presumption against territorial change should be overridden. A valid secessionist claim will in effect also imply a change in boundaries. And, as I will argue here, we must also sometimes acknowledge a state's right to go to war to take back territory that it considers its own. When such a state succeeds, and the territory is returned to its possession, the outcome of the war is morally preferable to the prewar situation.

What then are the characteristics of wars that should lead to a change of borders? First, the state that lays claim to the area must have a strong moral claim to the territory in question. That is to say, the state must be able to argue that the territory and the population in the area should be governed by it, and not the state that is currently in control. The passage of time is a key element here. The longer the territory has been "lost," the weaker the territorial claim most likely is. Second, the war must plausibly be said to uphold the principle of territorial integrity. That is, the war must be a response to a previous territorial aggression. Again, there is an important time element. We must be able to say that the war is a response to a recent illegitimate territorial aggression. If it is not, then the war to reclaim the territory will itself be a case of territorial aggression.

WARS FOR LOST TERRITORY

There is general agreement among contemporary just war scholars that starting a war to acquire or recover long-lost territory is not acceptable. The presumption against territorial wars can be explained by the fact that modern technology has made wars extremely deadly for all of those involved, and by the way in which such wars can escalate by drawing other states into the conflict. We also have to worry about the consequences of accepting a general rule that states can go to war to bring about territorial change. Such a rule would "encourage war and endlessly imperil international peace and security."[75]

According to some just war scholars, however, there are situations in which wars for territory are justified. Early just war thinkers such as Saint Augustine held that a just cause for going to war was to redress a wrong. That included taking back territory others had wrongfully occupied. Contemporary just war thinkers mostly agree that under certain conditions a state has the right to counter territorial aggression and take back territory that was unjustly taken from it. Iraq's invasion and annexation of Kuwait was met with international condemnation, and when Iraq did not pull out, an international coalition led by the United States went to war in order to force Iraq out and reestablish the territorial *status quo ante bellum*. Richard Regan defends this type of war by noting that "to argue that nations may not justly initiate hostilities to vindicate claims to lost territories is not to argue that nations may not justly resort to military action to recover territory recently occupied by an aggressor."[76]

Sometimes, however, it is argued that wars for territory are wars of self-defense, even if the territory was "lost" years earlier. In Argentina's view, its resort to force was defensive because the intention was to restore its previously held territory. By some accounts, the notion of self-defense in international law provides this kind of "loophole." A state can argue that an attack on another state is a war for self-defense if that territory previously belonged to the attacker.[77] The argument implies that there is a

continuing right of self-defense that extends beyond a response to
a military attack. But scholars reject the validity of this interpretation of international law. As Oscar Schacter argues, self-defense
does not extend to cases in which the use of force is not a response
to a very recent attack. If we were to allow self-defense in the
absence of such attacks, he points out, "self-defense would sanc-
tion armed attacks for countless prior acts of aggression and conquest. It would completely swallow up the basic rule against use
of force."[78]

How do we distinguish the cases in which the resort to war to
take back territory is justified from the cases in which it is not?
When, as Regan asks, "should territory be considered 'lost' and
not a just cause for waging war for its recovery, and when should
territory be considered 'recently occupied' and a just cause for waging war?"[79] In Regan's mind, it is difficult to pin down the length
of the period of time that should pass before a state no longer has
the right to initiate war to recover lost territory. He says,

> A generation would certainly seem long enough, but a single year
> might be a preferable limit from the viewpoint of international
> peace and security. That would give the victim nation and sup-
> porting nations, ideally with the approval of the Security Council,
> sufficient time to mobilize military forces to expel the occupying
> power without encouraging wars to reclaim longer-lost territory.[80]

But the one-year mark seems a bit arbitrary. By this criterion,
Croatia's military offensive to take back Krajina was wrong, and
thus presumably the outcome of it was wrong too. Rather, I think
our judgment must be based on balancing two different considerations: the territorial integrity principle and the strength of the
territorial claim. The first refers to the goal of promoting international stability and peace, the second to the robustness of the
territorial claim.

Territorial Integrity and *Uti Possidetis*

We should, I have argued, assume that a state has a moral right
to territory based on the material and cultural bonds that exist
between its population and the land. That creates a moral presumption against wars for territorial change. There is a similar legal presumption against territorial change, based on what is sometimes

referred to as the "territorial integrity" norm. According to this norm, wars to change interstate boundaries are illegal, and must be considered a case of territorial aggression.[81]

The outlaw of wars for territorial gain is somewhat of a novelty. From a historical perspective, conquest, the taking possession of territory by force with the intention and ability to retain it, was an important mode of acquiring territory. In fact, it was considered a valid form of territorial acquisition as late as in the nineteenth century.[82] With the mass violence of the First and Second World Wars, states sought to limit the use of force by defining the first use of force as illegal. The signatories of the Kellogg-Briand Pact of 1928 paved the way by condemning the use of war and demanding that international disputes be solved by pacific means.[83] The Charter of the United Nations cemented this norm by making war illegal, except in cases of self-defense. As noted by Mark Zacher, attitudes and practice among contemporary states show a widespread support for the territorial integrity norm.[84]

When states break up, and new states are formed, the norm of *uti possidetis* supplements the territorial integrity norm. According to this norm, the territory of new states is defined by prior administrative boundaries. *Uti possidetis* was originally a concept in Roman law and was used in the resolution of conflict over private property. The phrase *uti possidetis, ita possideatis* ("as you possess, you may possess") meant that the individual holding the property was assumed to be its rightful owner.[85] The principle of *uti possidetis* was first coupled with the emergence of new states when countries in Latin American gained independence. It meant that colonial administrative boundaries were converted into international boundaries.[86] It was also adopted as the favored principle of decolonialization in Africa.

The International Court of Justice explained the purpose of the principle in the following way:

> The essence of the principle lies in its primary aim of securing respect for the territorial boundaries at the moment when independence is achieved. Such territorial boundaries might be no more than delimitations between different administrative divisions or colonies all subject to the same sovereign. In that case, the application of the principle of *uti possidetis* resulted in administrative boundaries being transformed into international frontiers in the full sense of the term.[87]

The principle was also applied in the dissolutions of Yugoslavia, Czechoslovakia, and the Soviet Union.[88] With respect to the former Yugoslavia, for instance, the so-called Badinter Commission, named after the French judge who headed it, proposed that the internal boundaries of Yugoslavia should become the international borders of the successor states.[89] This opinion had a great impact, as the commission advised the European Community on legal questions relating to the disintegration of Yugoslavia.

The principle of *uti possidetis* has the effect of maintaining the territorial *status quo*. By avoiding extensive, and most likely disputed, boundary revisions through the transformation of administrative or colonial boundaries into international ones, *uti possidetis* has been seen as a way to avoid conflict.[90] According to Mark Zacher, in all of the nine state breakups that have taken place since 1945, the former internal administrative boundaries have been turned into international boundaries. And if new states have been reluctant to accept this principle, they have been put under pressure from other states to do so.[91]

There are good reasons for embracing the territorial integrity principle. When trying to alter the territorial *status quo*, states often argue that they are attempting to recover territory that was previously theirs.[92] They will go to great lengths to explain why their claim is the better one. For instance, through the use of "propaganda cartography"—maps that seek to illustrate a state's claimed historical connection to a territory—states hope to garner domestic and international support for their claim.[93] But such claims must be viewed with a great deal of skepticism. They may have more to do with what states believe will be considered an acceptable reason for the war by other states, than what is actually the real motive. As the norms surrounding the legitimate use of force have become more restrictive, the effort to justify the first use of force as an act of belated self-defense and the recovery of historical territory has become more common. Not surprisingly, restitution claims for territory became particularly widespread after the Second World War.[94] As Alexander Murphy notes, state "leaders rarely make speeches declaring that they are seeking to incorporate a neighboring territory into their domain because there is a valuable bauxite deposit in the area or because the territory would provide better access to the sea or because the state is too small to compete effectively with its neighbors."[95]

The Strength of Territorial Claims

Using one year as the mark between justified and unjustified recovery of territory, as Regan suggests, clashes quite strongly with what justice seems to require. In the justifications for territorial rights discussed above, there is an assumption that it takes time to build a territorial claim, and it takes time to lose one.[96] If a group is expelled from its territory, its territorial claims will eventually weaken, but this will not happen quickly.

There are several reasons why territorial rights might fade, one of which has to do with the very basis of these rights. The passage of time plays an essential part in the creation of valid territorial claims. As Miller notes,

> It should be clear, I hope, that if nation B expels nation A from the territory it has occupied historically and begins to occupy and cultivate that land, it does not immediately acquire territorial rights, according to my account. On the contrary, nation A's claim to be returned to its homeland is plainly the stronger when we consider the various factors that I have canvassed as relevant to such rights (the cultural fit between people and land, the value they have added, and the symbolic significance it holds for them). On the other hand, as time passes nation B will begin to have claims that resemble those of A (nation A may or may not develop occupancy claims in some other place). Who has the better title at any moment will be a matter of judgment.[97]

As time goes by and a society forms its own attachment to a particular piece of land—by building houses and infrastructure on it, by farming it, by using it for industrial purposes, and by giving it cultural significance—its claim grows stronger. And since it takes time to generate a valid connection to land, a displaced society does not immediately lose its claim. On the other hand, a displaced society cannot argue, years later, that the territory it previously possessed is still vital to its sustenance and way of life. As Waldron says, as time goes on "people are likely to have developed new modes of subsistence, making the claim that the land is crucial to their present way of life less credible."[98] Religious and cultural claims, on the other hand, have more staying power in Waldron's account, because the idea that a lost land "forms the center of a present way of life—and remain sacred objects despite their loss—may be as credible a hundred years on as it was at the time of dispossession."[99]

Jeff McMahan makes a slightly different argument with a similar conclusion. He agrees that if a state seizes another state's territory, it does not immediately acquire rights to it.

> If, following an unjust seizure of territory, enough time passes for a new society with its own infrastructure to arise within the territory, the members of that society may acquire an increasingly strong moral claim to stay, particularly as new generations who are entirely innocent of the initial aggression establish their own lives there.[100]

For McMahan, the decisive factor is not the strength of the territorial claim, but the degree to which the population is complicit in the aggression. When, for instance, Israeli settlers build on land Israel has unjustly occupied, they knowingly took part in the Israeli aggression. That invalidates their claim to the land, and their aggression also makes them liable to defensive attack. However, their children, who had no knowledge or say in the aggression, and therefore are innocent, have a right not to be evicted from the land.[101] Here too the argument seems to suggest that a generation marks the tipping point between justified and unjustified recovery of territory.

Clearly, a people will not lose their territorial right during the course of a year. If we are interested only in what justice requires, we should want the territorial outcome of a war to correspond more closely to people's territorial rights. The problem, of course, is that we do not want a general rule that says that a state that has lost its territory at some point in the past 40 years or so has the right to go to war to take it back. That might have unfortunate consequences and generate further conflict.

The Falkland Islands and the Krajina

The strength of the territorial claim and the territorial integrity principle together constitute the basis on which we must make judgments regarding wars over territorial change. In many cases the two norms will generate the same conclusion. It follows from the discussion so far, for instance, that it was not a bad thing,

morally speaking, that Argentina did not succeed in taking the
Falkland Islands. Argentina claimed that it was not acting as an
aggressor when it went to war because the military action took
place inside its own territory. But by any reasonable meaning of the
term, this was not a case of self-defense. Argentina's main claim
was that Great Britain had unjustly dispossessed the Argentinean
population in 1830. After having inhabited the islands for decades,
Britain withdrew in 1774, but returned to the islands in 1830 and
threw the Argentine settlers out. Since then, the islands have been
in British possession. This long and uninterrupted occupation of
the islands is a strong argument for acknowledging the British
claim. What is more, the population on the islands has expressed a
desire to remain British, and thus, Britain could also refer to self-
determination as a further justification for their possession.[102] In
addition to a weak territorial claim, the territorial integrity principle was not on the Argentinean side. Given Britain's long-lasting
control over the islands, Argentina's invasion was clearly a violation of the territorial integrity norm.

The case for Croatia's recovery of the Krajina is less clear-cut.
Before the war, the Krajina, a territory bordering Bosnia in the
eastern part of Croatia, had a mixed population consisting both
of ethnic Croats and ethnic Serbs. The Serbs were, in fact, more
numerous than the Croats. In the beginning of the war, Serb paramilitary forces, assisted by the Yugoslav National Army (JNA), took
control of the Krajina and proclaimed it an independent republic.
Here, as in Eastern and Western Slavonia, the Serb forces violently
pushed out much of the Croatian population. When a cease-fire
was signed in January 1992, about 10,000 were dead, over ten
percent of Croatia's houses had been destroyed, and the country housed 700,000 refugees.[103] The cease-fire established four
United Nations Protected Areas in Eastern and Western Slavonia
and in the Krajina, but low-level conflict continued.

Clearly, both ethnic Croatians and ethnic Serbs had valid territorial claims to the Krajina. Both groups had lived in this border
region for centuries. Thus, it was an area to which neither group
could claim sole possession. If we only were to base the judgment
on the strength of the territorial claim, we might not get very far.
However, when we supply the analysis with the principle of territorial integrity, and the subsidiary principle of *uti possidetis,* it seems
that Croatia had a better claim to the Krajina. Since the Krajina

had been part of Croatia when it was a republic in Yugoslavia, there is a presumption against giving another state sovereign rights over it. This was for the most part the position that the European states took at the beginning of the war.[104] The United States also insisted on converting the prior administrative boundaries to international boundaries. Thus, it supported Croatia's claims to the Krajina and Slavonia, while also insisting that Croatia must respect the territorial integrity of the other former republics of Yugoslavia. There was, for instance, no US support for Croatia's territorial ambitions in Bosnia.[105]

The territorial integrity principle promotes stability, but this case shows that this principle is important also for more straightforward moral reasons. Had we accepted the Serbian takeover of the Krajina, it seems that we would also be condoning the methods the Serbs used to gain control. These methods are now well known: it was only through violence against civilians, by forcing them out of their homes, killing and torturing them, and looting and burning their houses, that the Serbs could take control of the Krajina. This process of ethnic cleansing flagrantly violated the laws of armed conflict. As Norman Naimark has pointed out, ethnic cleansing was an attempt to remove the civilian population from an area and thereby secure control over the territory.[106] Thus, many would agree with the American diplomat Richard Holbrooke that to accept Serb rule of the Krajina would be the same as to legitimize Serb aggression.[107]

There is an obvious paradox here. When Croatia took the Krajina back, much of the Serb population left the Krajina. Operation Storm has, in fact, been called "the largest single instance of 'ethnic cleansing' of the Yugoslav war."[108] About 150,000 Serb civilians fled from the area right before or during the offensive, leaving their possessions and homes behind.[109] Many appeared to have left in a rush. A cable sent to the US Department of State from the American Embassy in Zagreb, a week after the offensive started, reported that "throughout Knin's homes, food was on the tables, clothing was hanging on the lines, toys remained outside, and all of the ostensible signs of life remained, except for the presence of human life."[110] In 1991, Serbs had accounted for about 12 percent of Croatia's population, but now the number was down to around 3 percent.[111] Tudjman had encouraged the Serbs to stay, but did not seem too upset about their departure.

"They disappeared ignominiously," he said, "as if they had never populated this land. We urged them to stay but they did not listen to us. Well, then, *bon voyage*."[112] Yet it seems that the Croatian military committed more human rights violations after Operation Storm than during it. Dozens of Serb villages were burned, empty homes were looted and destroyed, and old and disabled people who had not managed to flee were executed or forced out of their homes.[113]

If accepting a Serb claim to the Krajina implies condoning aggression, would not accepting a Croatian claim to it also be to condone aggression? It might seem inconsistent to accept Croatian control over the Krajina when it too violated fundamental *in bello* principles. However, there is one important difference between the two military actions. It was the Serbs who first used ethnic cleansing to gain control over the Krajina. That does not make the Croatian methods less blameworthy, but Croatia could plausibly argue that their military campaign sought to counter the results of a recent aggression. The Croatian Serbs could not use the same argument.

Yet, given the way the Krajina was taken back, it does not seem right to judge the outcome "just." It was morally preferable to a continued Serb control of the area, but the manner in which Croatian control was regained made the outcome less than ideal. Had the Croatian government done more to convince the Krajina Serbs that it would be safe for them to stay, and had the Croatian military not targeted Serbian civilians, our judgment that Croatian sovereignty was the right outcome would be much more whole-hearted. Clearly, we want to accord ethnic Serbs a right to still reside in the area, and if the Croatian government does not accommodate Serbian refugees' right to return, we might also have to reevaluate its claim to territorial sovereignty. This is so because, as I have argued above, in order for a state to have the right to territorial sovereignty, it has to protect the interests of the populations under its control. If a state systematically and persistently violates the rights of parts of its population, its territorial right will erode.

Gray Areas

In both of the two cases I have discussed, considerations of the strength of the territorial claim and the territorial integrity pulled in the same direction. After about 150 years, Argentina's claim to the Falkland Islands, which was not very strong to begin with, had clearly faded. To go to war to recover them was not a case of justified recovery. Respect for territorial integrity argues for the same conclusion. In the Krajina case, two national groups had historical rights to the same piece of land. But Croatia could claim that its military offensive sought to uphold the principle of territorial integrity. The way it took the area back, while clearly wrong, did not invalidate its claim to territorial sovereignty. Thus, we cannot reasonably claim, for instance, that violations of *in bello* principles serve to nullify Croatian territorial rights.

There will be cases where it will be more difficult to make a judgment about the right outcome to a war over territory. These hard cases arise when not enough time has passed for the territorial claim of the dispossessed group to fade, but when respect for territorial integrity argues against a change of borders. As it was, it took four years from the Serb takeover of the Krajina until Croatia was able to reclaim it. During this period, the Croatian military was built up considerably—its soldiers and officers received training, and military equipment was smuggled in. But what if it had taken longer? What if the Croatian Serbs had held possession of the Krajina for another 10 years, or 20? It might not be possible to come up with general guidelines for how such cases should be judged.

It is worth pointing out again that when we judge the beginning of a war, we are making a different kind of judgment than when we judge its end. When we judge how a war has started, we are concerned both with questions of justice (including whether the war has a just cause) and with whether the war realistically can achieve a just aim (i.e., reasonable hope). We also have to take into account the consequences that generalizing a particular judgment would have. We cannot say that State X is justified in going to war to recover territory, but that State Y is not, unless there is a morally relevant difference between the two cases. At the end of the war, the war is an established fact. Since the war has happened, we want to make sure it ends well, from the point of view of both justice and future stability. We might therefore be allowed to worry a bit less about unfortunate incentives than when we judge the beginning of a war. That will allow us to give a bit more weight to justice demand.

Part III: Preemptive Conquest

Wars, as a general rule, should not end in a change of territorial boundaries. One exception to this rule, I have argued, is when a state takes back a piece of territory that was very recently annexed. Another exception is when there is a strong moral reason to accept the claim to statehood by a secessionist group. In this section I discuss a third possible exception to this rule: the taking of territory as preemptive self-defense. The idea here is that a state can, under certain circumstances, take a piece of territory from another state in order to promote its own security.

Sharon Korman asks whether it would not be a violation of international justice if one prohibits, "the right of acquiring by force territory which has repeatedly been used as a base for attacking the state that emerges victorious in a war of self-defense?"[114] Buchanan, while not fully embracing the argument, presents the case for conquest as preemptive self-defense in the following way:

> There is, however, one possible exception to the general principle that conquest is not a legitimate mode of acquiring territory according to liberal theory. Pre-emptive self-defense might under certain highly constrained circumstances justify the forcible taking of territory for the purpose of incorporation.[115]

Buchanan asks us to imagine the following hypothetical example:

> Country X has repeatedly been the innocent victim of aggression by its neighbor to the North, country Y. There is good reason to believe that if country X's border with country Y were pushed forward sixty miles, to coincide with a formidable natural boundary such as a mountain range or major river, the threat of future successful invasions by Y would be greatly diminished.[116]

Since country Y has repeatedly attacked X, Buchanan asks, should X not have the right in this case to prevent future attacks by taking Y's territory?

Buchanan immediately suggests a problem with accepting a more general principle of preemptive conquest: such a principle would have harmful incentives. It could be misused in an effort by states to mask their own territorial ambitions under the disguise of preemptive self-defense. If we were to accept a case of preemptive conquest as valid, Buchanan holds, it would have to be only if it were impossible to control Y's aggression in other ways, for instance, through an international organization, and if other ways of defense short of conquest, like demilitarization, had been explored.[117]

The problem of harmful incentives is not likely to convince a country that feels that territorial annexation could aid in its defense. Such a state might agree that we should not accept a *general* principle of preemptive annexation, but argue that the circumstances it is in are so unique that we should make an exception. And, maybe such a state could be right. I would therefore like to challenge the idea of conquest as preemptive self-defense by more directly engaging with the arguments that such a state might use.

In order, then, to judge the moral acceptability of annexation as preemptive self-defense, I think we have to take two types of considerations into account. First, we have to accept the idea that preemption is sometimes morally acceptable. Then, granted that people have an important interest in security, we must ask whether the taking of a particular piece of territory will actually significantly help improve the state's security situation. That means that we must weigh the possible military utility of the occupation against the costs of it.

Preemptive Self-Defense

Virtually everyone agree that states, as individuals, have a right to self-defense. However, there is considerable debate about the temporal dimension of this right. Does the right of self-defense only apply to cases in which an attack is already underway? Or does it extend to cases in which the attack is imminent, but not actually a materialized fact? What if a neighboring state has gathered its troops along the borders, evacuated its civilian population, and pointed its weapons in the right direction—all that is lacking is the actual attack itself. Should we not accept that states have a right of preemption, that is, to respond militarily to an attack that is imminent?[118]

There is a large body of literature written by international lawyers and just war scholars about the legal and moral acceptability of preemption.[119] The legal debate often takes as its point of departure the ambiguity in the notion of self-defense in the Charter of the United Nations. Chapter VII, Article 51, reads:

> Nothing in the present Charter shall impair the inherent right
> of individual or collective self-defense if an armed attack occurs

against a Member of the United Nations, until the Security Council has taken measures necessary to maintain international peace and security.

But it is not fully clear how the phrase "if an armed attack occurs" should be interpreted in international law. Does it mean that the attack has to be already underway, or does it also justify anticipatory action if a state knows that an attack is imminent?[120] Some international lawyers will argue that since there is a general prohibition against the use of force in international law, we have to interpret Article 51 literally and rule out any right to preemptive self-defense. Others argue that customary international law allows for states to strike first in the face of an impending attack. Those who argue for the acceptance of preemption will often claim that such action must be limited in the ways suggested by U.S. Secretary of State Daniel Webster. In response to the so called Caroline incident in 1837, Webster established four criteria for the justifiable use of preemptive force: it must be "overwhelming" in its necessity, there must be no "choice of means," the threat must be so imminent that there is "no moment for deliberation," and it must be proportionate.[121]

The moral right to preemption can be explained in the following way: although the preemptive attack is a first use of force, it is a defensive action because it is a response to an "impending unjustified attack."[122] While the enemy has not yet attacked, it is so close to doing so that the right of self-defense has kicked in. Thus, Michael Walzer argues, a country's right to anticipatory self-defense seems justified when it is under a threat so credible that it virtually "has been forced to fight" and when failure to strike first might seriously risk its "territorial integrity or political independence."[123] Walzer represents a large group of people who believe Israel's first strike in the 1967 war against Egypt was a case of legitimate anticipation.[124]

Although that seems to be Buchanan's suggestion, I am not certain that the taking of territory in order to ward off future attacks actually qualifies as a preemptive action. Preemptive self-defense, as I now have explained, is justified in cases where the attack is imminent and where not acting would put the country at a severe disadvantage. But the scenario Buchanan describes above does not seem like such a case. Here the problem is that the country has been repeatedly attacked in the past and that there is good reason to believe the enemy will attack again in the future. But the future attack is not "imminent," which is a requirement for preemption. Buchanan's scenario seems more like preventive war, that is, a war that "aims to forestall a military threat that is distant rather than imminent."[125] Yet, the claim to preemptive self-defense is not implausible if these attacks have happened repeatedly, if they have happened recently, and if there is no sign that they will cease. Let us therefore proceed on the assumption that what Buchanan describes can be viewed as a case of preemption, and that the taking of territory in principle can be justified.

TERRITORY AND SECURITY

According to the traditional realist view of international politics, threats to a state's security are military based and arise from the actions of other states. A state's security is achieved by defending its territorial integrity, by maintaining physical barriers and buffer zones and, perhaps also, by forming military alliances. Borders protect the state and must therefore be defended by military force, and some borders are better, that is more defensible, than others.[126] As General Wesley Clark recently has said:

> From a military perspective we would want to divide the ground along defensible lines, avoiding the kinds of isolated pockets and peninsular-type arrangements that could encourage renewed conflict later or that would simply prove unenforceable in practice.[127]

Robert Gilpin has shown that states throughout history have sought to take territory in part to protect their interest in security.[128] But this practice might be increasingly flawed. Take the case of the Israeli-occupied territories after 1967.

Israel and the Idea of Defensible Borders

There has been a sense in Israel that the pre-1967 borders were "indefensible." Foreign Minister Abba Eban once called Israel's old borders "Auschwitz borders," and argued immediately after the 1967 war that Israel needed "a better security map, a more spacious frontier, a lesser vulnerability."[129] The perceived vulnerability was a function of several geographical features. According to Yigal Allon, who served as foreign minister from 1974 to 1977, the borders that existed before the June war in 1967 were to a large degree "without any topographical security value; and, of no less importance, the lines fail[ed] to provide Israel with the essential minimum of strategic depth."[130] The lack of strategic depth was a result of the short distance between important Israeli populations centers, such as Tel Aviv and Jerusalem, and its international borders. The distance from the border with Jordan to the Mediterranean Sea, for instance, was in parts only 10 miles. Another problem for Israel was the Golan Heights, a plateau raised 300 to 1,200 meters above the surrounding areas. In the northern parts of the plateau there is a steep descent westward toward Galilee and eastward toward Damascus.[131] When Syria held the Golan Heights, its artillery could easily reach Israeli targets in the valley below. Add to that that the Arab soldiers far outnumbered Israeli and were better equipped. Before 1967, therefore, Israel adopted a preemptive strategy so that it could fight its wars outside its own borders.[132]

The war in 1967 had dramatic territorial consequences as Israel captured the West Bank, including the Old City of Jerusalem, and Gaza, as well as the Sinai Peninsula and the Golan Heights. But it would be wrong to suggest that the motives for the 1967 territorial gains were only security based. In the immediate aftermath of the war there was in fact no consensus in Israel about what to do with the newly gained land.[133] By some accounts, it was thought that the territories could be "bargaining chips" that could be used in negotiations to extract concessions from the Arab states.[134] And in Israeli discussions of which territories to hold on to, religious and economic reasons were mixed together with the security arguments.[135] Moreover, while Israeli politicians mostly agreed that the old borders were "insecure," there was no actual agreement about what would make for secure borders.[136] Minister of Defense Moshe Dayan, who claimed that Syria did not pose much of a threat to Israel, did not regard an occupation of the Golan Heights as vital to Israeli security. But other Israeli military leaders made the case for keeping a substantial part of the Golan Heights for security reasons, and politicians quickly started making plans for the building of Jewish settlements there.[137] By doing so, they embarked on the road that Avi Shlaim has called a "creeping annexation."[138]

I cannot here make a full assessment of the possible military benefits and disadvantages of the occupied territories for Israel's security. Suffice it to point to a few different factors. In a review essay, David Rodman argues that the new territorial acquisitions have been an asset in Israel's defense:

> These territorial acquisitions provided Israel with a measure of strategic depth for the first time in its history. Its major population centers, industrial assets and military bases no longer remained within easy reach of Arab armies or terrorist organizations. Furthermore, despite the extent of Israel's territorial conquests, it now had defensible borders. Not only did these borders follow militarily impressive topographical obstacles, such as the Suez Canal and the Jordan River, and not only did they incorporate militarily significant high ground, such as the Judean and Samarian highlands, but the total length of the borders had also been shortened.[139]

Noting that Israel initiated two of the three full-scale wars it fought before 1967, and that it only initiated one after this war (the war against Lebanon in 1982), Rodman says that "the acquisition of defensible borders and strategic depth in the post-1967 era has curbed, to a certain extent, Israel's propensity to engage in preventive and pre-emptive war."[140] He also argues that in the war in 1973, both the Sinai and the Golan Heights provided buffer zones, which gave the Israeli military the time to mobilize its forces.[141]

But the 1967 territorial occupations have also led to some very obvious problems for Israeli security. Martin van Creveld, a military historian and strategist, points to several. First, he disputes the assumption that Israel's military strategic situation was as problematic as people have argued. He agrees that the pre-1967 borders "were completely without logic" and "cut right across countless streams, valleys, and transportation arteries."[142] But that, according to van Creveld, was not a huge problem. Take the West Bank. Van Creveld agrees that Jordan's control of the West Bank gave them "excellent starting positions from which to cut off Jerusalem, dominate and harass the costal plain, and invade Israel from the east." But, as he maintains, "the border between Jordan and Israel was no longer than the one between Israel and Jordan."[143] By that, he presumably means that if the borders between Israel and Jordan left Israel vulnerable, they also left Jordan vulnerable. The idea that Israel needed better and more defensible borders is therefore something of a puzzle. As van Creveld says,

> Given that the June 1967 War provided a spectacular demonstration of Israel's ability to defeat its enemies, how on earth did its leaders convince themselves that the country's security could not be guaranteed unless the Territories it had just occupied were retained?[144]

Considering that Israel had not lost any of the conventional wars it fought with its neighbors, van Creveld might have a point.

Israel's occupation of the territories also introduced new security challenges. First, Israel's occupation led to a wish in Syria and Egypt to reclaim their "lost" territory. In the three years after the 1967 war, Egypt and Israel fought a limited war of attrition over the Sinai Peninsula. More importantly, perhaps, in 1973 a coalition of Arab states, led by Syria and Egypt, initiated a war to take back the Golan Heights and the Sinai Peninsula. Secondly, a more long-lasting and difficult security challenge has come from inside the occupied territories. Because Israel built settlements in the occupied territories, it now needed to provide for the safety of the settlers. This was no simple task. As van Creveld notes, "The more settlements that were built, the more important it became to defend them and the less conceivable a withdrawal. Thus it was the tail that came to wag the dog."[145]

Another problem was that the occupation created hostility and caused Israel to become involved in a counterinsurgency campaign against the Palestinians. The Israeli military occupation of the West Bank and Gaza was harsh and repressive, and prompted a new chapter in the conflict between Israel and the Arabs. The First Intifada (or uprising), which began at the end of 1987, was a spontaneous mass revolt against Israeli occupation. It grew out of the poverty and miserable living conditions endured by the Palestinians there, as well as their feelings of humiliation and hatred of the occupation, which deepened with the founding of many Israeli settlements in the occupied territory.[146] Israeli soldiers were confronted by civilians, especially young men, throwing stones and burning tires, and by demonstrations and strikes. The Palestinian Liberation Organization (PLO) and other political groups quickly got behind these protests. The Intifada was a cry of anger, not a programmatic statement, but it did feed demands for Palestinian self-determination and the establishment of a Palestinian state.[147]

David Rodman notes that the strategic advantage of being in control of the West Bank and the Gaza was seriously undermined by the problems created by hostile populations.[148] By comparison, the Golan Heights has been a much easier annexation, because the population there is almost exclusively Israeli, and because there are no terrorists or holy sites to worry about.[149] Even if we accept that these annexations did provide Israel with some strategic advantages, it seems far from clear that the benefits outweighed the costs. In addition to having to provide for the safety of settlers in the new territories, the occupations prompted retaliatory wars for the recovery of territory and alienated and radicalized an already hostile population. This fact has led Israel's former foreign minister Shlomo Ben-Ami to conclude that, "Israel was wrong to assume that she could acquire new lands and have peace at the same time."[150]

CONCLUSION

Some borders are easier to defend than others. Yet, the idea that security corresponds intimately to the defense of a particular piece of territory does not reflect the type of threats most states face today. Now, arguably, transnational actors such as terrorists pose more of a challenge to state security than interstate military invasions. There is, as Peter Andreas has noted, "a widening gap between the traditional realist conception of security and borders and what many states are actually doing in the realm of security and border defense."[151] The military utility of borders seems to have declined considerably.[152]

The declining importance of borders as a way to protect a state's security does not mean that borders are unimportant. Nor does it mean that conquest can never be advantageous from a military point of view. But I doubt we need to make an exception to the principle that borders should remain intact based on a considerations of preemptive self-defense. When a war is fought over territory, we should in most cases hope for the restoration of *status quo ante bellum*. This conclusion is based on a consideration of both the robustness of territorial claim and of the principle of territorial integrity. If a state goes to war to undo a recent military conquest of its territory, we should hope it succeeds. And if a federal state breaks up, we should hope that the new borders follow old administrative borders. The main reason for accepting a change in sovereign territorial rights is in the cases where we should support a secessionist claim to sovereign statehood.

5

OUTCOMES OF WARS OVER
GOVERNMENT

At the heart of all civil war endings is the question of institutional choice. At stake in these conflicts, in the most general sense, is the configuration of the political system. The question is not (or no longer) the boundaries around the state, but what type of government should rule its population. At stake too, in the aftermath of war, is the issue of rebuilding a viable political system that reduces, not exacerbates, conflict. A civil war can destroy a country's infrastructure as well as administrative and political institutions, and typically cause a high degree of conflict and distrust between different population groups. Such conditions are not fertile grounds for the establishment of democracy. Thus, determining the appropriate political system for a country emerging from an internal war is just the first step— the second, and often more difficult, step is determining the appropriate process of establishing a viable democracy.

In keeping with the overall goal of this book, this chapter first discusses what we should regard as a just outcome to a war fought over government. The moral baseline in these types of conflicts is a democratic political system. Individuals have basic political rights, such as the right to vote, the freedom to assemble and associate with others, and the right to participate in the political process. These rights are best protected in a democracy. Thus, one would be hard pressed to explain why a war fought over government should not end in some kind of democracy. Who started the war and how it was fought seem irrelevant to this baseline judgment. It is implausible, for instance, to argue that if a substate group starts an armed rebellion to gain political rights, it should be denied these rights at the end of the war. The question is rather what kind of democracy is best for a country that has just been through a war, especially if the country has not had an established and well-functioning democracy before.[1] I give a qualified defense of the power-sharing model of democracy, and argue that while there are clear problems with this type of political system, it seems better than all the alternatives.

Michael Walzer has said that the beginning of peace is the restraint of war.[2] By the same token, the beginning of a stable democracy will often require the restraint of democratic procedures and rights. Because postwar democratization can exacerbate conflict, we have to ask what types of restraints we should accept in order to lay the foundations for a healthy political system. I will discuss two broad strategies that seek to enable the transition to democracy. First, the international community, especially through the United Nations, has sought to strengthen the political institutions of war-torn countries. These statebuilding operations temporarily set aside democratic principles in order to promote democracy and stability in the long run. Operated by unelected foreigners, statebuilding missions are by their very nature a paternalistic intrusion in the domestic affairs of a country. There are obvious and good moral reasons to embrace such operations—without them chances are that the country in question will revert back to repressive politics and violent conflict. Yet, the nondemocratic nature of these operations is problematic, and we should consider ways to lessen their most troublesome aspects. The goal of the second part of the chapter, is to discuss the dilemmas involved in statebuilding operations and some of the ways they can be managed and abated.

Second, the practice of lustration, or vetting as it is sometimes also called, also restrains democratic rights in order to enable a political transition. A form of lustration has been carried out in places like post–Second World War Germany, in many of the former eastern European countries, and more recently in Bosnia and Iraq. Lustrations usually target individuals or groups with close ties to a former repressive regime, or people suspected of war crimes, and deny their rights to participate in the political process and their right to work in the public sector. I discuss lustrations both as a punitive measure and as a way to promote postwar political legitimacy, and argue that the moral acceptability of this practice depends in important ways on how it is carried out. A careful consideration of lustration measures is important because they are common and valuable tools for postwar justice, and because they are part of the more general question of the ethics of foreign occupations.

Part I: Acceptable Postwar
Political Institutions

It is sometimes argued that the resolution to a civil war involves solving the Hobbesian problem, that is, creating or reestablishing political order.[3] But we do not only want to establish order, we also want to establish a stable order that is morally acceptable. These twin goals pose a formidable challenge for postwar societies.

The problem of stability stems in part from the emotional, physical, administrative, and political destruction that marks post–civil war societies. The infrastructure has been damaged; people's livelihoods have been destroyed or interrupted; human resources have been depleted; and the economy is often impoverished because resources have been diverted to support the warring armies.[4] The political system is usually in ruins and administrative institutions are ineffective or weak.[5] Citizens will often lack confidence in the government's ability to do its job, including providing for their security and welfare. The lack of trust not only taints the relationship between the government and the people, but also the relationships within and between different population groups, and it stems not only from the war but also from the societal conditions that led to the war in the first place.[6] Memories of prewar discrimination, human rights abuses, and political exclusion continue to taint postwar relationships. The breakdown of these relationships means that even the best strategies for rebuilding peace might fail.[7]

Post–civil war societies are often what scholars refer to as deeply divided, where nationality or ethnicity is strongly politicized and has created hostile, long-lasting societal divisions.[8] In these societies, there is one overarching layer of identity, in contrast to most other societies where other markers, such as class, race, gender, and religion also serve to set people apart from each other. In a deeply divided society, ethnicity organize the way in which political difference is perceived, and it shows up in voting behavior, in the organization of political parties, and in how a diverse set of issues is structured.[9]

How, then, does one reestablish political order in a country emerging from civil war, and how can that order meet fundamental demands of justice? At least three possibilities present themselves—partition, winner-takes-all, and some form of power-sharing democracy. Of these, I will argue, only the latter is a viable option. Partition is usually not a feasible alternative, especially if the warring populations are intermixed. In Bosnia, for instance, the international community regarded it as an immoral and unviable solution, which would have led to even more conflict and suffering. Another possibility is a winner-takes-all solution where the victorious belligerent takes full control over the state institutions. Some commentators claim that this can be a good solution to civil wars, "since there cannot be two governments ruling over one country, and since the passions aroused and the political cleavages opened render a sharing of power unworkable."[10] But the winner-takes-all outcome is only an option if one of the adversaries is able to beat the other on the battleground, and that, of course, is not always a possibility. This solution is also grossly undesirable, because military victories can come at a very high cost and are often coupled with acts of genocide.[11] There can be strong moral reasons to not want a military victory to end civil wars.

The Argument for Democracy

The core ideals of democracy have been absorbed and articulated by international organizations such as the UN, and they are also a fundamental component of important international treaties. Article 21 in the Universal Declaration of Human Rights, for instance, states that

(1) Everyone has the right to take part in the government of his country, directly or through freely chosen representatives.
(2) Everyone has the right of equal access to public service in his country.
(3) The will of the people shall be the basis of the authority of government; this will shall be expressed in periodic and genuine elections which shall be by universal and equal suffrage and shall be held by secret vote or by equivalent free voting procedures.

A war must end in the creation or re-creation of a legitimate political system, and that means democracy. As Kofi Annan notes, "At the centre of virtually every civil conflict is the issue of the State and its power—who controls it, and how it is used. No conflict can be resolved without answering those questions, and nowadays the answers almost always have to be democratic ones, at least in form."[12] This widespread acceptance of democracy as the most desirable political system, and the lack of other viable alternatives, has meant that the default approach of the international community has been to "encourage the warring parties to reach a comprehensive, negotiated settlement featuring a transition to democracy."[13]

I will shortly turn to the many challenges of establishing a well-functioning and stable democracy after war. But first it is worth spelling out why it is that we should hold the democratic ideal in high regard. For all its faults and problems, democracy is the political system that is most likely to be both procedurally just, in that it gives citizens an equal chance to affect a political outcome, and meet minimum standards of outcome justice.[14]

Democracy has three related core features: competition for power, political participation by citizens, and a system of political rights and liberties.[15] In Joseph Schumpeter's influential conception, democracy is "that institutional arrangement for arriving at political decisions in which individuals acquire the power to decide by means of a competitive struggle for the people's vote."[16] Competition for power is essential because it gives leaders the incentive to be open to the preferences of voters as well as the incentive to be responsive to a large quantity of voters, since both of these things are necessary in order to win an election. That encourages political leaders to take people's expressed interests into account. Competition reduces the likelihood of abuses of power.[17]

More recent definitions of democracy emphasize not only the competitive process but also the participation of citizens and a set of civil and political liberties.[18] According to Robert Dahl, democracy consists of a combination of rights (the right to vote, the right to run for office, the existence and right to alternative sources of information, freedom of expression, freedom of association), and the election of officials through free and fair elections.[19] This combination of rights and procedures is echoed in Samuel Huntington's definition. He sees a political system as democratic, "to the extent that its most powerful collective decision-makers are selected through fair, honest and periodic elections in which

all candidates freely compete for votes and in which virtually all
the adult population in able to vote."[20]

The value of participation is based on the underlying value
of equality.[21] Will Kymlicka notes that the idea that each person
matters equally is a fundamental component of modern political
thought.[22] We would immediately regard as implausible a theory
based on the idea that people are of unequal worth or that some
people matter more than others. One of the political implications of equality is that the government "treat[s] its citizens with
equal consideration; each citizen is entitled to equal concern and
respect."[23] More specifically, a general concern with equality
and the companion value of liberty, as John Rawls has successfully shown, can justify a *principle of (equal) participation*. This
principle consists of some basic procedural requirements for a just
political system. It requires that every citizen have the right to participate in the making of laws, through participation in elections
of a representative body that is accountable to the electorate.[24] The
clearest way to secure this right to participation is the rule of "one
elector, one vote." The right to participation also implies a right
to take part more directly in the political decision-making process.
As Rawls argues,

> All citizens are to have an equal access, as least in the formal sense,
> to public office. Each is eligible to join political parties, to run for
> elective positions and to hold places of authority.[25]

Furthermore, a concern with equality means that political procedures must be free and fair.[26] Because we should respect people's
opinions and interests, and because they have a right to participate in political decision making, we have to provide them with
the fundamental freedoms that make such participation possible.
That necessitates the protection of fundamental liberties, such as
the right to vote, the freedom of association, and the freedom
of speech. Democracy is preferable to other forms of government
because its secures formal political equality and fundamental
political rights.

If we only rely on a procedural conception of justice, we run into
what we can call the "problem of tyranny." The problem is effectively described by James Fishkin in his book on tyrannical policies: in 1972, the President of Uganda, Idi Amin, ordered around

50,000 Asians to leave the country within 90 days. Many of these people had worked for generations to build a life in Uganda, and many of them became stateless when they were expelled. Those who refused to leave were threatened with military imprisonment, and many were severely mistreated by Ugandan authorities. As Fishkin points out, Amin's decision enjoyed a large degree of support among black Ugandans.[27] It is quite possible that had Amin held a referendum on the issue, he would have acquired a sufficient majority to justify the decision on procedural grounds. If all we care about is procedural principles, we cannot guarantee that some portion of the population is not severely deprived or that their rights are not violated.[28] Just because a decision rule is morally acceptable, the outcome does not have to be morally acceptable. The problem of tyranny is especially prevalent in countries with clearly defined majorities and minorities, because, as one of the Federalist papers points out, if a majority is "united by a common interest, the rights of the minority will be insecure."[29] Thus, it is especially important to guard against the problem of majority tyranny in countries where politics is defined to a large degree by ethnicity.[30]

MAJORITARIAN OR
POWER-SHARING DEMOCRACY?

What type of democratic system is best for a deeply divided country emerging from war? Institutional choices—the choice of electoral system, of parliamentary or presidential systems, and of the degree of decentralization—have important consequences for the way conflict will be managed.[31] Before I discuss two prominent models of democracy, it is worth noting that some scholars believe that a system of hegemonic control is best for a country marked by ethnic conflict. In fact, this model is perhaps the most common form of ethnic conflict management.[32] South Africa under apartheid, Rwanda before 1993, the Soviet Union and a number of the other communist states until 1991, Iraq, and Kosovo are all examples of societies that have been stabilized through the dominant use of power by one group over the others.[33] John McGarry and Brendan O'Leary describe hegemonic control as a system that makes an "overtly violent ethnic contest for state power either 'unthinkable' or 'unworkable' on the part of the subordinated communities."[34] The dominating group manages conflict through its control of the political system, and often also through its monopolization of the military and the police. As a result, it is able to wrest compliance from the other groups. The subordinate groups are "held down" into obedience and submission. Hegemonic control is, in other words, essentially a system of political domination.[35]

From the point of view of justice, it is difficult to defend this solution to ethnic conflict. By its very definition, hegemonic control is a strategy that either formally or informally denies large segments of the society basic political rights and opportunities, thus violating the principles of participation and political equality.[36] Given the clear moral problems connected with this type of political system, the only reason why hegemonic control would be acceptable is if it proved to be a superior model for conflict resolution.[37] But there is little evidence to suggest that hegemonic control actually promotes stability. Especially when it is instituted for a longer period of time, it creates injustice and grievances that in turn can create violent opposition to the regime. As Arend Lijphart claims, "Not only have non-democratic regimes failed to be good nation-builders; they have not even established good records of maintaining intersegmental order and peace in plural societies."[38]

Majoritarian Democracy

Majoritarian democracy is sometimes also referred to as the Westminster model. The core features of this model are an electoral system based on concentration of executive power in one party, the exclusion of the minority opposition from the cabinet, and a unitary and centralized government.[39] The electoral system in these types of democracies ensures that "the winning candidate gains an absolute majority (i.e., more than 50 per cent), not just a plurality (i.e., more than any other contestant) of eligible votes."[40] How exactly this happens can vary. One method is a first-past-the-post system (often abbreviated as FPTP) in which the person who gains a majority in a single-member district wins, but other types of electoral methods can also be classified as majoritarian.[41] Regardless of the exact form of voting method, a majoritarian system is essentially a winner-takes-all system.

The problem with majoritarian democracy in a deeply divided society is that it often results in a majoritarian tyranny. When parties are organized around ethnicity and the ethnic groups are of unequal size, the consequences of a plural vote system can be dramatic. The minority can in these cases be excluded from power and influence altogether.[42] For many countries, of course, it is not a problem that a minority is excluded from power. The majority model of democracy is built on the assumption that political parties will alternate in the executive power and that the opposition is loyal. In countries where "political 'majorities' constantly fluctuate, as people change their minds on the key policy or political issues of the day, then majority rule is a sensible decision rule."[43] But in deeply divided societies, political allegiances do not fluctuate. When voting behavior is determined by national or ethnic affiliation, the minority group faces a situation of always being excluded from political power.

When minorities are excluded from power they are not only put in vulnerable position but the incentive for cooperation is also removed. As Timothy Sisk points out, "without an assurance that the electoral system will not lead to permanent exclusion, why *should* a minority group that perceives a threatening environment be willing to accept the inherent risks of electoral competition?"[44] The winner-takes-all presidential election after the 15-year-long civil war in Angola, for instance, did not give the smaller UNITA faction any incentive to function as a loyal opposition. The result was that the war started up again.[45] If ethnic groups are territorially separated, the minority might opt for secession, but if they are territorially intermixed, the violence might take the form of rioting or an attempted coup.[46] Thus, Lijphart concludes that, in divided societies "majority rule spells majority dictatorship and civil strife rather than democracy."[47] This is also the conclusion of Ian Shapiro, who notes that the experience with the Westminster model in postcolonial Africa was catastrophic:

> Constitutions were swept away, ignored, or buried in systemic nepotism and corruption, leaving subjected populations at the mercy of self-appointed or (at most) once-elected leaders, and of single-party states. Within only a few decades the continent found itself awash in the blood of war and civil war, with millions living in abject suffering and poverty and having little hope for improvement in the foreseeable future.[48]

The Power-Sharing Model

As a general term, power sharing can be defined as "practices and institutions that result in broad-based governing coalitions generally inclusive of all major ethnic groups in society."[49] The aim of power sharing is to make sure that each of the main groups in a society are part of the decision-making process, as well as given some autonomy over the issues that are important to them.[50] What all power-sharing models share is an inclusive coalition of segmental groups in the executive, the acceptance of nationality or ethnicity as the defining social cleavage, and decentralization either through federalism or autonomy.[51] The most well-known form of power sharing is the consociational model associated with Lijphart, but an alternative is provide by Donald Horowitz's integrative model.[52] Since there is limited experience with Horowitz's model, I will primarily talk here about power sharing in its consociational form.

As described by Lijphart, consociationalism has four defining characteristics.[53] It is a political system where the government is run by a grand coalition of political leaders from all the significant segments of society.[54] The exact way the grand coalition is arranged institutionally is not so important as long as the leaders of all main segments of the society are part of it.[55] There must be a sharing of executive power.[56] To further protect vital segmental interests, consociationalism is defined by mutual vetoes for the partners in the coalition. For the same basic purpose, consociationalism also calls for proportionality as the chief standard of allocating seats to decision-making institutions.[57] Proportionality aims to make sure that each societal group will have a corresponding number of votes in the parliament.[58] And finally, consociationalism is marked by a high degree of autonomy for each of the major segments in society, which is thought to further ensure that the interests of all groups are protected. Usually this form of segmented autonomy will take the form of a federal system.[59]

From the perspective of both procedural and outcome justice, the great advantage of the consociational model is that it ensures access to political power for all segments of society. Unlike the majority model of democracy, there is no risk that one group will be permanently kept out of the decision-making arena. The principle of proportional representation helps to make sure that all segments in the society get their share of political power, and autonomy and minority vetoes ensure that no issue of vital interest to a group is decided against its preferences.[60] The principles of consociationalism, in short, seek to protect "the rights, identities, freedoms and opportunities of all ethnic communities."[61] According to Lijphart this means that consociationalism is not only the best, but simply the *only* viable political system for a divided society. He writes, "For many plural societies of the non-Western world, therefore, the realistic choice is not between the British model of democracy and the consociational model, but between consociational democracy and no democracy at all."[62]

PROBLEMS FACING POWER-SHARING DEMOCRACIES AFTER WAR

A negotiated settlement after a civil war will usually contain power-sharing provisions. Power-sharing peace accords have formally ended the wars in countries as different as Afghanistan, Columbia, Burundi, Kosovo, Sudan, South Africa, and Bosnia.[63] According to one overview, more than 20 post–Cold War conflicts resulted in a peace agreement containing power-sharing provisions.[64] Power-sharing arrangements are arguably a good idea from a war termination point of view. Barbara Walter argues, for instance, that former enemies are 38 percent more likely to commit to a peace agreement if it guarantees them a position of power in the future government.[65] The reason is obvious—no adversary wants to sign off on a peace agreement that will exclude it from power in the postwar order. As belligerents consider putting down their weapons, they are naturally worried about their future security and about whether their interests will be protected after the war.[66] Power-sharing provisions are therefore positively associated with peace. By reassuring adversaries that their interests will not be jeopardized in the postwar order, such provisions increase "the likelihood that peace will endure and democratic practices will be embraced."[67]

The experiences of many postwar societies suggest that beyond formally ending the war, power sharing will neither lead to much democracy nor to much peace. To some degree, this can be attributed to the very process of trying to democratize a postwar society, but the power-sharing model also has some important drawbacks.[68] To take the general problem of democratization first: a well-functioning democracy requires the presence of a number of societal and political conditions. First of all, there has to be a minimal level of security. Without that, it will be impossible to achieve free competition among political rivals and the participation of the electorate at the ballot box.[69] A democracy, as Roland Paris successfully has argued, is also dependent on a functioning state apparatus; on a diverse media not dominated by hate speech; on courts and police that can maintain order, uphold basic rules, and manage disputes; and on a civil society that promotes cooperation and cohesion between groups.[70] But a war-torn society usually lack these basic conditions, and democratization can therefore be detrimental to the peace effort. In his study of 11 peacebuilding operations between 1989 and 1998, Paris concludes that democratization worked against the establishment of peace, either by exacerbating societal discord or by reproducing historical patterns of conflict.[71]

One of the reasons for this is that democracy thrives on competition. While this is not a problem for well-established democracies, it is a problem for countries that are conflict prone. Instead of channeling conflict into healthy political competition, democratization has "the potential to stimulate higher levels of societal competition at the very moment (immediately following the conflict) when states are least equipped to contain such tensions within peaceful bounds."[72] Another problem is the holding of elections. Elections, as Benjamin Reilly points out, are often an integral part of contemporary peace agreements. In Namibia, Angola, Cambodia, El Salvador, Mozambique, Liberia, Haiti, Bosnia, Kosovo, and East Timor, elections have been thought to help a country transition from war to peace. The hope is that elections will transform belligerent groups into peaceful political parties, and help set up a legitimate governing authority.[73] Peace builders, as Paris laments, have therefore had a tendency to "portray elections as simply serving the cause of peace."[74] This is a problematic assumption, because elections do not necessarily promote peaceful competition, nor do they necessarily produce governments that are interested in peaceful dispute management and compromise.[75]

Take the case of Bosnia, which at the end of the war emerged as a new country with novel political institutions. The Dayton Peace Accords, brokered under the auspices of the United States, established Bosnia as a parliamentary republic with three "constituent peoples"— Bosniaks, Serbs and Croats—and two entities, the Federation of Bosnia and Herzegovina (the Federation) and Republika Srpska (RS). It also called for a political system with many of the hallmark features of a consociational democracy: executive power sharing, proportionality, veto powers for the constituent groups, and autonomy. The first elections were held in September 1996, less than a year after the signing of the Dayton agreement.[76] If not surprising, the result was nonetheless depressing. There was an enormous amount of nationalistic agitation in the political campaign leading up to the elections. Members of the Serb Democratic Party, for instance, were reported to be campaigning under the slogan "Vote for the Republic of Srpska, vote for peace, vote for Serbhood!"[77] The three nationalist political parties that had dominated the political scene in the years immediately leading up to the war won a large majority of the votes. The elections in the next few years did little to produce moderate candidates. It seemed that the most relevant factor for both the candidates and the voters was ethnic loyalty and not a definite political platform.[78] Commenting on the election results of 1998, the International Crisis Group concluded:

> The results are simply the latest manifestation of a political system which panders to extremists and does not afford Bosnians the luxury of forsaking nationalism. Electors fear living under the ethnic rule of another community and therefore vote for the most robust defense of their own interests, thus sustaining a vicious cycle of fear and insecurity.[79]

The Croat and Serb political parties in particular simply worked to undermine the consolidation of Bosnia's democracy.[80]

Some problems of democratization are more directly related to the power-sharing model itself.[81] The consociational model accepts ethnic difference as both legitimate and permanent.[82] This is reflected especially in the electoral system, where each group can form political parties that represent the specific interests of that group. In its efforts to promote democracy and peace, the international community has generally embraced both ethnic parties and proportional representation. The Organization for Security and Cooperation in Europe (OSCE), for instance, "explicitly affirm[s] the right of ethnic minorities to form their own parties and compete for office on an ethnic basis."[83] And a majority of UN-supported postwar elections—in Namibia, Cambodia, Kosovo, Bosnia, and Iraq, to mention a few examples—have made use of a permissive proportional representation system. But, as Benjamin Reilly notes, in deeply divided societies, this has had "the effect of fragmenting the legislature and encouraging ethnic polarization."[84] When politicians rely on votes only from people in their own ethnic group, the incentive for moderation and cooperation across ethnic groups does not exist. The electoral system has the effect of rewarding ethnic extremism, rather than discouraging it. The result is that "democratization itself can too easily lead to an increase in ethnic tension and, in some cases, the outbreak of ethnic conflict."[85]

Another problem with a power-sharing model is the idea of elite cooperation. For consociational systems to work, elites have to work together to bridge ethnic divisions and stabilize the society. Moderation and willingness to compromise are, as Lijphart notes, prerequisites for consociationalism.[86] But this is a problematic assumption for countries that have been marked by just the opposite, elite conflict. Horowitz holds that the consociational model is simply motivationally inadequate, and argues that no evidence suggests that elites are any more accommodating than their followers. In fact, the opposite might be true.[87]

Again, Bosnia can serve as an illustration. In postwar Bosnia, the three ethnic groups showed little interest in working together. In the period leading up to the elections in 1996, cooperation between the federation and Republika Srpska was virtually nonexistent.[88] This was due not least to the influence of Radovan Karadzic, who remained an important figure in the RS. The Serbian hard-liners refused to implement major provisions in the Dayton accords, such as the return of refugees, and sabotaged cooperation with the central institutions. On February 5, 1996, for instance, the Bosnian government arrested eight Serb soldiers for alleged war crimes. The next day, Serb leaders suspended all contact with the Bosnian government.[89] The assumption that elites are willing to cooperate is especially flawed in a postwar society in which most of the leaders that brought the country to war also are responsible for implementing the peace.[90]

For a power-sharing democracy to succeed, according to Donald Rothchild and Philip Roeder, a number of societal conditions have to be present: ethnic elites have to be able to dominate their respective groups; there has to be a culture of accommodation; leaders have to be sincere about the commitments that they make; the central government and the administrative bureaucracy have to be effective and legitimate; the ethnic groups have to be roughly equal with respect to economic wealth; the demographic composition has to be relatively stable; and there has to be a constructive relationship between internal and external actors.[91] These are unlikely conditions in a post–civil war society. Yet, the fact remains that when former adversaries consider signing on to a peace agreement, they will want to have some guarantee that their interests will be served in the postwar order.[92] Thus, power sharing might be a necessary compromise in order to get to any peace at all.

Possible Solutions—Political Engineering and International Intervention

There are several possible ways to tackle some of the problems that power-sharing democracies face. First, one might try what is sometimes referred to as "political engineering," that is, tweaking the design of the political institutions. The goal is to encourage moderation among political parties and voters, as well as among politicians.[93] In order to achieve this, one can institutionalize electoral incentives for moderation, decentralize in a nonethnic-based way, and encourage the development of nonethnic or multiethnic political parties.[94] To help promote multiethnic parties, one might, for instance, ask that political parties demonstrate a crossethnic or crossregional composition before they participate in elections, or forbid the participation of ethnic parties all together.[95]

A related strategy is to design the electoral system in a way that encourages moderation. One suggestion is so-called vote pooling, where candidates or parties have to rely on the support of voters from other ethnic groups in order to win. One electoral system that encourages vote pooling is the alternative vote (AV) system, which is essentially a majority system that requires the candidate to win an absolute majority of votes. A proportional representation system such as the single transferable vote system can also encourage such pooling.[96] The goal is to reduce ethnic extremism "by making politicians reciprocally dependent on the votes of members of groups other than their own."[97] These measures are based on the assumption that political leaders are rational actors seeking power, and that they will do what it takes to get elected, even if that means having to rely on the votes of people belonging to other ethnic groups.[98]

The jury is still out on how effective these and other similar measures are. Some studies suggest that electoral systems encouraging
vote pooling can produce more moderation.[99] But, as Sisk points
out, "The debate over which electoral system is best is complicated
because electoral system design can be a very technical matter; the
outcomes that flow from a specific choice are highly dependent on
unknowns such as the spatial distribution of votes, shifting party
alignments and interparty pacts, voting behavior, ballot design,
and myriad other variables."[100] Because there are so many variables
that come into play, we cannot predict with complete accuracy
whether a particular solution will work or not. There is no one
solution that will solve the great variety of problems that postwar
societies face.[101] A final problem is that wartime leaders might not
be very interested in supporting measures that require them to
gain support from hostile ethnic groups.[102] If we assume that the
political system is established in negotiations after the war is over,
we have to ask whether political leaders will accept a model that
calls for interethnic cooperation at the ballot box.

Robert Keohane has noted "that people who are in endemic
conflict with one another, and mutually suspicious, are typically
unable to solve the problem of order by themselves [and] from a
human rights perspective, effective rule by an international institution is preferable to Leviathan."[103] This seems to have been the
conclusion of the international community as well. Therefore, the
other main strategy for dealing with the problem of democratic
instability after war has been to establish a peacebuilding operation. Since the end of the Cold War, there have been more than
20 major such operations, in places like Namibia, East Timor,
Bosnia, Kosovo, and Afghanistan.[104] Recognizing that not only
is a democracy dependent on stability, but stability is in part a
function of legitimate political institutions, the main goal of these
operations has increasingly been to help create and strengthen
postwar political institutions.[105]

Part II: Postconflict
Statebuilding Operations

Let me briefly return to the implementation of democracy in postwar
Bosnia, where the first few years after the war proved disheartening
indeed. The first rounds of elections enabled wartime nationalistic

leaders to remain in positions of power, but these leaders showed little interest in the conciliation or cooperation that a genuine political transition would require. Faced with political deadlocks, delays in legislation, inflammatory nationalistic propaganda, and the political manipulation of the media, the international community grew steadily more frustrated. The Peace Implementation Council (PIC) decided to take a more aggressive stance in the implementation of the Dayton accords, and consequently broadened the powers of the Office of the High Representative (OHR) considerably.[106] This office could now decide the "timing, location and chairmanship of meetings of the common institutions," and was given ability to take "interim measures...when parties are unable to reach agreement."[107] These increased powers, often referred to as the "Bonn powers" from the location of where they were adopted late in 1997, came to mean two things in particular: that the High Representative had the power to impose laws and that he could dismiss any public official from office.[108] The OHR repeatedly took advantage of its new authority. From December 1997 to January 2000, for instance, approximately 50 laws were imposed in areas concerning citizenship and state symbols, economic reform, property issues, and judicial reform.[109]

The increased international involvement in Bosnia is emblematic of a shift in international peacebuilding strategies. In the late 1990s and early 2000s, both practitioners and scholars realized that rapid democratization would often not help nurture a stable and lasting peace. Instead, they started to emphasize the need for international involvement in *statebuilding*. This strategy meant that outside peace builders took on a more active role in running the wartorn country. The idea was to rebuild the political system by taking over "some or all governmental powers on a temporary basis."[110]

Postconflict peacebuilding missions, most generally speaking, aim to "strengthen and solidify peace in order to avoid a relapse into conflict."[111] This necessitates a social transformation, as well as an economic and a political transformation. The social transition refers to the change away from destructive communal relationships and toward cooperation and stability. The economic transition refers to a move away from "war-warped accumulation and distribution to equitable, transparent postwar development that in turn reinforces peace."[112] And the political transition consists of a shift away from a wartime belligerent regime to a stable, democratic postwar government. These transformations are naturally interlinked, but statebuilding refers primarily to the political transition. Statebuilding, then, can be seen as a distinct approach to the goal of peacebuilding.[113]

The strategy of statebuilding is founded on the idea that in order for peace to take hold, government institutions have to be "capable, autonomous and legitimate."[114] It is a strategy that directs attention to the machinery of the state and seeks to ensure that institutions like the legislative, the executive, and the courts work well. Statebuilding seeks to build and strengthen legitimate government institutions in wartorn countries.[115]

Peacebuilding missions that take the form of statebuilding constitute by their very nature a substantial and serious intrusion into the domestic affairs of the country in question. These intrusions are ethically problematic. In order to evaluate justice after wars fought over government, we need to understand these contradictions and how to make them less problematic.

Fundamental Contradictions in Statebuilding Operations

At the most fundamental level, statebuilding operations set aside democratic principles in the short run in order to promote a viable and stable democracy in the long run. By taking over core legislative and executive political tasks, they are by their very nature an invasive interference in the domestic affairs of another state. By restricting the political freedom of domestic political actors, they set aside the principle of popular self-determination, which in this context means that each people should "work out *their own* institutions and governance structures."[116] There is a paternalistic component to such missions too, as the international actors assume that they know what is in the best interest of the country in question.[117]

When local political actors are not fully involved in the design and running of political institutions, they are alienated from the process that is vital for the democratic and peaceful future of their country. In the statebuilding literature, this problem is often discussed under the heading of "local ownership." Local ownership refers to the degree of participation and consent of the local population in the process of statebuilding. It is also often defined as the end goal of such missions.[118] Lack of ownership is problematic from both a practical, moral, and legitimacy point of view. The practical problem concerns how local self-government can be promoted when local political groups are excluded from the political process.[119] The moral problem is connected to the intrusive and paternalistic quality to such operations, which in turn can lead to a legitimacy problem. Lack of domestic support for the statebuilding mission can also result in a reversion to violence.[120] Unless the local population has a stake in the creation of new political institutions, the effectiveness and the durability of the political transformation might simply be in jeopardy.[121]

A related problem is that international statebuilding missions are not accountable to the populations that they are trying to help. Accountability, as Richard Caplan points out, "refers to the various norms, practices, and institutions whose purpose is to hold public officials (and other bodies) responsible for their actions and for the outcomes of those actions."[122] Accountability seeks to prevent abuses of power and make sure that those in charge answer to the population they govern. But the local population does not elect the international peace builders and cannot remove them either.[123] In Bosnia, for instance, the OHR and the other international agencies did not answer to the population that they were trying to help, but to the organizations that had appointed them (that is, the Peace Implementation Council, the Council of the European Union, and the North Atlantic Treaty Organization [NATO]).[124] This is problematic. By what authority, we might ask, do outside agencies make political decisions, if the people have not elected them and cannot remove them from office? As the Council of Europe's Parliamentary Assembly observed in the case of Bosnia,

> The scope of the OHR is such that, to all intents and purposes, it constitutes the supreme institution vested with power in Bosnia and Herzegovina. In this connection, the Assembly considers it irreconcilable with democratic principles that the OHR should be able to take enforceable decisions without being accountable for them or obliged to justify their validity and without there being a legal remedy.[125]

Statebuilding missions, in short, are morally problematic because they are paternalistic and intrusive and because they set aside important democratic principles like self-determination, participation and accountability.

Yet, there are good moral reasons for wanting an international agency like the UN to take control of the political reconstruction of a war-torn society. Post–civil war countries are often in a situation of "extreme emergency."[126] The consequences of not trying to stabilize war-torn countries can be nothing short of disastrous, leaving people in lawlessness, fear, and chronic violence. That is not only a problem for the countries in question but also for the international community, because the problems faced by weak or failed states can spread to stable countries as well. As Paris and Sisk point out, "State weakness and state failure are global concerns because of the spillovers, contagious, instabilities, and vitiation of international norms that occurs when authority and order disappear."[127]

It is not difficult then, to offer a broad justification for statebuilding operations. But it matters greatly that the moral dilemmas involved in these operations are understood and explicitly handled. In particular, it is important to consider what it takes to make statebuilding missions morally acceptable in the eyes of the local population, because legitimacy is a core component of the overall success of the mission. The question of legitimacy will naturally depend on specific aspects of the conflict and the peacebuilding mission in question, so here I will point only to a few general norms that might help abate the moral contradictions that these missions entail.

Ways to Abate the Contradictions

In order to create legitimate political institutions, the peacebuilding mission must be disinterested and benefit the population it serves. Such operations should not be undertaken for the advantage of the intervening states or organizations. The economic benefits of peacebuilding missions, and of occupations, must not go to one country in particular. As Walzer has argued, "If resources accumulated for the occupation end up in the hands of foreign companies and local favorites, then the occupation is unjust."[128] That statebuilding missions are regarded as disinterested is not only important for the mission in question, but for how they are viewed more generally by postconflict states. If they are seen as "an imperial project, local actors in postconflict countries that could benefit from international assistance might think twice about inviting or accepting this assistance, and the result might be more cease-fire collapses, renewed fighting and zones of chronic violence."[129]

The problem of legitimacy can to some extent be dealt with by making sure the mission is authorized and carried out as a multilateral operation, whether that is by the UN or some other multinational organization. This minimizes the risk of self-interested interference and "usurpation by powerful states."[130] We have to acknowledge, however, that there can be a trade-off between legitimacy and efficiency. In Iraq, for instance, the United States had enormous resources and a large degree of cohesion, which UN-led operations most often do not have. But lack of legitimacy was clearly a problem in Iraq, and was one of the reasons why the US sought to expand the international involvement in the Coalition Provisional Authority (CPA).[131] The problems connected to statebuilding operations run by the UN are of a different kind. It is limited, as David Harland notes, "by the compromises of its huge membership," and the need to "accommodate a broad spectrum of views and constituencies."[132] On the other hand, the UN's broad international support ensures that problems of legitimacy are less pressing in the operations it is responsible for.

One of the most difficult challenges for an international statebuilding operation is striking the right balance between foreign intrusion and local involvement. Local ownership, as I have pointed out, concerns to the degree to which domestic political groups are involved in the creation and running of their own political institutions.[133] It is worth stating explicitly that these operations would not be necessary if local political actors were capable of running the country in a way that met basic requirements of stability and justice.[134] Statebuilding is a necessary response to the failure of the political system to take care of the fundamental needs and interests of its own population. The handing over of power too early can be destabilizing.[135] That said, the foreign intrusion must not be unnecessarily excessive. Stefano Recchia suggests, therefore, that these missions must be guided by a principle of proportionality of interference. The principle implies that the size of the international presence and the degree of intrusiveness should be carefully measured against the local capacity to govern. As Recchia says,

"Any intrusive measures aimed at redressing a wrongdoing or an undesirable situation ought to be proportional to that wrongdoing or the seriousness of the situation."[136] It is only in severely perilous situations that full-scale international trusteeship is justified. As the country moves away from a highly precarious situation and toward increasing stability, the degree of the international presence must be progressively reduced. And as the local capacity for self-government surfaces, international state builders should gradually retreat.[137] Although very general, this principle reminds us that the goal of these operations must be stability and the capacity for self-government. In order to increase local understanding and popular support of a peacebuilding mission, it is also important that the mission has a clearly defined final outcome as well as subsidiary benchmark goals.[138]

In order to reduce unnecessary intrusiveness and the alienation of the local population, peace builders should encourage processes of consultation.[139] By having regular conversations with political groups and allowing for their input, international peace builders can foster domestic political knowledge and capability as well as promote the legitimacy of the mission as a whole.[140] According to Recchia, consultation with local stakeholders and the broader population is desirable to the greatest extent possible.[141] But this cannot always be the case. International state builders will have difficult choices to make about whom to bring into the political process in this way.[142] There are good reasons, as I will discuss further below, to exclude extremist politicians and hypernationalist parties from the postwar political process. In order not to send the signal that violence pays, it might be especially important to shut out former warring parties. On the other hand, international state builders must seek to prevent the creation of spoilers. Spoilers are "leaders and parties who believe the emerging peace threatens their power, world view, and interests and who use violence to undermine attempts to achieve it."[143] If former wartime leaders enjoy wide-spread popular support, there are good reasons to make sure they are not alienated from the peace process.[144] It is probably impossible to come up with general rules for how to strike the balance between these different considerations. Rather, these trade-offs have to be worked out on a case-by-case basis by international peace builders with extensive local knowledge and political experience.

Finally, there are ways to reduce the accountability problem. In Bosnia, for instance, international administrators had to report to the organizations that mandated their work; the local media acted as a watchdog, albeit an unreliable one; and nongovernmental organizations like the International Crisis Group, the International Institute of Democracy and Electoral Assistance, and Human Rights Watch kept an eye on the international state builders.[145] Another way to increase accountability is through the institution of the ombudsperson. Kosovo is an example in this regard. Any person in Kosovo could file complaints if they felt that the United Nations Mission in Kosovo (UNMIK) had abused its authority or violated human rights.[146]

Part III: Lustrations

In Republika Srpska, one of the two entities in Bosnia-Herzegovina, individuals suspected of being involved in ethnic cleansing, sexual violence, mass murder, and other war crimes during the 1992–1995 war remained in positions of power years after the war was over. They worked in the local police, in the bureaucracy, as town majors, and as representatives in municipal assemblies. After the April 2000 elections to the Bratunac Municipal Council, for instance, seven of the thirteen candidates elected were alleged war criminals.[147] In several cases, individuals who had taken part in ethnic cleansing were in charge of overseeing the return of the very refugees they had driven away. Many of these local officials worked actively against the implementation of the Dayton Peace Accords, and some of them even denied that well-documented war crimes, such as the massacre in Srebrenica, had ever happened.[148]

A number of countries have in one way or another used lustrations to promote the transition from war to peace, or from a repressive regime to a democratic one. These measures have also become a common feature of postwar occupations and of international peacebuilding operations.[149] Most famously, perhaps, Germany underwent a process of denazification after the Second World War. It was a policy initiated by the Allied powers for the purpose of completely eradicating the influence of Nazi policies and ideas in postwar Germany.[150] After the Cold War ended, a number of the eastern European countries went through a process of purging people who had collaborated with or worked for the former communist regimes.[151] More recently, in Iraq, the CPA called for the de-Baathification of Iraqi society.[152] The CPA recognized "that the Iraqi people have suffered large scale human rights abuses and deprivation over many years at the hands of the Baath Party," and declared that full members of the Baath Party would be "removed from their positions and banned from future employment in the public sector."[153] It was estimated that the US Office of Reconstruction and Humanitarian Assistance would forbid 15,000 to 30,000 former Baath party members from joining future Iraqi governments or holding other public positions.[154] Later, de-Baathification was expanded to include people who "had committed or incited violence against the coalition forces," and people who were "reasonably suspected of having committed, participated in, ordered, or permitted war crimes, genocide, crimes against humanity, atrocities, or gross violations of human rights."[155]

On a number of occasions, the High Representative in Bosnia sought to help the implementation of the Dayton accords by removing elected politicians from power. For instance, Wolfgang Petritsch, the High Representative from 1999 to 2002, dismissed 66 officials because they were seen to obstruct the implementation of the peace agreement. Political parties, like the Bosnian wing of the Serb Radical Party (SRS), were also prevented from taking part in the political process.[156] In addition, Bosnia saw two comprehensive vetting processes. During the war, police officers had served as soldiers and took part in ethnic cleansing together with military and paramilitary forces. Rather than giving people a sense of security, Bosnian "police forces continued to discriminate against, harass and intimidate citizens who were not of their own ethnicity."[157] Between 1999 and 2002, the United Nations Mission in Bosnia and Herzegovina (UNMIBH), which was in charge of police reform, screened about 24,000 police officers in order to weed out those suspected of being involved in wartime violations. The screening sought to make sure the police met "international standards of professional and personal integrity."[158] When the screening was over, about one-third of the officers had been prohibited from serving in law enforcement.[159] And between 2002 and 2004, about one thousand judges and prosecutors were screened for wartime activities in order to make the judicial and prosecutorial services more competent and ethnically diverse.[160]

This practice, which I will here primarily call "lustration," but which is also referred to as purges, vetting, screening, administrative justice, and disqualifications, aims essentially at purifying state institutions.[161] The practice of lustration tries to draw a line between the state of war and the state of peace, and between an old regime and the new one. Lustration consists of screening people for jobs in the public sector, preventing them from taking up positions in the public sector, and removing people from positions they already hold.[162] It is a practice that suspends an individual's right to participate in the political decision-making process and to work in the government. Thus, it violates the right to participation—the right each individual has to run for elected positions and to occupy appointed places of power in the government.[163] Lustrations might also infringe on basic principles of the rule of law, such as the right a person has to be presumed innocent until proven guilty, and to have one's case heard in an impartial court of law.[164] By precluding people from taking up certain positions, or removing them from office, lustration violates the internationally recognized right to work.[165]

How, then, can lustrations be justified, and what principles should govern this practice? The first thing to note is that any attempt to assess the moral acceptability of lustrations has to take into account the differences in how such lustrations have been carried out. These differences relate to the targets of lustration, what type of conduct the lustrations aim to screen for, the design and scope of the lustration process, the timing and duration of it, the justification for it, the sanctions applied to lustration subjects, and how lustration relates to other transitional justice measures.[166] As I will discuss further below, there is an important moral difference between a process that aims to screen individuals for public-sector jobs and purges that summarily exclude people on the basis of membership in a political party or some other group.[167]

In looking at the underlying justification for lustrations, I make a distinction between backward-looking reasons and forward-looking reasons.[168] The backward-looking justification sees lustration as a form of punishment, while forward-looking reasons see lustration as a way to build trust, democracy, and stability in a transitional phase.

Lustration as a Punitive Measure

There is a clear punitive dimension to lustration practices. It violates the principle of participation which gives citizens the right to take part in the political process and work in the public sector.[169] By preventing a person from running for office or working in the public sector, lustrations infringes on rights that ought to be fundamental to any political system. Furthermore, as Pablo de Greiff points out, losing a job and an income is in itself a penalty.[170] In a postconflict society where the economy most often is in crisis and where it is difficult to find alternative employment, the loss of a job can be a harsh punishment. Lustrations, especially when made public, can also be seen as a shaming public condemnation.[171]

While lustrations are punitive sanctions, and in that sense resemble criminal justice, they do not rely on a judicial process.[172] Being a form of administrative justice, lustrations will almost inevitably violate important principles of the rule of law. The rule of law—at least in its formal conception—concerns primarily how the law is enforced and applied.[173] The precept "treat like cases alike" asks that cases that are the same in legally relevant ways also should also be judged the same way.[174] The rule of law also implies that defendants should receive an open and fair trial; that the legal process should seek to establish the truth about the alleged offense; that the defendant has a right to a lawyer; and that laws should be applied in the correct way by unbiased and impartial judges. There is also the presumption that a person is innocent unless proven otherwise. The rule of law, as Rawls points out, requires some degree of due process.[175]

There are clear problems connected with lustrations from a rule of law point of view. Administrative sanctions cannot take into account individual considerations such as degrees of guilt or mitigating circumstances. In the legal system, it is common to make a distinction between degrees of seriousness of the crime—the more serious the crime, the harsher the punishment. Lustrations, on the other hand, mete out the same punishment for crimes that may vary substantially in content and severity. Furthermore, such sanctions cannot accommodate the fact that there might be mitigating circumstances. In the absence of individual trials one cannot probe into the reasons why, and the circumstances under which, the wrongful acts were committed.[176] A related problem is that lustrations are often based on membership in organizations. The Provisional Authority in Iraq decided that every member of the previously ruling Baath party should be barred from political participation. The problem with this is obvious. It does not allow for the individual determination of guilt but establishes it instead by association to a political group or party. Thus, it is a form of punishment that is "overinclusive" because the "category of individuals actually stigmatized or otherwise treated as criminal would include some who could successfully defend themselves, if given the chance to do so."[177]

Because lustrations risk ascribing guilt by association and punishing innocent people, many scholars and human rights activists have rejected them as an appropriate form of punishment. Federico Andrau-Guzmán argues that the principle of individual responsibility cannot be ignored when the vetting procedures target conduct that can be described as criminal.[178] And according to Roman Boed, as "long as lustration is an administrative measure, not one relying on criminal procedure, it could not be justifiably endowed with the role of identifying the guilty and punishing them, through the loss of a job or otherwise."[179]

In an ideal world we would want individuals suspected of war crimes and other human-rights violations tried in front of a court of law. However, for postconflict societies the legal option is often nonexistent or very limited. Criminal proceedings through international courts will likely abide by the principles of the rule of law, but these tribunals can only handle a small percentage of the cases. The International Criminal Tribunal for the Former Yugoslavia (ICTY) illustrates the problem. Initially marred by a lack of funds, organization, and staff, it took several years before the ICTY was in full operation. The ICTY had by 1999 over 700 employees, which in 2006 had grown to over 1,100. Yet, in the first six years of operation, the ICTY only tried 6 offenders. By 2006, the ICTY had put 51 offenders on trial and indicted a total of 161 people.[180] International courts inevitably have to focus on the most serious violations which means ignoring defendants at lower levels.[181] National legal systems, which often are heavily politicized and which lack legal expertise and resources, cannot necessarily solve this capacity problem in a way that upholds the rule of law. Postconflict societies are simply ill-equipped to handle the challenge of large-scale criminal trials.

Lustrations can be seen as a way to avoid the problem of mass impunity and delayed justice. Whether lustrations are an appropriate form of punishment, I would argue, depends to a large degree on how they are carried out. Take the example of police reform in Bosnia. During the war, many police officers, as I have mentioned, were intimately involved in the war effort and committed a number of atrocities, including establishing and running concentration camps, conducting illegal arrests, and killing and torturing civilians.[182] When UNMIBH sought to reform the police in Bosnia, they established a three-step process.[183] First, all personnel in the law-enforcement sector had to register with UNMIBH. Secondly, all of those who had registered went though an initial screening to get a provisional authorization. This screening sought to make sure that the person met certain requirements with respect to age, education, and citizenship. If a person had a criminal record or were indicted, he or she would not receive provisional authorization.[184] The finally step was to perform extensive background checks on the people who had received the provisional authorization. Offenses that would result in exclusion included evidence of serious breaches of law or duty, violations of property laws, and acts during the war "which demonstrate the inability or unwillingness to uphold internationally recognized human rights standards."[185] In order to make judgments, UNMIBH made use of data compiled by the ICTY, statements of victims and witnesses, and information provided by nongovernmental organizations, as well as the data provided by the certification subjects themselves.[186] If "reasonable, rounded suspicion of criminal liability" was found, the officer would be deauthorized.[187] Among those deauthorized were police officers who had served as concentration camp guards and officers during the war. Merely by having held such positions, UNMIBH assumed that there was enough ground to suspect that the officers had committed serious human rights violations.[188] Deauthorized police officers were not allowed to have their case heard or to defend themselves, and the possibility to appeal a decision was limited.[189]

Ideally, one would want any punitive sanctions to observe fundamental legal principles like individual hearings. The lack of these in Bosnia led senior officials in the Ministry of Interior and union representatives to argue that deauthorized police officers had not been fairly treated.[190] But there are ways to mitigate some of the negative consequences that lack of due process implies. According to the United Nations Secretary-General, lustrations should be conducted with some basic procedural guarantees: individuals must be informed that they are under investigation, be notified of the allegations against them, be given an opportunity to respond, as well as have the right to appeal the decision.[191] This latter demand, that individuals are given the opportunity to appeal a vetting decision, seem particularly important because it makes it possible for a person who has been wrongfully charged to have the decision overturned.[192]

Lustrations can be an acceptable way to deal with the problem of past crimes in the nonideal situation in which a war-torn society usually finds itself. It might be necessary to accept some modifications of rule of law principles as a way to deal with the impunity problem. It seems a greater injustice that a large group of war criminals are not punishment than that some are unfairly punished, especially if it is possible for individuals to appeal the decision. As Gregory L. Naarden concludes, the vetting of police officers in Bosnia "represented a balancing between the purging of violators and the making of fair, accurate determinations."[193]

Lustration and Political Legitimacy

Many countries face the challenge of, on the one hand, dealing with a violent or repressive past and, on the other hand, establishing a viable and legitimate democracy. How, one might ask, can a political system emerging from a devastating war enjoy legitimacy if people responsible for atrocities during the war are still in positions of power? It has been argued that the way in which the new regime deals with former crimes and abuses has an important impact on the degree to which the new political order will be regarded as legitimate.[194] This is the forward-looking element of lustration, which sees it as a way to effect a political transformation.[195] Should we accept lustrations as a forward-looking measure? There are several reasons for doing so, although much will depend, again, on how lustrations are carried out.

Lustrations are important because they provide a symbolic and actual break with the past. Administrative lustration, as Arthur Stinchcombe points out, draws a boundary between people connected to the old regime and those who are to establish the new one.[196] If a regime does nothing about past crimes, it seems to send the message that human rights violations and war crimes are tolerated. This might undermine the trust that people have in political institutions. As Neil J. Kritz asks with respect to Bosnia, "What confidence can returning refugees be expected to have in the new order if the current mayor personally helped torch their homes in the campaign of ethnic cleansing?"[197]

A related concern is that if wartime leaders are allowed to continue in positions of power after the war, they might seek to cover up or deny the crimes of the war. This was a problem in Bosnia, where politicians in Republika Srpska for a long time denied that well-documented war crimes had happened. For instance, it was not until five years after the war that a high-ranking official in Republika Srpska officially acknowledged that a genocide had been perpetrated in Srebrenica.[198] Because former war criminals are unlikely to admit to or publicly denounce their own crimes, it is also unlikely that the truth about what has happened will be officially acknowledged. This brings up the point that lustration is one out of several transitional justice measures that a country emerging from war can make use of. Other alternatives include granting a general amnesty; bringing out the truth about what happened through an investigatory committee or a truth commission; holding perpetrators accountable by legally prosecuting them in a national or international court; and compensating the victims.[199] Lustrations and vetting procedures are related to these other measure in important ways. If war criminals continue to occupy positions in the public administration, it might be difficult to initiate other transitional justice measures, such as criminal prosecutions and truth telling.[200]

Whether or not lustrations promote legitimacy is in the end an empirical question. It has to be investigated, not assumed. According to a report by the United Nations Secretary-General, if vettings "are seen to function fairly, effectively and in accordance with international human rights standards, they can play an important role in enhancing the legitimacy of official structures, restoring the confidence of the public and building the rule of law."[201] I pointed above to some of the ways in which the fairness of such measures can be improved. Let me here then focus on some pitfalls. One problem is that those who are removed may seek to undermine the new regime. As Claus Offe points out, "Dismissals may provoke hostile attitudes on the part of those affected by such measures, leading to acts of sabotage, revenge, obstruction, resentment and conspiracies on their part."[202] This might be a particular problem in deeply divided countries. If one ethnic group was more at fault for the war than the others, or was responsible for a larger share of war crimes, lustrations might be interpreted as acts of hostility and revenge.[203]

A policy of lustrations can also mean that people with important expertise is removed. As Offe argues, "Countries which rely extensively on disqualification may deprive themselves of significant portions of the managerial and administrative manpower and talent that they depend upon in the process of economic reconstruction."[204] The debate over de-Baathification in Iraq can provide an example. Although it was admitted that this process would make the running of government less efficient, US officials argued that "that is the price we're willing to pay."[205] But the policy of de-Baathification was soon criticized by politicians, military personnel, and administrators, both in the United States and in Iraq, for shutting "out the skilled technocrats and intellectuals."[206] UN envoy Lakhdar Brahimi made the point in the following way:

> It is difficult to understand that thousands upon thousands of teachers, university professors, medical doctors and hospital staff, engineers and other professionals who are sorely needed, have been dismissed within the debaathification process.[207]

A spokesman for the coalition, Dan Senor, later admitted that the policy of de-Baathification was taken too far. He argued that the policy sometimes had excluded "innocent, capable people who were Baathist in name only from playing a role in reconstructing Iraq."[208] For this reason, the policy of barring former Baath party members was later relaxed.

There are good reasons to think that lustrations can help promote postwar legitimacy. By removing people closely associated with the violent past, such measures help create a symbolic break between the wartime and the peacetime regimes. But lustrations will not have the intended effect if they are seen as a form of victor's justice or if they remove large groups of people with needed expertise. Making a clean break with the past will not automatically facilitate a new, legitimate order.

Conclusion

We cannot find the answer to how wars fought over government should end in judgments about how the war started or how it was fought. *Jus ad bellum* and *jus in bello* considerations have little to contribute to our understanding of postwar justice in these types of conflicts. Instead we must seek answers in political theories of democracy, and in judgments about how a legitimate and stable postwar order is to be created. But even with a solid footing in democratic political theory, the contradictions involved in the democratization of postwar societies abound. Some type of power-sharing system is most likely to be accepted by belligerents who consider putting down their weapons. They want to secure a place in the postwar order. But a country marked by conflict and distrust does not provide fertile ground for such a democratic system, as it relies heavily on the cooperation among political elites. And while elections are necessary in order to establish a postwar regime, they can increase discord if they are held too soon.

International statebuilding missions might solve the problem of stability, but only by setting aside democratic rights and principles. Even as a temporary measure, this is problematic. Some of the most troublesome aspects of these statebuilding missions can be reduced, however, especially through multilateralism and the principles of proportionate intrusion. Consulting with local political groups and establishing different types of accountability mechanisms go some way toward abating the dilemmas that such missions inevitably pose. Lustration practices, which withdraw an individual's rights to participate in the political system and to work in the public sector, are often necessary in order to mark a new beginning and promote political legitimacy. But if carried out the wrong way, such measures might undermine the new order too. In order to minimize some of the most problems related to lustration, we must as a minimum limit their scope and build in room for appeals.

In well-established democracies, as numerous studies have pointed out, the goal of peace and the goal of democracy seem to be mutually reinforcing. But in postwar societies, uniting peace and justice is complicated indeed.

CONCLUSION

In thinking about *post bellum* justice there are no giants on whose shoulders to stand. The absence of an intellectual tradition is especially striking when compared to the resources available to us if we contemplate *ad bellum* and *in bello* justice. Encompassing scholars who wrote in sharply different historical circumstances and from widely different philosophical points of view—think, for instance, of all that separates Saint Augustine, Hugo Grotius, and Michael Walzer—the just war tradition is immensely useful. It helps us to ask the right questions about justified warfare and provides an abundance of concepts, opinions, and principles on which to draw. The framework offers a set of moral and prudential criteria by which wars must be judged, and even if people in the tradition end up with substantially different views about, for instance, what constitutes a just cause, they agree on the importance of the just cause criterion. *Post bellum* discussions have no comparable body of thought to turn to. To be sure, thinkers like Francisco de Vitoria, Grotius, and John Locke have not ignored the question of postwar justice completely.[1] And, as I noted in the introduction, during the last decade there has been something of an explosion of interest in the topic. But for *post bellum* discussions, there is still nothing comparable to the just war tradition—there is no historical consensus about the scope of *jus post bellum*, about what the most important issues at the end of war are, or about how we should go about addressing them. Especially by comparison with *ad bellum* and *in bello* discussions, it seems that *post bellum* discussions have to start from scratch.

In the absence of a shared framework for thinking about justice after war, the way we make our way into this subject—what questions we ask and how we conceive of the answers—will inevitably be colored by specific historical cases. Say, for instance, that we start to think of *jus post bellum* in terms of the Gulf War. When Iraq invaded Kuwait in August 1990, it crossed a well-established international border, and so committed the paradigmatic act of aggression. An international coalition led by the United States sought to push Iraq back out of Kuwait and quickly succeeded. By all accounts, the war ended with a just peace: the aggression was reversed, and international borders were restored. In this case of international aggression, justice was done when the *status quo ante bellum* was restored. *Jus post bellum* appeared to be a mirror image of the just cause criterion, in particular. But this type of war is the exception, not the rule. It is rare indeed for a war to begin with one state crossing an established international boundary in an attempt to take control of another state's territory. Common instead are intrastate wars fought, for instance, over regime type, or wars over statehood and independence.

The 2003 invasion of Iraq brings other questions to the fore, as well as the need to seek their answers in places other than *ad bellum* considerations alone. Although there were good reasons for wanting Saddam Hussein removed from power, the 2003 US-led invasion lacked a clear just cause. When the war succeeded in removing him from power, there was certainly no returning to the *status quo ante bellum*. Instead the questions revolved around postwar reconstruction and occupation. What responsibility did the victorious United States now have for getting Iraq back on its feet? More generally, what rights and obligations fall to an occupying power? What type of political system should the postwar order be built on? What principles should govern this type of statebuilding operation? And how should one deal with the remnants of the former regime? Closely related to these was the question of how to achieve postwar stability in a country fragmented by hostile population groups, who became increasingly hostile, in turn, to the foreign presence. The answers to these questions seems far more difficult to extract from the concepts and ideas of the just war tradition.

The wars in the former Yugoslavia also raised the question of the role and responsibility of outside states, albeit in a different way. Western states were implicated as bystanders, as peacekeepers and mediators, but not until the very end, when the North Atlantic Treaty Organization (NATO) bombed Bosnian Serb positions, were they involved in the war as active participants. One of the most pressing questions for the international community in this war was what kind of peace deal it should work for, especially in Bosnia. The mediators involved in trying to find a solution—among them Cyrus Vance, David Owen, Thorvald Stoltenberg, Peter Galbraith, and Richard Holbrooke—all wrestled with the question of how to come up with an agreement that was both morally acceptable and likely to be accepted by adversaries who had very different visions of Bosnia's future. A foundational question concerned the configuration of the Bosnian state itself. Could outsiders endorse the Bosnian Serbs' wish for partition? If not, how should the substate borders be drawn? Did some towns, like Sarajevo and Srebrenica, belong to one ethnic group in particular? The negotiations over the map were among the most explosive and stickiest issues during this process. And then there was the question of the political system. What type of democracy would be best for Bosnia, divided as it had now become between hostile ethnic groups and by the events of a terrible war? What peace terms, in the end, would be morally acceptable?

The wars in the former Yugoslavia did much to color my own way into the topic of postwar justice. Some of the Serbian aggression in Bosnia and Croatia defied fundamental principles of humanity. The warfare waged by Bosnian Croatians was hardly better. Like so many postwar countries, Bosnia brought into relief the question of how to build peace in a country that has been brutally ravaged by war. How can we provide justice for the victims of aggression, ethnic cleansing, and genocide? How can reconciliation be fostered? And how can we make sure that those who were driven from their homes during the war can return to them in safety? Although I have not discussed these concerns in any detail in this book, questions of restitution, punishment, and compensation are clearly a core component of postwar justice.

The wars in the former Yugoslavia also brought up basic questions about statehood, territory, and government. When does a national group have a strong claim to independence, and what is a solid territorial claim? And what types of political institutions are best for a war-torn society divided between hostile population groups? Alongside questions of justice, and what justice meant at the end of this war, there was the question of stability and how to achieve it. Neither value could be ignored or subordinated to the other. For outside peacebuilders, the question was how to restrict democratic rights in the short run in order to build a solid foundation for a stable democracy. Few answers to the questions this war posed and created could be found in the prewar order. A return to prewar Yugoslavia was flatly impossible. Instead, the starting point for any of these judgments, I have argued, must first be sought in political theories of statehood and secession, in theories of territorial rights, and in democratic theory.

Jus ad Bellum, Jus in Bello, and Jus post Bellum

It is common in the just war tradition to see *jus ad bellum* as a category distinct from the category of *jus in bello*. As Walzer has argued, these two kinds of judgments are logically independent.[2] The *jus in bello* criteria require that the warfare distinguish between combatants and noncombatants and be proportionate. These demands apply regardless of whether the adversaries met the previous *ad bellum* requirements. A war might be just from the point of view of *jus ad bellum*, but be fought in blatant violation of the laws of war. And conversely, a war can be undertaken for the wrong reasons and therefore be unjust, but still be fought in accordance with *jus in bello*.

Throughout this book I have suggested that a judgment of *post bellum* justice is distinct from our judgment of *ad bellum* and *in bello* justice. The final stage of the war must, at least initially, be judged on its own merits, independent of the way the war came about and how it was fought. When we judge whether a war is justified, we ask not only questions about just cause, right intention, and right authority, but also whether the war can achieve its desired aim. Even with a just cause, a belligerent should not go to war if that cause can be achieved by other, less violent means, or if there is little hope of succeeding. To go to war without a reasonable hope of success not only wastes military power, but unnecessarily put soldiers and civilians in harm's way. Given the destruction and trauma that inevitably follows in war's path, a war should only be begun when it both seeks to redress grave injury and might actually succeed in doing so.

Once the war has been fought, our focus must shift. Now we must look ahead, and ask what the best outcome is, both in terms of justice and in terms of stability. We want to avoid a return to the situation that led to the conflict in the first place. Some injustices are not large enough to justify a war, but once the war is fought, we might nonetheless seek to redress them. Say an adversary had a just cause for going to war, but should have refrained because there was little chance that the war would succeed in that cause. That state of affairs would have made it wrong to initiate a war. But if at the end of the war there is a chance to redress that injury, then we should take it, according to my argument. The end of the war can be an opportunity to set things right, and it would be wrong not to do so.

There will be cases where our judgment of how the war should end will correspond with our judgment of whether it was justified. Sometimes postwar justice will, at least in part, consist of establishing the *status quo ante bellum*. I have argued, for instance, that the *status quo ante bellum* was the right outcome to the territorial conflict over the Falkland Islands. But it was the right outcome not only because Argentina was fighting an aggressive war and England was fighting a defensive war. It was the right outcome because England had a solid territorial claim to the islands, and because considerations about stability argue for upholding long-standing and well-established boundaries. In other cases, the *status quo* is either impossible to achieve or glaringly undesirable. When that is the case, we can only answer the question of what justice requires by looking at the issues over which the war was fought, and how best they can be solved.

I am not suggesting that the questions asked by the just war tradition are entirely different from the questions raised at the end of war. For instance, just war discussions of just authority and theories of secession both examine the relationship between a population and its government. Theories of secession, as I showed in chapter 3, ask when a state or a government no longer can be said to have the rightful authority to govern a population group. For just war scholars, the question of right authority concerns both to whom it is that the right of going to war belongs and how that right can be justified. Here, too, the question arises of when a government is the rightful representative of a population. Or to take another example: when just war scholars examine the question of just cause, they ask what values are worth fighting a war for. That question is, of course, not unrelated to the question of what the values are upon which we should build the postwar order. There are clear connections, then, between *ad bellum* and *post bellum* judgments, but these two types of judgments are also different in important respects.

One might worry that my argument implicitly rewards aggression. I have argued, for instance, that a secessionist group should only go to war if it is the subject of severe and systematic human-rights violations. A democratically expressed desire for statehood is not a just cause of war. Yet, such democratically expressed preferences are not irrelevant once we judge the end of war. There are grievances that do not justify war, but that should be redressed at its end. But if we, at the end of war, argue that justice demands securing the goals for which an unjust war was fought, are we then implicitly condoning aggression? I think not, for the following reasons.

The crimes of aggression and unjust warfare lie with political leaders and military officers. These crimes must be punished, but not by denying the civilian population what they have a justified claim to. We should punish aggression by putting those responsible for the aggression on trial, and not the population for which they claim to speak. This position is complicated, of course, by wars where aggressive leaders enjoy a large degree of popular support. But even in these cases we cannot reasonably deprive a population of essential rights as a way to punish the aggression of its leaders. Because we want to avoid a reversion to war, it is to be hoped that the rights and privileges established by the postwar order are not merely a temporary arrangement. Given the hoped-for permanence of peace, we should not mete out collective punishment for the leaders' crimes, but rather build the postwar order on people's legitimate claims and interests.

Given the destruction and suffering that always accompany war, we want to discourage its inception. That is why the bar for justified war is set high. There are a number of injustices that we want to eliminate—indeed, we will often have a moral responsibility to get rid of them. But not many of these injustices justify war. Yet, I have argued that we want the war to end with a more just order than the one that existed before the war. Exactly because we want to avoid the return to war, we must try to reduce the number of wrongs that can undermine future stability. At the end of war, our concern must be to lay the building blocks of a legitimate and just postwar order.

Peace or Justice Revisited

Throughout this book I have tried to show that the relationship between peace and justice is not always conflictual. A minimum degree of justice is often a prerequisite for peace. Unfairness and grievances lead to discontent, conflict, and violence. The reverse is also true: a minimum level of security, for example, is plainly necessary if we are to carry out key democratic practices like elections. I am not arguing that the goals of peace and justice are invariably intermeshed, or even that they are almost always compatible. Peace and justice are not two faces of a single good. They are, however, two values that prove much easier to support than to undermine one another.

That said, there will be those difficult cases in which peace and justice do seem to clash. So let me close by returning to a concern I introduced in the beginning of this book. The worry was that if we focus too much on justice at the end of war, we might reject an acceptable, if not a just, peace, and thereby produce more war and more suffering. My argument should not be taken to mean that I am against compromises for peace, even if they imply compromising over important principles of justice. Seeking the best can mean turning down the good, which in itself can be an injustice. Therefore, as Avishai Margalit notes, "peace can be justified without being just."[3] There will be cases, most likely many cases, where we should accept peace terms that are far from ideal but have the great advantage of ending the war.

The question is actually not only whether we should sacrifice peace for the sake of justice, but also whether we should sometimes sacrifice peace for the sake of a stabler peace. The following can serve as an illustration. In the days leading up to Operation Storm, the large-scale military operation launched by the Croatian military to take control of the Krajina, the American ambassador to Croatia, Peter Galbraith, finally secured an agreement with Croatian Serb leaders. At a meeting in Belgrade two days before the offensive, Galbraith convinced Milan Babic, the President of the Serb Krajina Republic, to accept the key provisions in the Z-4 plan. The plan implied that Krajina would be reintegrated into Croatia and that Serb forces would have to withdraw from the town of Bihac.[4] This was a major concession on the part of the Bosnian Serbs. Babic was under great pressure. He knew that Operation Storm was about to be launched by the Croatian military forces, and he had more to lose by not agreeing than by agreeing. Yet, while the deal gave Croatia much of what it had sought in earlier negotiations, the Croatian leadership did not want it any longer. Instead they wanted settle the issue by a military victory.

Key American diplomats, like Richard Holbrooke, had much sympathy with the Croatians' desire to beat the Serbs on the battleground. The Croatian Serb leaders had time and time again proven to be temperamental and unreliable. There was little reason to assume that they would be true partners in peace. It was also broadly assumed that in order to bring about a realistic prospect for a negotiated peace in Bosnia, any impression of Serb invincibility had to be shattered.[5] That was why President Clinton said after Operation Storm that he was hopeful it would "turn out to be something that will give us an avenue to a quick diplomatic solution."[6] The NATO air strikes during the next couple of months, along with a joint Croatian and Bosnian military offensive against Bosnian Serb territorial holdings, pushed the Serbs into an even weaker position. It was against the background of these defeats that the negotiators in Dayton succeeded in getting the parties to sign a peace agreement.

Here, then, was a situation where a peace deal was turned down, in part at least, for the sake of a stabler peace. But as I discussed in chapter 4, this stability came at a terrible cost. Most of the Serbian civilians fled the Krajina as the military operations started, but those who stayed were badly mistreated, if not killed, and empty homes were looted and burned down. These war crimes made the return of the Krajina Serbs improbable, as did the words and actions of the Croatian political leadership, which after the war worked against such return.[7] Coming to a judgment in a case like this is also made harder by the impossibility of knowing what would have happened if the Croatian military had accepted the peace deal that Galbraith negotiated. It requires not only that we weigh the good that refusing the peace brought against the harm that it wrought, but also that we take into consideration what would have happened if the peace had been accepted. There are no simple theoretical answers to these sorts of problems.

So what compromises of justice should we be willing to accept for the sake of peace? Margalit argues that a truly rotten compromise—one that we always will be obliged to avoid—is "an agreement to establish or maintain an inhuman regime." Inhuman regimes are cruel, barbarous, and humiliating, and for that reason they define the limits of compromise.[8] Fortunately, in the world of peace negotiations it hardly ever comes to this. Instead mediators try to secure a set of peace terms that are as unproblematic as possible and that will also be acceptable to the parties. Let me pose the question a bit differently, then: what issues should we feel most worried about compromising on? Some of the issues I have discussed lend themselves more readily to compromise than others.

The principles we should be most reluctant to bargain with are those established by democratic institutions and participatory rights. The set of rights that form a core part of any true democracy—the right to vote, the right to assemble, freedom of association, and rights to participate in the political process more broadly—are at the core of justice, too. We should be very careful about signing a deal that means people will be stripped of those kinds of political influence, because they protect fundamental values such as equality and liberty. We have to make sure we are not agreeing to a deal that leads, with something like inevitability, to systematic repression. It is easier to make compromises for the sake of peace over the other two issues I have discussed. In both cases there might be good alternatives. Some form of autonomy or decentralization can meet many of the legitimate concerns that a secessionist group may have. In most instances a degree of self-determination will not require independent statehood. That said, we should be very reluctant to compromise on this question, if the secessionist group will be systematically oppressed and discriminated against in the larger state. The alternative to the full set of rights of territorial sovereignty is a right to reside. In many conflicts, guaranteeing this right will go some way toward meeting the legitimate territorial claims of a group. But we should hesitate to make concessions on territorial issues if the proposed outcome would permanently block a group's access to a culturally and historically important territory.

There are many concessions we should accept for the sake of peace. War always brings about suffering and destruction, but as the just war tradition reminds us, there are situations where war is justified and even required. That also means that some peace terms are simply too unjust to be acceptable. As desirable as peace is, it can come at a cost that is too high. It is a good thing, then, that the values of peace and justice rarely collide in such devastating ways, but more often mutually reinforce and strengthen each other.

NOTES

1 INTRODUCTION

1. B. H. Liddell Hart, *Strategy*. 2nd rev. ed. (New York: Meridian, 1991), 338; Michael Walzer, *Just and Unjust Wars: A Moral Argument with Historical Illustrations*, 3rd ed. (New York: Basic Books, 1977), 121.
2. Because I am interested in a war's issue, I do not look specifically at either peace agreements or post-war constitutions. A war's issue can be settled even if it is not the result of an agreement between the adversaries or specified in an agreed upon text. In my understanding, the secessionist issue involved in the war in Sri Lanka, for instance, was settled (at least temporarily) when the government forces defeated the Tamil Tigers.
3. For a discussion of the Peel Plan, see Ahron Bregman, *A History of Israel* (Basingstoke, UK: Palgrave Macmillan, 2003), 29–31.
4. Ibid., 30–31.
5. Yossi Beilin, "Just Peace: A Dangerous Objective," in *What Is a Just Peace?*, ed. Pierre Allan and Alexis Keller (New York: Oxford University Press, 2006), 143.
6. Ibid., 148.
7. In fact, Beilin's argument rests on some wobbly counterfactual reasoning. It is by no means clear, for instance, that an Israeli state established according to the Peel Plan would not have gone to war to expand its territory and that a similar refugee catastrophe as the one in 1948 would then have occurred. In fact, many of the Jewish politicians who agreed to the Peel Plan considered it a temporary first step towards an expanded Israeli state. Bregman, *A History of Israel*, 30.
8. Anonymous, "Human Rights in Peace Negotiations," *Human Rights Quarterly* 18, no. 2 (1996): 258. See also, Roy Licklider, "Ethical Advice: Conflict Management vs. Human Rights in Ending Civil Wars," *Journal of Human Rights* 7, no. 4 (2008): 376–387.

9. See, for instance, I. William Zartman et al., "Negotiations as a Search for Justice," *International Negotiation* 1, no. 1 (1996): 79–98.

10. Bregman, *A History of Israel*, 29.

11. Monica Duffy Toft, *Securing the Peace: The Durable Settlement of Civil Wars* (Princeton: Princeton University Press, 2010), 5–6.

12. Christine Bell, *On the Law of Peace: Peace Agreements and the Lex Pacificatoria* (Oxford: Oxford University Press, 2008), 5.

13. Donald M. Snow, *Uncivil Wars: International Security and the New Internal Conflicts* (Boulder, CO: Lynne Rienner Publishers, 1996), 25. The best translation of Clausewitz's *On War* remains Carl von Clausewitz, *On War*, ed. Michael Howard and Peter Paret, trans. Michael Howard and Peter Paret (Princeton: Princeton University Press, 1976). Donald Snow argues, however, that many recent civil wars cannot be characterized in this way, because the belligerents seem to lack the desire to achieve clearly defined political goals, and because the warfare is conducted in a vicious and uncontrolled way. See, Snow, *Uncivil Wars: International Security and the New Internal Conflicts*, 1–2. My conceptualization of war, and of peace, will have little to say about such wars. I believe, however, that for most wars it is possible to detect a genuine political disagreement, even if the war itself is fought, at least in part, by people who do not have a clear political objective.

14. Adam Roberts, "Just Peace: A Cause Worth Fighting For," in *What Is a Just Peace?* ed. Pierre Allan and Alexis Keller (Oxford: Oxford University Press, 2006), 59. As Adam Roberts points out, "there is real strength in the liberal position as expressed by Hedley Bull, that 'order in international relations is best preserved by meeting the demands for justice, and that justice is best realized in a context of order.'" Quoting a lecture given by Hedley Bull at the University of Waterloo, Ontario, in 1983, reprinted in Kai Alderson and Andrew Hurrell, eds., *Hedley Bull on International Society* (Basingstoke, UK: Macmillan, 2000), 227; Roberts, "Just Peace: A Cause Worth Fighitng For," 60.

15. Kalevi J. Holsti, *Peace and War: Armed Conflicts and International Order 1648–1989* (Cambridge: Cambridge University Press, 1991), 341.

16. For a collection of a number of classical and contemporary texts on just war, see Gregory M. Reichberg, Henrik Syse, and Endre Begby, eds., *The Ethics of War: Classic and Contemporary Readings* (Oxford: Blackwell Publishing, 2006).

17. James Turner Johnson, "The Idea of Defense in Historical and Contemporary Thinking about Just War," *Journal of Religious Ethics* 36, no. 4 (2008): 544–545.

18. Mona Fixdal and Dan Smith, "Humanitarian Intervention and Just War," *Mershon International Studies Review* 42 (1998): 283–312.

19. James F. Childress, "Just-War Criteria " in *Moral Responsibility in Conflicts: Essays on Nonviolence, Wars and Conscience* (Baton Rouge: Lousianna State University Press, 1982), 63–94. He is supported by Richard B. Miller, "Aquinas and the Presumption against Killing and War," *The Journal of Religion* 82, no. 2 (2002): 178. According to James Turner Johnson among others, however, this statement is not an accurate description of the classical just war tradition. Johnson believes this "the presumption against war" describes pacifism, but that, "the just war tradition is about responding to injustice and aiming to establish justice." The just war tradition, we might say, expresses instead, "a presumption against injustice." James Turner Johnson, "Comment," *The Journal of Religious Ethics* 26, no. 1 (1998): 221–222.

20. Walzer, *Just and Unjust Wars*, 21.

21. Thomas Aquinas, *Summa Theologica*, trans. Fathers of the English Dominican Province, vol. 2 (New York: Benziger Brothers, 1947), 1359 (Question 40: Of War). Later scholars in the just war tradition added a few more requirements to these three criteria. The most central of these are that a just war must be *proportionate*, that is, it should not do more good than harm; that there must be *reasonable hope* that the goal of the war can be achieved, otherwise, soldiers would have fought in vain; and that the war must be a *last resort*, that is, that there is no other way of achieving the goal than going to war. For a discussion of these and other criteria, see Richard B. Miller, *Interpretations of Conflict: Ethics, Pacifism, and the Just War Tradition* (Chicago: Chicago University Press, 1991), 13–15.

22. James Turner Johnson, *Ideology, Reason, and the Limitation of War: Religious and Secular Concepts 1200–1740* (Princeton: Princeton University Press, 1975), 218.

23. Johnson, "The Idea of Defense in Historical and Contemporary Thinking About Just War," 549.

24. James Turner Johnson, *Just War Tradition and the Restraint of War: A Moral and Historical Inquiry* (Princeton: Princeton University Press, 1981), 23.

25. Johnson, "The Idea of Defense in Historical and Contemporary Thinking about Just War," 550.

26. St. Augustine, *City of God*, trans. Henry Bettenson (London: Penguin Books, 1972), 862 (bk. 19, chap. 9).

27. Johnson, "The Idea of Defense in Historical and Contemporary Thinking about Just War," 548.

28. Francisco de Vitoria, *Political Writings*, ed. Anthony Pagden and Jeremy Lawrence (Cambridge: Cambridge University Press, 1991),

303 ("On the Law of War," Question 1, article 3). Emphasis removed.

29. Hugo Grotius, *The Law of War and Peace*, trans. Francis W. Kelsey, bks. 1–3 (Indianapolis: Bobbs-Merrill Company, 1925): 170 (bk. 2, chap. 1, sec. 1, par. 4).

30. Francisco de Vitoria, *Political Writings*, 302–304 ("On the Law of War," Question 1, article 3).

31. For instance, in Chapter VII, Article 51 of the Charter of the United Nations.

32. For a discussion of the emerging principle of the Responsibility to Protect, see, Alex J. Bellamy, *Responsibility to Protect: The Global Effort to End Mass Atrocities*. Malden, MA: Polity Press, 2009.

33. Augustine, *City of God*, 866 (bk. 19, chap. 12).

34. Francisco Suárez, *Selections from Three Works of Francisco* Suárez, vol. 2. Trans. Gwladys L. Williams, Ammi Brown, and John Waldron (Oxford: Clarendon Press, 1944), 836 (Disp. XIII, Sect. VII).

35. The term "laws of war" refers to not only "international law on the conduct of armed conflict and military occupation, but also the law on genocide and on crimes against humanity." Adam Roberts and Richard Guelff, *Documents on the Laws of War*, 3rd ed. (Oxford: Oxford University Press, 2000), 2. The laws of war are sometimes used synonymously with the term "international humanitarian law," which can be defined as "the law governing the conduct of armed conflict." Steven R. Ratner and Jason S. Abrams, *Accountability for Human Rights Atrocities in International Law: Beyond the Nuremberg Legacy*, 2nd ed. (Oxford: Oxford University Press, 2001), 10. International criminal law is defined as "a body of international rules designed both to proscribe international crimes and to impose upon States the obligation to prosecute and punish at least some of those crimes." Antonio Cassese, *International Criminal Law* (Oxford: Oxford University Press, 2003), 15. It includes war crimes, crimes against humanity, and genocide, as well as other international crimes, such as aggression, torture, and terrorism.

36. For a discussion of *jus post bellum* ideas among classical just war thinkers such as Francisco de Vitoria, Francisco Suárez, Hugo Grotius, John Locke, Emmerich de Vattel, and Jean-Jacques Rousseau, see Pablo Kalmanovitz, "Justice in Postwar Reconstruction: Theories from Vitoria to Vattel" PhD diss., Columbia University, 2010. A short survey of both historical and current writings on *jus post bellum* can be found in Mark J. Allman and Tobias L. Winright, *After the Smoke Clears: The Just War Tradition & Post War Justice* (New York: Orbis Books, 2010).

37. Charles W. Jr. Kegley and Gregory A. Raymond, *How Nations Make Peace* (New York: Worth Publishers, 1999), 243.
38. Mark Evans makes a distinction between restricted and extended conceptions of *jus post bellum*. A restricted conception of *jus post bellum* is concerned with war termination and the immediate period after the war. An extended conception of *jus post bellum* is concerned with the issues that arise in, for instance, long-term occupations. In Evans's view, most *jus post bellum* theories, including Brian Orend's influential work, are examples of a restricted approach. Mark Evans, "Balancing Peace, Justice and Sovereignty in *Jus Post Bellum*: The Case of 'Just Occupation',," *Millennium—Journal of International Studies* 36, no. 3 (2008): 539–540.
39. David Rodin calls this topic "terminatio law," and argues that we should spell out "the transition from fighting to peace and give guidance to combatants on when they are permitted or required to quit hostilities and sue for peace." See David Rodin, "Two Emerging Issues of *Jus Post Bellum*: War Termination and the Liability of Soldiers for Crimes of Aggression," in *Jus Post Bellum: Towards a Law of Transition from Conflict to Peace*, ed. Carsten Stahn and Jann K. Kleffner (The Hague: T.M.C. Asser Press, 2008), 54.
40. Walzer, *Just and Unjust Wars*, 110.
41. George Bush and Brent Scowcroft, *A World Transformed* (New York: Vintage Books, 1999), 488.
42. Ibid., 489. David Rodin holds that there are cases in which one should stop the war even before a justified goal has been achieved. He takes the case of a war fought in self-defense in order to regain a territory invaded by an aggressive state. If war termination is guided strictly by the criteria of a just cause, the war should end when the territory is recaptured. But what if taking the territory requires a large amount of sacrifice? If we agree that the rule of proportionality has to govern the war effort, that is, that the good of the war has to outweigh the harm, it can be difficult to insist that the war should continue until the whole territory is recaptured. See, Rodin, "Two Emerging Issues of Jus Post Bellum: War Termination and the Liability of Soldiers for Crimes of Aggression," 55–56.
43. Brian Orend, "*Jus Post Bellum*: The Perspective of a Just-War Theorist," *Leiden Journal of International Law* 20, no. 3 (2007), 576.
44. Walzer, *Just and Unjust Wars*, 123.
45. The prosecution of war crimes is part of a larger subject often referred to as "transitional justice." Transitional justice involves both legal and nonlegal mechanisms that states can adopt to address crimes that were committed during a war or during the rule of an oppressive regime, and include truth-commissions,

reparations, amnesties, and various forms of purges. The literature on this topic is extensive, but one good place to start is the three-volume collection of writings on the topic offered in Neil J. Kritz, ed. *Transitional Justice: How Emerging Democracies Recon with Former Regimes*, 3 vols. (Washington, DC: United States Institute of Peace Press, 1995). A shorter, but excellent, discussion of different ways in which people might respond to past violence is provided by Martha Minow, *Between Vengeance and Forgiveness: Facing History after Genocide and Mass Violence* (Boston: Beacon Press, 1998).

46. Brian Orend, *"Jus Post Bellum:* The Perspective of a Just-War Theorist," 574.

47. For a discussion, see Kalmanovitz, "Justice in Postwar Reconstruction: Theories from Vitoria to Vattel." A discussion of the history and politics of international war crimes tribunals is offered by Gary J. Bass, *Stay the Hand of Vengeance: The Politics of War Crimes Tribunals* (Princeton: Princeton University Press, 2000).

48. Walzer, *Just and Unjust Wars*, 287.

49. The International Criminal Court does not yet exercise jurisdiction over the crime of aggression. Until 2010, the Rome Statute, the treaty that established the Court in 1998, had not defined the crime of aggression or specified the conditions for the Court's jurisdiction over the crime. The Rome Statute was amended in 2010 to define the crime of aggression, but the Court will not begin to exercise jurisdiction over this crime until 2017 at the earliest. For a discussion of the process that led to this amendment, see Jennifer Trahan, "The Rome Statute's Amendment on the Crime of Aggression: Negotiations at the Kampala Review Conference," *International Criminal Law Review* 11, no. 1 (2011): 49–104. The ICC has only sought to put two sitting political leaders on trial. In 2009, the ICC indicted the Sudanese President Omar Hassan al-Bashir for crimes of genocide, crimes against humanity, and war crimes in Darfur, and in July 2011, the ICC issued a warrant of arrest for Libyan leader Muammar Gaddafi for crimes against humanity.

50. Ratner and Abrams, *Accountability for Human Rights Atrocities*, 126.

51. Kalmanovitz, "Justice in Postwar Reconstruction: Theories from Vitoria to Vattel," 4. For a justification of war crimes trials, see Davida E. Kellogg, *"Jus Post Bellum*: The Importance of War Crimes Trials," *Parameters* 32, no. Autumn (2002): 87–99.

52. Walzer, *Just and Unjust Wars*, 309–327; Brian Orend, *The Morality of War* (Peterborough, Ont.: Broadview Press, 2006), 170–179.

53. Amnesty International, "Rwanda: The Troubled Course of Justice," April 25, 2000. Available at: http://www.amnesty.org/en/library /info/AFR47/010/2000/en.

54. Sally Marks, *The Illusion of Peace: International Relations in Europe 1918–1933* (New York: St. Martin's Press, 1976), 12.

55. John Maynard Keynes, *The Economic Consequences of the Peace* (New York: Harcourt, Brace and Howe, 1920/1988), 225. Later assessments of the Versailles Treaty have been more positive. According to Sally Marks, for instance, "the real difficulty was not that the Treaty was exceptionally unfair but that the Germans thought it was, and in time persuaded others that it was." Marks, *The Illusion of Peace: International Relations in Europe 1918–1933*, 16. An excellent discussion of reparations in the wake of the First World War is also provided by Mark Trachtenberg, *Reparations in World Politics: France and European Economic Diplomacy, 1916–1923* (New York: Columbia University Press, 1980).

56. Gary J. Bass, "*Jus Post Bellum*," *Philosophy and Public Affairs* 32, no. 4 (2004): 410–411. For a discussion of how the right to reparations is viewed by contemporary international law and practice, see, De Feyter, Koen, Stephan Parmentier, Marc Bossuyt, and Paul Lemmens, eds., *Out of the Ashes: Reparations for Victims of Gross Human Rights Violations* (Antwerp: Intersentia, 2005). A clear overview of reparations is also provided by Marco Sassòli, "Reparation," in *Post-Conflict Peacebuilding: A Lexicon*, ed. Vincent Chetail (Oxford: Oxford University Press, 2009).

57. Haig Khatchadourian, "Compensation and Reparations as Forms of Compensatory Justice," *Metaphilosophy* 37, no. 3–4 (2006): 429–431. Reparations can be contrasted with compensation, which can be called for in cases where no identifiable party has committed the wrongdoing, for instance, in floods and earthquakes. For further elaboration on the distinction between reparations and compensation, see ibid., 430–433.

58. Allman and Winright, *After the Smoke Clears: The Just War Tradition & Post War Justice*, 124–125.

59. Walzer, *Just and Unjust Wars*, 297; Bass, "*Jus Post Bellum*," 408.

60. Walzer, *Just and Unjust Wars*, 297.

61. Bass, "*Jus Post Bellum*," 408–409. For a discussion of how governments, national and international courts, and other institutions have sought to establish reparation schemes for victims of genocide, crimes against humanity, and war crimes, see Carla Ferstman, Mariana Goetz, and Alan Stephens, eds., *Reparations for Victims of Genocide, War Crimes and Crimes against Humanity: Systems in Place and Systems in the Making* (Leiden: Martinus Nijhoff Publishers, 2009).

62. Michael Walzer, *Arguing about War* (New Haven, CT: Yale University Press, 2004), 19.

63. For a discussion of how classical just war thinkers, such as Francisco Vitoria, Francisco Suárez, and Hugo Grotius defined the responsibilities of postwar reconstruction, see Kalmanovitz, "Justice in Postwar Reconstruction: Theories from Vitoria to Vattel." In Brian Orend's view, Immanuel Kant was one of the first to systematically address issues of postwar justice. See Brian Orend, "*Jus Post Bellum*: The Perspective of a Just-War Theorist," 574–575.

64. This is part of what Walzer refers to as the "legalist paradigm," which defines his core theory of aggression. See Walzer, *Just and Unjust Wars*, 61–62.

65. Ibid., 86. Bass also presents a cultural objection to reconstruction. He asks, "what right does one have to impose one's political or cultural values on a conquered country?" Bass, "*Jus Post Bellum*," 394–395.

66. Bush and Scowcroft, *A World Transformed*, 488–489.

67. Bush and Scowcroft suggest another reason why attempting to oust Saddam Hussein from power would have been wrong. Extending the war, they claim, "would have incurred incalculable human and political costs." It would have implied a prolonged occupation, which probably would have alienated the Arab states and some of America's allies. Evoking the principle of reasonable hope, there was also no guarantee that the attempt to create a better regime in Iraq actually would have worked. Bush and Scowcroft argued, therefore, that not only could they not guarantee that an extended war would have created a better peace, but the cost of such a peace was unacceptable. See ibid., 489.

68. Walzer, *Arguing About War*, 19.

69. Ibid.

70. Walzer, *Just and Unjust Wars*, 114.

71. Bass, "*Jus Post Bellum*," 399.

72. Ibid., 397.

73. Orend, *The Morality of War*, 204–208.

74. Walzer, *Arguing About War*, 165–166.

75. It is possible, as Orend argues, that the lack of attention to *jus post bellum* is in part a result of the assumed link between *jus ad bellum* and *jus post bellum*. When the rightful termination of war is defined by the justified reasons for going to war, *jus post bellum* does not need to be explored independently. *Jus post bellum* has, in this way, been subsumed under *jus ad bellum*. See Orend, "*Jus Post Bellum*: The Perspective of a Just-War Theorist," 573.

76. Orend, *The Morality of War*, 162. Orend attempts to define a set of principles that can guide a victorious state, which has been

the victim of another state's aggression, during the termination phase of the war. See primarily the discussion in ibid., 160–219. For Orend's earlier works on the subject, see Brian Orend, *Michael Walzer on War and Justice* (Cardiff: University of Wales Press, 2000); Brian Orend, *War and International Justice: A Kantian Perspective* (Waterloo, Ont.: Wilfrid Laurier University Press, 2000); Brian Orend, "*Jus Post Bellum*," *Journal of Social Philosophy* 31, no. 1 (2000): 117–137; Brian Orend, "Justice after War," *Ethics & International Affairs* 16, no. 1 (2002): 43–56.

77. See, for instance, Walzer, *Arguing About War*, 18–19.

78. Mark Evans, "Moral Responsibilities and Conflicting Demands of *Jus Post Bellum*," *Ethics & International Affairs* 23, no. 2 (2009): 155.

79. Walzer, *Arguing About War*, 163.

80. Orend, *The Morality of War*, 162.

81. Orend, "*Jus Post Bellum:* The Perspective of a Just-War Theorist," 575. Emphasis added. The same way of defining post-bellum justice can be found in Louis V. Iasiello, "*Jus Post Bellum*: The Moral Responsibilities of Victors in War," *Naval War College Review* 57, no. 3/4 (2004): 33–52.

82. Bass, "*Jus Post Bellum*."

83. Alex J. Bellamy, "The Responsibilities of Victory: *Jus Post Bellum* and the Just War," *Review of International Studies* 34, no. 4 (2008): 602.

84. Ibid., 611.

85. Toft, *Securing the Peace: The Durable Settlement of Civil Wars*, 5–6.

86. Mark Evans also argues that a theory of *jus post bellum* has to address different endings of just wars, not only those that end in victory for the just side, but also those that end in defeat for the just side, or in a stalemate See, Evans, "Moral Responsibilities and Conflicting Demands of *Jus Post Bellum*," 163–164. The same position is taken by Bellamy, who argues that when *jus post bellum* criteria are not tied directly to the just causes of war, it becomes possible also to also evaluate the peace after an unjust war. See, Bellamy, "The Responsibilities of Victory: *Jus Post Bellum* and the Just War," 612.

87. An important exception here is the so-called "independent thesis," which holds that combatants enjoy the same kinds of rights and obligations regardless of the *ad bellum* status of the state to which they belong. Modern just war theory is often also based on the "symmetry thesis," which states that belligerents on both sides of the conflict hold the same *in bello* rights and obligations. David Rodin, "The Moral Inequality of Soldiers: Why *Jus in Bello*

Asymmetry Is Half Right," in *Just and Unjust Warriors: The Moral and Legal Status of Soldiers*, ed. David Rodin and David Shue (Oxford: Oxford University Press, 2008), 44.

88. James Turner Johnson, *Morality and Contemporary Warfare* (New Haven, CT: Yale University Press, 1999), 208.

89. Or as Bass argues, "the aftermath of the war is crucial to the justice of the war itself." Bass, "*Jus Post Bellum*," 388. Walzer believes that it is quite possible to fight a just war in a just manner, but still "make a moral mess of the aftermath—by establishing a satellite regime, for example, or by seeking revenge against the citizens of the defeated (aggressor) state, or by failing, after a humanitarian intervention, to help the people you have rescued to rebuild their lives." Walzer, *Arguing about War*, 163.

90. Orend, *The Morality of War*, 195.

91. Ibid., 162.

92. Ibid., 162–163.

93. Boutros Boutros-Ghali, Introduction to *The United Nations and Rwanda, 1993–1996*. The United Nations Blue Books Series, Volume 10 (New York: United Nations, Department of Public Information, 1996), 11–13. Wm. Cyrus Reed argues, that "by legalizing political activities domestically and softening its stand on the right of return for refugees, the regime in Kigali was taking a major initiative on the two central demands of the RPF, without their participation." Wm. Cyrus Reed, "Exile, Reform, and the Rise of the Rwandan Patriotic Front," *The Journal of Modern African Studies* 34, no. 3 (1996): 487.

94. Boutros-Ghali, "The United Nations and Rwanda," 12.

95. Walzer, *Arguing About War*, 18. Bass says: "If one's goals are mere self-defense, the paradigmatic case of just war, then there is little justification for reshaping a defeated society. One does not have to completely change an enemy country's domestic arrangements in order to make sure it will not attack again." Bass, "*Jus Post Bellum*," 393–394. Williams and Caldwell concur: "*Jus post bellum*, in other words, requires in the case of a war against aggression the restoration of the *status quo ante bellum* with respect to the rights of the victims of aggression." Williams and Caldwell, "*Jus Post Bellum*: Just War Theory and the Principles of Just Peace," 317. In the case of a humanitarian intervention, they go on, a just peace requires "the securing of the rights of those whom the intervention was intended to assist." Ibid. According to Kalmanovitz's study, "the classical theory puts a strong emphasis on the connection between *jus ad bellum* and *jus post bellum*, and uses the just cause of war as the main guide to assess the justice of a war's aftermath." Kalmanovitz, "Justice in Postwar Reconstruction: Theories from Vitoria to Vattel," 14.

96. Orend, *The Morality of War*, 166.
97. Orend, "*Jus Post Bellum*," 122.
98. Walzer, *Just and Unjust Wars*, 121; Hart, *Strategy*, 338.
99. Walzer, Ibid.
100. H. E. Goemans, *War and Punishment* (Princeton: Princeton University Press, 2000), 170.
101. Jeff McMahan, "Just Cause for War," *Ethics & International Affairs* 19, no. 3 (2005): 2.
102. Kalmanovitz, "Justice in Postwar Reconstruction: Theories from Vitoria to Vattel," 71.
103. Walzer, *Arguing About War*, 163. A similar position is taken by Robert E. Jr. Williams Jr. and Dan Caldwell, "*Jus Post Bellum*: Just War Theory and the Principles of Just Peace," *International Studies Perspectives* 7, no. 4 (2006): 311–313.

2 Some Theoretical Considerations

1. Lotta Themnér and Peter Wallensteen, "Appendix 2a. Patterns of Major Armed Conflicts, 2001–10," in *SIPRI Yearbook 2011: Armaments, Disarmament and International Security* (Oxford: Oxford University Press, 2011), 69.
2. Margaret Thatcher, "Speech in a Debate on the Falkland Islands in the House of Commons, 3 April 1982," in *The Collected Speeches of Margaret Thatcher*, ed. Robin Harris (London: HarperCollins 1997), 149.
3. John A. Vasquez and Brandon Valeriano, "Territory as a Source of Conflict and a Road to Peace," in *The Sage Handbook of Conflict Resolution*, ed. Jacob Bercovitch, Victor Kremenyuk, and I. William Zartman (London: Sage Publications, 2009), 195–197.
4. Themnér and Wallensteen, "Appendix 2a. Patterns of Major Armed Conflicts, 2001–10," 69.
5. Kalevi J. Holsti, *Peace and War: Armed Conflicts and International Order 1648–1989* (Cambridge: Cambridge University Press, 1991), 311.
6. According to the UCDP the issue territory "refers to contested incompatible positions regarding the status of a territory and may involve demands for secession or autonomy (intrastate conflict) or the aim of changing the state in control of a certain territory (interstate conflict)." Themnér and Wallensteen, "Appendix 2a. Patterns of Major Armed Conflicts, 2001–10," 69–70.
7. In his investigation of 177 wars from 1648 to 1989, Kalevi Holsti makes a distinction between 24 different issues, including territory, state or regime survival, enforcement of treaty terms, national liberation, defense of ally, government composition, and balance

of power. His typology also includes values and stakes such as status and prestige. See, Holsti, *Peace and War*. Bercovitch et al. point out that one single war might be fought over more than one issue. Their typology consist of sovereignty, ideology, security, independence, and a residual category. Jacob Bercovitch, J. Theodore Anagnoson, and Donnette L. Wille, "Some Conceptual Issues and Empirical Trends in the Study of Successful Mediation in International Relations," *Journal of Peace Research* 28, no. 1 (1991): 14. For the argument that different issues dominate different historical periods, see Evan Luard, *War in International Society: A Study in International Sociology* (New Haven, CT: Yale University Press, 1986).

8. Louis Kriesberg, *Constructive Conflicts: From Escalation to Resolution* (Lanham, MD: Rowman & Littlefield, 2007), 7.

9. Robert L. Rothstein, "In Fear of Peace: Getting Past Maybe," in *After the Peace: Resistance and Reconciliation*, ed. Robert L. Rothstein (Boulder, CO: Lynne Rienner, 1999), 17.

10. Ibid.

11. Timothy D. Sisk, *Peacemaking in Civil Wars: Obstacles, Options, and Opportunities*, Occasional Paper Series No. 20:OP:2 (Notre Dame, IN: The Joan B. Kroc Institute for International Peace Studies, 2001), 11–12. See also, Caroline Hartzell, Matthew Hoddie, and Donald Rothchild, "Stabilizing the Peace after Civil War: An Investigation of Some Key Variables," *International Organization* 55, no. 1 (2001): 189.

12. It must be said, though, that in some cases ethnic differences do seem to be the stated incompatibility. This holds especially true in genocides, where the aim is to eradicate a whole population. In the 1994 genocide in Rwanda, for instance, segments of the Hutu population singled out the Tutsis with the aim of extinguishing them. In such cases the issue cannot be classified without distortion as either territorial or governmental. Thus, I do not directly address the issue of how to create a just peace after genocide.

13. Rothstein, "In Fear of Peace: Getting Past Maybe," 17–18.

14. Hidemi Suganami, *On the Causes of War* (Oxford: Clarendon Press, 1996), 33.

15. Ibid.

16. Holsti, *Peace and War*, 17.

17. Suganami, *Causes of War*, 33.

18. Jeffrey Dixon, "What Causes Civil Wars? Integrating Quantitative Research Findings," *International Studies Review* 11, no. 4 (2009): 709–710.

19. For the assertion that poor economic conditions is one of the most important underlying causes of internal armed conflict, see Dan

Smith, "Trends and Causes of Armed Conflicts," in *Transforming Ethopolitical Conflict—The Berghof Handbook*, eds. Alex Austin, Martina Fisher, and Norbert Roberts (Wiesbaden: VS Verlag, 2004), 111–127. On the flip side, according to Jeffrey Dixon, the "findings are almost entirely consistent in one direction—growth, prosperity and development reduce the risk of civil war." Dixon, "What Causes Civil Wars? Integrating Quantitative Research Findings," 714.

20. The work of Paul Collier and his colleagues at the World Bank has sparked new interest in the explanatory role of economic factors. Collier challenges the idea that grievances such as ethnic hatred, political domination, or economic inequality explains most internal conflicts. He suggested that the expression of such grievances are not the real motivation but must be understood as propaganda, aimed at the international community, and also as a way to recruit new soldiers. The true motivation of armed rebellion can be more accurately explained by economic incentives, in particular by the desire to capture primary commodities. While armed conflict might impoverish the society as a whole, smaller groups within it can benefit economically from the war. A society will especially be at risk for conflict if it has large amounts of natural resources, and a high proportion of young men lacking education. Paul Collier, "Doing Well out of War: An Economic Perspective," in *Greed and Grievance: Economic Agendas in Civil Wars*, ed. Mats Berdal and David M. Malone (Boulder, CO: Lynne Rienner, 2000), 92, 97, 110. See also, Karen Ballentine and Jake Sherman, Introduction to *The Political Economy of Armed Conflict: Beyond Greed and Grievance*, ed. Karen Ballentine and Jake Sherman (Boulder, CO: Lynne Rienner, 2003), 3–4. The greed thesis has been challenged on several scores. While the economic opportunities provided by conflict might play a role in the duration and intensity of the conflict, economic factors alone do not cause conflict. In most cases, conflict is rather caused by the interaction of economic incentives, socioeconomic and political grievances, ethnic animosities, and insecurity. See, Karen Ballentine, "Beyond Greed and Grievance: Reconsidering the Economic Dynamics of Armed Conflict," in *The Political Economy of Armed Conflict: Beyond Greed and Grievance*, ed. Karen Ballentine and Jake Sherman (Boulder, CO: Lynne Rienner, 2003), 260.

21. According to Dixson's survey of the statistical evidence on this topic, diamonds and oil do seem to increase the likelihood of war, while other gemstones and opiates actually seem to reduce the chances of a civil war. Dixon, "What Causes Civil Wars? Integrating Quantitative Research Findings," 713–714.

22. Global Witness, "A Rough Trade: The Role of Companies and Governments in the Angolan Conflict" (London: Global Witness, 1998). Available at: http://www.globalwitness.org/sites/default /files/pdfs/A_Rough_Trade.pdf.

23. Ibid., 4.

24. Philippe Le Billon, "Angola's Political Economy of War: The Role of Oil and Diamonds, 1975–2000," *African Affairs* 100, no. 398 (2001): 79.

25. Greg Cashman, *What Causes War? An Introduction to Theories of International Conflict* (New York: Lexington Books, 1993), 134.

26. Alastair Finlan, *The Gulf War 1991 (Essential Histories)* (Oxford: Osprey Publishing, 2003), 14.

27. David H. Finnie, *Shifting Lines in the Sand: Kuwait's Elusive Frontier with Iraq* (Cambridge: Harvard University Press, 1992), 168.

28. Cashman, *What Causes War? An Introduction to Theories of International Conflict*, 134.

29. Ibid., 134, 145–146.

30. This also means the question of how we should create economic justice falls outside the bounds of this book. I should point out, though, that it would be easy to accommodate other types of issues within the basic framework I construct.

31. Margaret Thatcher, *The Downing Street Years* (London: HarperCollins, 1993), 173.

32. For more on issue-based approaches to conflict, see Robert Randle, *Issues in the History of International Relations* (New York: Praeger, 1987); Paul F. Diehl, "What Are They Fighting for? The Importance of Issues in International Conflict Research," *Journal of Peace Research* 29, no. 3 (1992): 333–344; Paul R. Hensel et al., "Bones of Contention: Comparing Territorial, Maritime, and River Issues," *Journal of Conflict Resolution* 52, no. 1 (2008): 117–143.

33. Michael Howard, *The Causes of War* (Cambridge: Harvard University Press, 1984), 12.

34. John Rawls, *A Theory of Justice* (Cambridge: Harvard University Press, 1971), 7.

35. The Socialist Federal Republic of Yugoslavia was established in 1946.

36. At least for the time being: after a referendum, Montenegro declared independence in 1996.

37. Tim Judah, *Kosovo: War and Revenge* (New Haven: Yale Nota Bene, 2002), 1–32; Iain King and Whit Mason, *Peace at Any Price: How the World Failed Kosovo* (Ithaca: Cornell University Press, 2006), 25–46.

38. Thomas L. Carson and Paul K. Moser, Introduction to *Moral Relativism: A Reader*, ed. Paul K. Moser and Thomas L. Carson (Oxford: Oxford University Press, 2001), 1.

39. J. L. Mackie, *Ethics: Inventing Right and Wrong* (London: Penguin Books, 1977), 36. One might wonder why disagreement about other things, like human origins, does not lead to a similar conclusion that knowledge in that area can only be relative. For a discussion, see Sarah McGrath, "Moral Disagreement and Moral Expertise," in *Oxford Studies in Metaethics:* vol. 3, ed. Russ Shafer-Landau (Oxford: Oxford University Press, 2008): 89–90.

40. Carson and Moser, Introduction, 2.

41. An absolutist view of morality can be seen as the opposite of relativism. An absolutist position may be summed up in what Isaiah Berlin calls the "Platonic ideal." According to this ideal, all questions have one true answer, and "the true answers, when found, must necessarily be compatible with one another and form a single whole." Isaiah Berlin, *The Crooked Timber of Humanity: Chapters in the History of Ideas* (London: John Murray Publishers, 1990), 5–6.

42. Susan Wolf, "Two Levels of Pluralism," *Ethics* 102, no. 4 (1992): 789.

43. Ibid.

44. Pierre Allan, "Measuring International Ethics: A Moral Scale of War, Peace, Justice, and Global Care," in *What Is a Just Peace?*, ed. Pierre Allan and Alexis Keller (Oxford: Oxford University Press, 2006), 117.

45. Pierre Allan and Alexis Keller, "The Concept of a Just Peace, or Achieving Peace through Recognition, Renouncement, and Rule," in *What Is a Just Peace*, ed. Pierre Allan and Alexis Keller (Oxford: Oxford University Press, 2006), 209.

46. Ibid., 197–201.

47. Ibid., 209.

48. Ibid., 195.

49. Anonymous, "Human Rights in Peace Negotiations," *Human Rights Quarterly* 18, no. 2 (1996): 249–258.

50. Paul C. Szasz, "The Dayton Accord: The Balkan Peace Agreement," *Cornell International Law Journal* 30, no. 3 (1997): 762. I will not use the word "Muslim" to denote the population of Bosnia that did not identify itself as Serb or Croatian, because it overemphasizes the religious element of their national identity.

51. Laura Silber and Allan Little, *Yugoslavia: Death of a Nation*, Rev. and updated ed. (New York: Penguin Books, 1997), 218.

52. Noel Malcolm, *Bosnia: A Short History*, Rev. ed. (New York: New York University Press, 1996), 230.

53. The referendum had been recommended by the European Community, which also helped conduct it. See James Gow, *Triumph of the Lack of Will: International Diplomacy and the Yugoslav War* (London: Hurst and Company, 1997), 83–84.

54. David Rieff, *Slaughterhouse: Bosnia and the Failure of the West* (New York: Touchstone, 1995), 23. The European Community recognized Bosnia as a sovereign nation on April 6, 1992, and the United States followed suit the day after.

55. Anonymous, "Human Rights in Peace Negotiations," 252.

56. Ibid., 253. Anonymous is not entirely correct when he or she says that Western governments and media are to blame for the Bosnian government's repudiation of the deal. Lack of support for the plan, especially in the United States was a contributing factor, but there were many in the Bosnian government who were against it because it gave away too much to the Serbs and because it killed the hope of a multicultural Bosnia. See Steven L. Burg and Paul S. Shoup, *The War in Bosnia-Herzegovina* (Armonk, NY: M.E. Sharpe, 1999), 280–281.

57. Anonymous, "Human Rights in Peace Negotiations," 252.

58. Ibid.

59. Geoffrey Sayre-McCord, "Contractarianism," in *The Blackwell Guide to Ethical Theory*, ed. Hugh LaFollette (Oxford: Blackwell Publishers Ltd., 2000), 247. The largest branch of contractarian theories is interested in explaining the political legitimacy of the state.

60. Cecilia Albin, *Justice and Fairness in International Negotiation* (Cambridge: Cambridge University Press, 2001), 9.

61. In a democratic country, one can explain the obligation of political leaders with reference to the democratic process. The election of pubic officials is the source of rights and obligations for both citizens and the public officials. By choosing people to govern them, citizens relinquish some of their political independence (and, many would argue, take on a general duty of political obedience.) In exchange for the authority conferred on them, political leaders take on a duty to do what is in the interest of the people. For a critical discussion of this view, see Carole Pateman, *The Problem of Political Obligation: A Critique of Liberal Theory* (Berkeley: University of California Press, 1985). In a democratic country, then, political leaders and government officials can be seen as trustees; they have an obligation to promote the interests of the citizens. For the argument that this duty is based on a promise, see Raino Malnes, *National Interests, Morality and International Law* (Oslo: Scandinavian University Press, 1994). It is much more difficult to explain why political leaders who have not come to power through a democratic process have the right to make decisions on behalf of

the populations they claim to represent. What is the source of their authority? They might claim that they have the interests of their people at heart, but unless the citizens have given them some kind of mandate, their right to make decisions cannot be explained.

62. Allan and Keller, "The Concept of a Just Peace, or Achieving Peace through Recognition, Renouncement, and Rule," 197.

63. Susan Woodward, *Balkan Tragedy: Chaos and Dissolution after the Cold War* (Washington, DC: The Brookings Institution, 1995), 33. Bosniaks consisted of about 44 percent, Croats 17 percent, and "others" 8 percent.

64. Melanie C. Greenberg and Margaret E. McGuinness, "From Lisbon to Dayton: International Mediation and the Bosnia Crisis," in *Words over War: Mediation and Arbitration to Prevent Deadly Conflict*, ed. Melanie C. Greenberg, John H. Barton, and Margaret E. McGuinness (Lanham, MD: Rowman & Littlefield: 2000): 39.

65. Sabrina P. Ramet, *Balkan Babel: The Disintegration of Yugoslavia from the Death of Tito to the Fall of Milosevic* (Boulder, CO: Westview Press, 2002), 213.

66. See Mona Fixdal and Ingrid O. Busterud, "The Undiplomatic Diplomat: Peter Galbraith," in *Ways out of War: Peacemakers in the Middle East and Balkans*, ed. Mona Fixdal (New York: Palgrave Macmillan, 2012). Forthcoming.

67. David Owen, *Balkan Odyssey* (San Diego: Harcourt Brace & Company, 1995), 200.

68. Silber and Little, *Yugoslavia: Death of a Nation*, 303.

69. For a discussion of the ICTY, see for instance, William A. Schabas, *The UN International Criminal Tribunals: The Former Yugoslavia, Rwanda and Sierra Leone* (Cambridge: Cambridge University Press, 2006).

70. Kalevi Holsti, *The State, War and the State of War* (Cambridge: Cambridge University Press, 1996), 26–27. For a discussion of the distinction between Clausewitzian wars and "new" wars, see also Mary Kaldor, *New and Old Wars* (Stanford: Stanford University Press, 2007).

71. Holsti, *The State, War and the State of War*, 39. Whether such conflicts are defined as uprisings, insurgencies, guerrilla warfare, ethnic cleansing, or genocide, one of their consequences has been to drive up the number of refugees and internally displaced persons, and increased civilian deaths in comparison with military deaths. Kaldor, *New and Old Wars*, 9.

72. Quoted in Fixdal, "Peacemaking in Asymmetrical Conflicts."

73. Burg and Shoup, *The War in Bosnia-Herzegovina*, 280–281.

74. See the discussion in Joel Feinberg, *Social Philosophy* (Englewood Cliffs: Prentice-Hall, 1973), 99–102.
75. Tom L. Beauchamp, *Philosophical Ethics: An Introduction to Moral Philosophy*, 2nd ed. (New York: McGraw-Hill, 2001), 344.
76. Allen Buchanan and Deborah Mathieu, "Philosophy and Justice," in *Justice: Views from the Social Sciences*, ed. Ronald L. Cohen (New York: Plenum Press, 1986), 15.
77. Rawls, *A Theory of Justice*, 5.
78. Aristotle, *The Nicomachean Ethics* (Oxford World's Classics), trans. David Ross (Oxford: Oxford University Press, 1998), 114.
79. See Buchanan and Mathieu, "Philosophy and Justice," 18.
80. Buchanan and Mathieu, "Philosophy and Justice," 19.
81. Johan Galtung, "Violence, Peace, and Peace Research," *Journal of Peace Research* 6, no. 3 (1969): 168.
82. Martin Luther King Jr., "Letter from a Birmingham Jail," in *Approaches to Peace: A Reader in Peace Studies*, ed. David P. Barash (New York: Oxford University Press, 2000), 147.
83. Boutros Boutros-Ghali, "An Agenda for Peace" (New York: United Nations, 1992). Available at: http://www.un.org/Docs/SG /agpeace.html.
84. John A. Vasquez, "Understanding Peace: Insights from International Relations Theory and Research," in *A Natural History of Peace*, ed. Thomas Gregor (Nashville and London: Vanderbilt University Press, 1996), 274.
85. Kenneth E. Boulding, *Stable Peace* (Austin: University of Texas Press, 1978), 13.
86. Arie M. Kacowicz and Yaacov Bar-Siman-Tov, "Stable Peace: A Conceptual Framework," in *Stable Peace among Nations*, ed. Arie M. Kacowicz et al. (Lanham, MD: Rowman & Littlefield, 2000), 12. Kacowicz and Bar-Siman-Tov are describing international stability, but the same would also apply for domestic stability.
87. Ibid., 11.
88. Alexander L. George, Foreword to *Stable Peace among Nations*, ed. Arie M. Kacowicz et al. (Lanham, MD: Rowman & Littlefield, 2000), xii.
89. Ibid., xiii.
90. Stephen John Stedman, Introduction to *Ending Civil Wars: The Implementation of Peace Agreements*, ed. Stephen John Stedman, Donald Rothchild, and Elizabeth M. Cousens (Boulder, CO: Lynne Rienner, 2002), 2.
91. Hartzell, Hoddie, and Rothchild, "Stabilizing the Peace after Civil War: An Investigation of Some Key Variables," 187.
92. Monica Duffy Toft, *Securing the Peace: The Durable Settlement of Civil Wars* (Princeton: Princeton University Press, 2010): 2.

93. Roy Licklider, "The Consequences of Negotiated Settlements in Civil Wars, 1945–1993," *American Political Science Review* 89, no. 3 (1995): 681.

94. Michael W. Doyle and Nicholas Sambanis, *Making War and Building Peace: United Nations Peace Operations* (Princeton: Princeton University Press, 2006), 103–104.

95. Virginia Page Fortna, *Peace Time: Cease-Fire Agreements and the Durability of Peace* (Princeton: Princeton University Press, 2004), 29–30.

96. Ibid., 208.

97. Stedman, Introduction, 9.

98. Ibid., 10.

99. Roy Licklider, "Ethical Advice: Conflict Management vs. Human Rights in Ending Civil Wars." *Journal of Human Rights* 7, no. 4 (2008): 376–387.

100. Jack Snyder and Leslie Vinjamuri, "Trials and Errors: Principle and Pragmatism in Strategies of International Justice," *International Security* 28, no. 3 (2003/04): 43.

101. Licklider, "Ethical Advice: Conflict Management vs. Human Rights in Ending Civil Wars," 380, 379.

102. Daniel Druckman and Cecilia Albin, "Distributive Justice and the Durability of Peace Agreements," *Review of International Studies* 37, no. 3 (2010): 1158.

103. Stanley Hoffmann, "Peace and Justice: A Prologue," in *What Is a Just Peace?*, ed. Pierre Allan and Alexis Keller (Oxford: Oxford University Press, 2006), 16.

104. Kacowicz and Bar-Siman-Tov, "Stable Peace: A Conceptual Framework," 25.

105. Doyle and Sambanis, *Making War and Building Peace: United Nations Peace Operations*, 96.

106. Hartzell, Hoddie, and Rothchild, "Stabilizing the Peace after Civil War: An Investigation of Some Key Variables," 199.

107. Ibid.

108. Doyle and Sambanis, *Making War and Building Peace: United Nations Peace Operations*, 97–99.

109. Hartzell, Hoddie, and Rothchild, "Stabilizing the Peace after Civil War: An Investigation of Some Key Variables," 198.

110. Doyle and Sambanis, *Making War and Building Peace: United Nations Peace Operations*, 100–101.

111. George Downs and Stephen John Stedman, "Evaluation Issues in Peace Implementation," in *Ending Civil Wars: The Implementation of Peace Agreements*, edited by Stephen John Stedman, Donald Rothchild and Elizabeth M. Cousens (Boulder, CO: Lynne Rienner Publishers, 2002), 44.

112. Fortna, *Peace Time: Cease-Fire Agreements and the Durability of Peace*, 112–113, 211–212.

113. Ibid., 215.

114. Stephen D. Krasner and Carlos Pascual, "Addressing State Failure," *Foreign Affairs* 84, no. 4 (2005): 158–159.

115. Downs and Stedman, "Evaluation Issues in Peace Implementation," 44.

116. Michael W. Doyle and Nicholas Sambanis, "International Peacebuilding: A Theoretical and Quantitative Analysis," *The American Political Science Review* 94, no. 4 (2000): 780; Stephen John Stedman, "Spoiler Problems in Peace Processes," *International Security* 22, no. 2 (1997): 5.

117. Stedman, "Spoiler Problems in Peace Processes," 6.

118. Fortna, *Peace Time: Cease-Fire Agreements and the Durability of Peace*, 20–24.

119. Ibid., 211.

3 OUTCOMES OF SECESSIONIST WARS

1. Jon Lee Anderson, "Death of the Tiger: Sri Lanka's Brutal Victory over Its Tamil Insurgents," *The New Yorker*, January 17 (2011): 49.

2. Not all secessions are the result of violent conflict. For instance, Norway peacefully received independence from Sweden in 1905, and Czechoslovakia was formally split into Slovakia and the Czech Republic in 1993.

3. David Miller, "Secession and the Principle of Nationality," in *National Self-Determination and Secession*, ed. Margaret Moore (Oxford: Oxford University Press, 1998), 65. For another discussion of the problems connected to talking about rights to statehood, see Ronald S. Beiner, "National Self-Determination: Some Cautionary Remarks Concerning the Rhetoric of Rights," in *National Self-Determination and Secession*, ed. Margaret Moore (Oxford: Oxford University Press, 1998), 158–180.

4. Allen Buchanan, *Secession: The Morality of Political Divorce from Fort Sumter to Lithuania and Quebec* (Boulder, CO: Westview Press, 1991), 4.

5. Lea Brilmayer, "Secession and Self-Determination: A Territorial Interpretation," *Yale Journal of International Law* 16 (1991): 201, 178.

6. S. W. R. de A. Samarasinghe, introduction to *Secessionist Movements in Comparative Perspective*, ed. Ralph R. Premdas, S .W. R. de A. Samarasinghe, and Alan B. Anderson (London: Pinter, 1990), 8.

7. Buchanan, *Secession: The Morality of Political Divorce from Fort Sumter to Lithuania and Quebec*, vii.
8. This follows Allen Buchanan, "Theories of Secession," *Philosophy and Public Affairs* 26, no. 1 (1997); 34. Margaret Moore operates with a similar distinction, with slightly different labels. Her term for "remedial right only theories" is "just cause theories"; her term for "ascriptive right theories" is "national self-determination theories," and her term for "associative right theories" is "choice theories." See discussion in Margaret Moore, "The Ethics of Secession and a Normative Theory of Nationalism," *Canadian Journal of Law and Jurisprudence* 13, no. 2 (2000): 225–250; Margaret Moore, introduction to *National Self-Determination and Secession*, ed. Margaret Moore (New York: Oxford University Press, 1998): 1–13.
9. Buchanan, *Secession: The Morality of Political Divorce from Fort Sumter to Lithuania and Quebec*, 152; Buchanan, "Theories of Secession," 37.
10. Allen Buchanan, *Justice, Legitimacy, and Self-Determination: Moral Foundations for International Law* (Oxford: Oxford University Press, 2004), 364. It should be pointed out that establishing an acceptable international law on secession will involve other considerations than establishing a moral right to secession. These considerations include that the proposed legal rule is minimally realistic, consistent with other international norms, and that it does not create perverse incentives. For the distinction between a moral and legal right to secession, see Buchanan, "Theories of Secession," 32, 41–44.
11. See Wayne Norman, "The Ethics of Secession as the Regulation of Secessionist Politics," in *National Self-Determination and Secession*, ed. Margaret Moore (New York: Oxford University Press, 1998), 41.
12. "Ethics of Secession and a Normative Theory," 230.
13. Buchanan, *Justice, Legitimacy, and Self-Determination: Moral Foundations for International Law*, 281.
14. Ibid., 283.
15. Buchanan, *Secession: The Morality of Political Divorce from Fort Sumter to Lithuania and Quebec*, 67.
16. Buchanan points out that there might be difficulties in determining whether this principle applies if the would-be seceding group is not closely related to the group whose territory was unjustly annexed in the first place, or if the original group did not have a solid and undisputed claim to the land. Allen Buchanan, "Toward a Theory of Secession," *Ethics* 101, no. 2 (1991): 330.
17. Buchanan, *Justice, Legitimacy, and Self-Determination: Moral Foundations for International Law*, 354.
18. Ibid., 355.

19. Allen Buchanan, "Self-Determination, Secession, and the Rule of Law," in *The Morality of Nationalism*, ed. Robert McKim and Jeff McMahan (New York: Oxford University Press, 1997), 317.

20. Margaret Moore, "The Ethics of Secession and Postinvasion Iraq," *Ethics and International Affairs* 20, no. 1 (2006): 70.

21. Moore, "The Ethics of Secession and a Normative Theory," 231.

22. Sabrina P. Ramet, "Slovenia's Road to Democracy," *Europe-Asia Studies* 45, no. 5 (1993): 872.

23. Brenda Fowler, "Slovenes to Vote on Independence," *The New York Times*, December 23, 1990.

24. Ramet, "Slovenia's Road to Democracy," 870.

25. Ibid., 871.

26. Milica Z. Bookman, "War and Peace: The Divergent Breakups of Yugoslavia and Czechoslovakia," *Journal of Peace Research* 31, no. 2 (1994): 178.

27. Ibid., 177–178.

28. In the spring of 1991, the picture became more complicated as the Serb republic struggled to keep control over the federation. The Slovenian republic had not opted for complete independence at first, but sought, together with Croatia, to negotiate a loose confederation. The Serbs reacted by walking out of the negotiations, and then later declaring martial law. On June 24, 1991, after another failed attempt to reach a negotiated settlement between the republics, the prime minister of Yugoslavia warned authorities in Slovenia and Croatia that, "The Federal Government will use all means available to stop the republics' unilateral steps towards independence." Slovenia (and Croatia) declared independence the next day. See Marc Weller, "The International Response to the Dissolution of the Socialist Federal Republic of Yugoslavia," *The American Journal of International Law* 86, no. 3 (1992): 570. Thus, in the end their bid for statehood can be viewed as preemptive self-defense. The intuition that Slovenia had a claim to secession before it got to this point, however, still stands.

29. The idea of self-determination has gone through several different incarnations. It was present as a moral or political idea both in the American and French revolutions, where it was primarily a principle for democratic self-governance; it had a great impact on the peace settlement after the First World War, as the victors tried to redraw the map according to ethnic settlement patterns; and it has been used as a legal principle of independence for colonial peoples. I use it here as a principle for national self-government. For discussions of the various incarnations of self-determination, see, for instance, Brilmayer, "Secession and Self-Determination," 179–184; Alfred Cobban, *The Nation State and National Self-Determination* (London: Collins,

The Fontana Library, 1969); Diane F. Orentlicher, "Separation Anxiety: International Responses to Ethno-Separatist Claims," *Yale Journal of International Law* 23 (1998), 22–44.

30. Moore, "Ethics of Secession and a Normative Theory," 238.

31. Miller, "Secession and the Principle of Nationality," 65; Ralph R. Premdas, "Secessionist Movements in Comparative Perspective," in *Secessionist Movements in Comparative Perspective*, ed. Ralph R. Premdas, S. W. R. de A. Samarasinghe, and Alan B. Anderson (London: Pinter, 1990), 15.

32. David Miller, *On Nationality* (Oxford: Oxford University Press, 1995), 81. Unlike Buchanan, Miller does not aim to establish an institutional right to secession. Rather, his wish is to develop a theory of secession that can articulate principles that will help us when we assess secessionist claims. By "us" he means both those who wish to secede, those who might oppose it, and the international community. Miller, "Secession and the Principle of Nationality," 64.

33. For a discussion, see Alan Patten, "The Autonomy Argument for Liberal Nationalism," *Nations and Nationalism* 5, no. 1 (1999): 6. See also, Tamar Meisels, *Territorial Rights* (Dordrecht, Netherlands: Springer, 2009), 3–5.

34. Miller, *On Nationality*, 85–86.

35. Ibid., 49, 82–88.

36. Ibid., 87.

37. Yael Tamir, *Liberal Nationalism* (Princeton: Princeton University Press, 1993), 76.

38. Miller, "Secession and the Principle of Nationality," 71.

39. For a discussion, see Patten, "The Autonomy Argument for Liberal Nationalism," 7–8.

40. Christopher Heath Wellman, *A Theory of Secession: The Case for Political Self-Determination* (New York: Cambridge University Press, 2005), 100 103.

41. For a discussion of this objection, see ibid., 104–108.

42. Daryl J. Glaser, "The Right to Secession: An Antisecessionist Defense," *Political Studies* 51, no. 2 (2003): 375.

43. Orentlicher, "Separation Anxiety," 46.

44. Moore, "Introduction," 5.

45. Daniel Philpott, "In Defense of Self-Determination," *Ethics* 105, no. 2 (1995): 353.

46. See, Harry Beran, "A Liberal Theory of Secession," *Political Studies* 32, no. 32 (1984): 21–31; Wellman, *A Theory of Secession: The Case for Political Self-Determination*; Daniel Philpott, "Self-Determination in Practice," in *National Self-Determination and Secession*, ed. Margaret Moore (New York: Oxford University Press,

1998): 79–102; Philpott, "In Defense of Self-Determination," 352–385. These theories are also called plebiscitary right theories or choice theories of secession.

47. Allen Buchanan, "Democracy and Secession," in *National Self-Determination and Secession*, edited by Margaret Moore (New York: Oxford University Press, 1998): 15.

48. Philpott, "In Defense of Self-Determination," 352–385.

49. Allen Buchanan, "Democracy and Secession," 22.

50. Ibid.

51. Allen Buchanan, "The Making and Unmaking of Boundaries: What Liberalism Has to Say," in *States, Nations, and Borders: The Ethics of Making Boundaries*, ed. Allen Buchanan and Margaret Moore (New York: Cambridge University Press, 2003), 246–247.

52. Robert E. Goodin, "Enfranchising All Affected Interests, and Its Alternatives," *Philosophy & Public Affairs* 35, no. 1 (2007): 40.

53. Philpott, "In Defense of Self-Determination," 362.

54. Brilmayer, "Secession and Self-Determination," 185.

55. Harry Beran, "A Democratic Theory of Political Self-Determination for a New World Order," in *Theories of Secession*, ed. Percy B. Lehning (London: Routledge, 1998), 39. This procedure is supported by Wellman, *A Theory of Secession: The Case for Political Self-Determination*, 60–61.

56. This is Goodin's interpretation of the principle. Goodin, "Enfranchising All Affected Interests, and Its Alternatives," 52. It is a variation of the all affected interests principle discussed by Robert Dahl, which states: "Everyone who is affected by the decisions of a government should have the right to participate in that government." See Robert A. Dahl, *After the Revolution? Authority in a Good Society* (New Haven, CT: Yale University Press, 1990), 49.

57. Goodin, "Enfranchising All Affected Interests, and Its Alternatives," 52.

58. Dahl, *After the Revolution? Authority in a Good Society*, 51.

59. See, for instance, Daryl J. Glaser, "The Right to Secession: An Antisecessionist Defense," 369–386.

60. Beiner, "National Self-Determination: Some Cautionary Remarks Concerning the Rhetoric of Rights," 160.

61. Lee C. Buchheit, *Secession: The Legitimacy of Self-determination* (New Haven, CT: Yale University Press, 1978), 29–30.

62. Daniel Philpott, "Self-Determination in Practice," 90.

63. Anna Stilz, "Nations, States, and Territory," *Ethics* 121, no. 3 (2011): 594.

64. See Wellman, *A Theory of Secession: The Case for Political Self-Determination*, 3; Beran, "A Democratic Theory of Political Self-Determination for a New World Order," 37–39.

65. Daniel Philpott, "Self-Determination in Practice," in *National Self-Determination and Secession*, ed. Margaret Moore (New York: Oxford University Press, 1998), 80.
66. Brian Orend, *The Morality of War* (Peterborough, Ont.: Broadview Press, 2006), 162.
67. Ibid., 162–163.
68. It is worth noting that this position is similar to the *remedial right* theory, just more elaborated and even more demanding.
69. Neil DeVotta, "The Liberation Tigers of Tamil Eelam and the Lost Quest for Separatism in Sri Lanka," *Asian Survey* 49, no. 6 (2009): 1046–1047. According to Harvard Medical School and the University of Washington, this number is modest. They argue that the real number is at least 215,000 and possibly as high as 338,000. See, Neil DeVotta, "Sri Lanka's Civil War," in *The Routledge Handbook of Asian Security Studies*, ed. Sumit Ganguly, Andrew Scobell, and Joseph Chinyoung Liow (New York: Routledge, 2010), 169n.
70. Sumantra Bose, *Contested Lands: Israel-Palestine, Kashmir, Bosnia, Cyprus, and Sri Lanka* (Cambridge: Harvard University Press, 2007), 13. There is also a smaller Indian Tamil population, which came to Sri Lanka during the colonial period to work on coffee and tea plantations. Stanley Jeyaraja Tambiah, *Sri Lanka: Ethnic Fratricide and the Dismantling of Democracy* (London: I. B. Tauris, 1986), 4.
71. Tambiah, *Sri Lanka: Ethnic Fratricide and the Dismantling of Democracy*, 4–5.
72. Ibid., 6–7.
73. Bose, *Contested Lands: Israel-Palestine, Kashmir, Bosnia, Cyprus, and Sri Lanka*, 12.
74. See more in chapter 5.
75. DeVotta, "Sri Lanka's Civil War," 161.
76. Bose, *Contested Lands: Israel Palestine, Kashmir, Bosnia, Cyprus, and Sri Lanka*, 16–17. In 1957, Tamils were promised some regional autonomy in a pact between political leaders of the two groups, called the B–C Pact, but political pressure led the Sinhalese leader to abrogate it. See, Ibid., 18–19.
77. Ibid., 20.
78. Amita Shastri, "Ending Ethnic Civil War: The Peace Process in Sri Lanka," *Commonwealth & Comparative Politics* 47, no. 1 (2009): 78–79. See also, DeVotta, "The Liberation Tigers of Tamil Eelam and the Lost Quest for Separatism in Sri Lanka," 1027; Tambiah, *Sri Lanka: Ethnic Fratricide and the Dismantling of Democracy*, 17.
79. The Vaddukoddai resolution, printed in Appendix 2, Anne Noronha Dos Santos, *Military Intervention and Secession in South Asia: The*

Cases of Bangladesh, Sri Lanka, Kashmir, and Punjab (Westport, CT: Praeger 2007), 140.

80. DeVotta, "Sri Lanka's Civil War," 166.
81. Richard B. Miller, *Interpretations of Conflict: Ethics, Pacifism, and the Just-War Tradition* (Chicago: University of Chicago Press, 1991), 13.
82. This analogy between an individuals right of self-defense and a state's right of self-defense is what Michael Walzer coined the "domestic analogy." Michael Walzer, *Just and Unjust Wars: A Moral Argument with Historical Illustrations*, 3rd ed. (New York: Basic Books, 1977), 58. For a critical discussion of the relationship between individual and national self-defense, see David Rodin, *War and Self-Defense* (Oxford: Oxford University Press, 2002).
83. Walzer, *Just and Unjust Wars*, 62. Italics removed.
84. Jeff McMahan, "Aggression and Punishment," in *War: Essays in Political Philosophy*, ed. Larry May (New York: Cambridge University Press, 2008), 67.
85. Ibid., 75.
86. DeVotta, "Sri Lanka's Civil War," 163. The Tamil Tigers distinguish between different phases of their armed struggle: Eelam War I (1983–1987), Eelam War II (1990–1994), and Eelam War III (1995–2002). See, Bose, *Contested Lands: Israel-Palestine, Kashmir, Bosnia, Cyprus, and Sri Lanka*, 29. The last stage, Eelam War IV began in mid-2006 and ended with the victory of the government forces in 2009.
87. Tambiah, *Sri Lanka: Ethnic Fratricide and the Dismantling of Democracy*, 15; DeVotta, "The Liberation Tigers of Tamil Eelam and the Lost Quest for Separatism in Sri Lanka," 1028; DeVotta, "Sri Lanka's Civil War," 158.
88. Bose, *Contested Lands: Israel-Palestine, Kashmir, Bosnia, Cyprus, and Sri Lanka*, 28.
89. Tambiah, *Sri Lanka: Ethnic Fratricide and the Dismantling of Democracy*, 16.
90. G. E. M. Anscombe. "War and Murder," in *Ethics, Religion, and Politics,* The Collected Philosophical Papers of G. M. E. Anscombe, Vol. 3. Minneapolis: University of Minnesota Press, 1981, 52. Quoted in McMahan, "Aggression and Punishment," 75–76.
91. A. J. Coates, *The Ethics of War* (Manchester, UK, and New York: Manchester University Press, 1997), 161.
92. Jeff McMahan, "Just Cause for War," *Ethics & International Affairs* 19, no. 3 (2005): 12.
93. Ibid., 12–13.
94. Walzer, *Just and Unjust Wars*, 59. Walzer argues, for instance, that neither the United States nor Saddam Hussein's regime was

fighting a just war in 2003. See Michael Walzer, *Arguing About War* (New Haven, CT: Yale University Press, 2004), 160.

95. According to Bruno Coppieters' conclusion to a book on secession in places like Cyprus, Yugoslavia, Chechnya and Abkhazia, "None of the injustices described in this volume can be regarded as serious enough to constitute a just cause for unilateral secession." Bruno Coppieters, "Conclusion: Just War Theory and the Ethics of Secession," in *Contextualizing Secession: Normative Studies in Comparative Perspective*, edited by Bruno Coppieters and Richard Sakwa (Oxford: Oxford University Press, 2003), 260.

96. Alex J. Bellamy, *Responsibility to Protect: The Global Effort to End Mass Atrocities* (Malden, MA: Polity Press, 2009).

97. James Turner Johnson, "Just War, as It Was and Is," *First Things* 149, January (2005): 23.

98. James Turner Johnson, *The War to Oust Saddam Hussein: Just War and the New Face of Conflict* (Lanham, MD: Rowman & Littlefield, 2005), 62.

99. Coates, *The Ethics of War*, 129.

100. Ibid.

101. Michael Walzer points to yet another problem: "The problem with a secessionist movement is that one cannot be sure that it in fact represents a distinct community until it has rallied its own people and made some headway in the 'arduous struggle' for freedom. The mere appeal to the principle of self-determination isn't enough; evidence must be provided that a community actually exists whose members are committed to independence and ready and able to determine the conditions of their own existence." Walzer, *Just and Unjust Wars*, 93.

102. Bertram I. Spector, "Negotiating with Villains Revisited: Research Note," *International Negotiation* 9, no. 1 (2003): 616.

103. Coates, *The Ethics of War*, 161–162.

104. John Rawls, *The Law of Peoples* (Cambridge: Harvard University Press, 1999), 96.

105. Johnson, "Just War, as It Was and Is," 23.

106. David Rodin, "The Ethics of Asymmetric War," in *The Ethics of War: Shared Problems in Different Traditions*, ed. Richard Sorabji and David Rodin (Aldershot, Hampshire, UK: Ashgate, 2006), 157.

107. DeVotta, "Sri Lanka's Civil War," 166.

108. DeVotta, "The Liberation Tigers of Tamil Eelam and the Lost Quest for Separatism in Sri Lanka," 1029.

109. Neera Chandhoke, "Exploring the Right to Secession: The South Asian Context," *South Asia Research* 28, no. 1 (2008): 15.

110. Shantha K. Hennayake, "Sri Lanka in 1992: Opportunity Missed in the Ethno-Nationalist Crisis," *Asian Survey* 33, no. 2 (1993): 160.
111. Chandhoke, "Exploring the Right to Secession: The South Asian Context," 15.
112. Hennayake, "Sri Lanka in 1992: Opportunity Missed in the Ethno-Nationalist Crisis," 161.
113. DeVotta, "The Liberation Tigers of Tamil Eelam and the Lost Quest for Separatism in Sri Lanka," 1023.
114. Ernest Gellner, *Nations and Nationalism*, 2nd ed. (Ithaca, NY: Cornell University Press, 2006), 2.
115. As cited in Victor S. Mamatey, *The United States and East Central Europe, 1914–1918: A Study in Wilsonian Diplomacy and Propaganda* (Princeton: Princeton University Press, 1957), 174.
116. Donald L. Horowitz, "The Cracked Foundations of the Right to Secede," *Journal of Democracy* 14, no. 2 (2003): 9.
117. His argument is presented in two articles: Chaim Kaufmann, "Possible and Impossible Solutions to Ethnic Civil Wars," *International Security* 20, no. 4 (1996): 136–174; Chaim Kaufmann, "When All Else Fails: Ethnic Population Transfers and Partitions in the Twentieth Century," *International Security* 23, no. 2 (1998): 120–156. Partition can be defined as "a civil war outcome that results in territorial separation of a sovereign state." Nicholas Sambanis and Jonah Schulhofer-Wohl, "What's in a Line? Is Partition a Solution to Civil Wars?" *International Security* 34, no. 2 (2009): 84.
118. Chaim Kaufmann, "Possible and Impossible Solutions to Ethnic Civil Wars," ibid. 20, no. 4 (1996): 137.
119. Ibid., 138–39.
120. Ibid., 137.
121. Matthew Hoddie and Caroline Hartzell, "Signals of Reconciliation: Institution-Building and the Resolution of Civil Wars," *International Studies Review* 7, no. 1 (2005): 22. A classic description of the problem of international anarchy is provided by Robert Jervis, "Cooperation under the Security Dilemma," *World Politics* 30, no. 2 (1978): 167–214.
122. Kaufmann, "Possible and Impossible Solutions to Ethnic Civil Wars," 147.
123. Roy Licklider, "The Consequences of Negotiated Settlements in Civil Wars, 1945–1993," *American Political Science Review* 89, no. 3 (1995): 681.
124. Kaufmann, "Possible and Impossible Solutions to Ethnic Civil Wars," 137.
125. Ibid., 139. Matthew Hoddie and Caroline Hartzell believe that institutions can play an important role in managing conflict. In

their view, the security dilemma is not as prominent as Kaufmann assumes. They believe that adversaries have strong incentives to end conflict and negotiate a settlement, but that misinterpretations and uncertainty often prevent them from doing so. Drawing on neoliberal institutionalism, they believe it is important to design institutional rules that can manage conflict in the postwar state. Hoddie and Hartzell, "Signals of Reconciliation: Institution-Building and the Resolution of Civil Wars," 26. They also argue that third parties can help achieve stability by reducing uncertainty about the adversaries' intentions. Third parties can also observe and verify compliance with agreements, and help enforce them. Ibid., 25.

126. Kaufmann, "When All Else Fails: Ethnic Population Transfers and Partitions in the Twentieth Century," 122.
127. Ibid., 155.
128. Stability is in these studies usually operationalized as the absence of "war recurrence."
129. Thomas Chapman and Philip G. Roeder, "Partition as a Solution to Wars of Nationalism: The Importance of Institutions," *American Political Science Review* 101, no. 4 (2007): 689.
130. Nicholas Sambanis and Jonah Schulhofer-Wohl, "What's in a Line? Is Partition a Solution to Civil Wars?" *International Security* 34, no. 2 (2009): 83, 86, 103–106.
131. Ibid., 110.
132. Ibid., 118.
133. Donald L. Horowitz, *Ethnic Groups in Conflict* (Berkeley: University of California Press, 1985), 589.
134. Richard Holbrooke, *To End a War* (New York: Random House, 1998), 363.
135. Moore, "The Ethics of Secession and Postinvasion Iraq," 65.
136. Sambanis and Schulhofer-Wohl, "What's in a Line? Is Partition a Solution to Civil Wars?" 116.
137. Jayadeva Uyangoda, "Sri Lanka in 2009: From Civil War to Political Uncertainties," *Asian Survey* 50, no. 1 (2010): 104–105. For a discussion of the international reactions to the Sri Lankan effort to defeat the LTTE, see ibid.
138. DeVotta, "Sri Lanka's Civil War," 167.

4 Outcomes of Territorial Wars

1. John A. Vasquez and Brandon Valeriano, "Territory as a Source of Conflict and a Road to Peace," in *The Sage Handbook of Conflict Resolution*, ed. Jacob Bercovitch, Victor Kremenyuk, and I. William Zartman (London: Sage, 2009), 195–197.

2. More exactly, 43 out of the 79 wars, that is, 54.4 percent, were over territory. John A. Vasquez and Brandon Valeriano, "Classification of Interstate Wars," *The Journal of Politics* 72, no. 2 (2010): 300. How many wars can be considered territorial depends obviously on how such conflicts are classified. Included in Vasquez and Valeriano's category "territorial wars" are wars associated with the formation or unification of new states, and wars over adjacent territory of established states. The other issues in their study are policy disagreements, regime, and other. See ibid., 299–300.

3. This number also includes conflicts that did not lead to war. See Paul K. Huth, *Standing Your Ground: Territorial Disputes and International Conflict* (Ann Arbor: University of Michigan Press, 1996), appendix A.

4. Lotta Themnér and Peter Wallensteen, "Armed Conflict, 1946–2010," *Journal of Peace Research* 48, no. 4 (2011): 525, 533–535. None of these conflicts were categorized as international, but nine of them were considered internationalized, meaning that other states were militarily involved with troop support. Ibid., 528. It is worth noting that Themnér and Wallensteen's categorization of territory also includes what I classify as conflicts over statehood.

5. John A. Vasquez, *The War Puzzle Revisited* (Cambridge: Cambridge University Press, 2009), 344.

6. Vasquez and Valeriano, "Classification of Interstate Wars," 295.

7. Barbara F. Walter, "Explaining the Intractability of Territorial Conflict," *International Studies Review* 5, no. 4 (2003): 137.

8. Vasquez, *The War Puzzle Revisited*, 351. See also, Paul R. Hensel, "Charting a Course to Conflict: Territorial Issues and Interstate Conflict, 1816–1992," *Conflict Management and Peace Science* 15, no. 1 (1996): 43–73. On the other hand, when territorial disputes are settled, the chances of a renewal of the militarized international dispute are much lower.

9. Walter, "Explaining the Intractability of Territorial Conflict," 138.

10. Vasquez and Valeriano, "Territory as a Source of Conflict and a Road to Peace," 194–195.

11. David Miller, *On Nationality* (Oxford: Oxford University Press, 1995), 1–2.

12. Tomis Kapitan, "Historical Introduction to the Philosophical Issues," in *Philosophical Perspectives on the Israeli-Palestinian Conflict*, ed. Tomis Kapitan (Armork, NY: M. E. Sharpe, 1997), 9.

13. See, for instance, Hillel Steiner, "Territorial Justice," in *National Rights, International Obligations*, ed. Simon Caney, David George, and Peter Jones (Boulder, CO: Westview Press, 1996), 139–148.

14. David Miller, "Territorial Rights: Concept and Justification" *Political Studies* 60, no. 2 (2012): 2–3. Forthcoming.

15. Ibid., 2.

16. Lea Brilmayer, "Consent, Contract, and Territory," *Minnesota Law Review* 74, no. 1 (1989–1990): 15.

17. David Miller, "Secession and the Principle of Nationality," in *National Self-Determination and Secession*, ed. Margaret Moore (Oxford: Oxford University Press, 1998), 65.

18. Miller, "Territorial Rights: Concept and Justification," 7.

19. Anna Stilz, "Nations, States, and Territory," *Ethics* 121, no. 3 (2011): 579.

20. Ibid., 574.

21. Anna Stilz, "Why Do States Have Territorial Rights?," *International Theory* 1, no. 2 (2009): 187.

22. Chaim Gans, *The Limits of Nationalism* (Cambridge: Cambridge University Press, 2003), 103.

23. Cara Nine, "Superseding Historic Injustice and Territorial Rights," *Critical Review of International Social and Political Philosophy* 11, no. 1 (2008): 82.

24. Indigenous peoples commonly argue that they have a claim to a particular piece of land because they occupied the land first, or at least before the current state system was erected. Contemporary political theorists generally reject this type of indigenousness claim, because it is implausible to claim that being first occupants in and of itself should give rise to a land claim. That is not to say that there are not other good reasons why we should give indigenous populations special land rights. One could argue that such groups should receive land rights as a compensation for injustices they suffered in the past or because they are often discriminated against and disadvantaged. For a discussion, see Gans, *The Limits of Nationalism*, 104–109. For an influential discussion of how to compensate for historic injustice, see Jeremy Waldron, "Superseding Historic Injustice," *Ethics* 103, no. 1 (1992): 4–28. The claim of indigenousness is similar to the legal principle of discovery. Discovery was never regarded as sufficient grounds for title to territory—it had to be coupled with occupancy to give rise to title. See discussion in Surya P. Sharma, *Territorial Acquisition, Disputes and International Law* (The Hague: Kluwer Law International, 1997), 40–46.

25. Gans, *The Limits of Nationalism*, 110.

26. Ibid., 100–101; Stilz, "Nations, States, and Territory," 575.

27. Gans, *The Limits of Nationalism*, 100.

28. For a discussion of Kosovo Polje and its meaning for the Serb nationhood, see George W. White, *Nationalism and Territory:*

Constructing Group Identity in Southeastern Europe (Lanham, MD: Rowman & Littlefield, 2000), 217–218; Malcolm, Noel, *Kosovo: A Short History* (New York: Harper Perennial 1999), 58–80.

29. For a description of Milosevic's visit to Kosovo and the impact it had on his career, see Laura Silber and Allan Little, *Yugoslavia: Death of a Nation*, Rev. and updated ed. (New York: Penguin Books, 1997), 37–40.

30. E. A. Hammel, "Demography and the Origins of the Yugoslav Civil War," *Anthropology Today* 9, no. 1 (1993): 5.

31. Margaret Moore, *The Ethics of Nationalism* (Oxford: Oxford University Press, 2001), 190.

32. Margaret Moore, "The Territorial Dimension of Self-Determination," in *National Self-Determination and Secession*, ed. Margaret Moore (Oxford: Oxford University Press, 1998), 137.

33. A similar position is taken by Moore in *The Ethics of Nationalism*, 190.

34. John Locke, *Second Treatise of Government*, ed. C. B Macpherson (Indianapolis: Hackett, 1980), 19 (§28).

35. Ibid., 21 (§32).

36. David Lyons, "The New Indian Claims and Original Rights to Land," *Social Theory and Practice* 4, no.3 (1977): 254.

37. For a different interpretation, see Jeremy Waldron, "Enough and as Good Left for Others," *The Philosophical Quarterly* 29, no. 117 (1979): 319–328.

38. Locke, *Second Treatise of Government*, 19 (§27).

39. Ibid., 21 (§ 33).

40. Ibid. (§ 31).

41. Ibid., 23 (§ 37).

42. For a more thorough discussion of these and other questions, see, for instance, John T. Sanders, "Justice and the Initial Acquisition of Property," *Harvard Journal of Law and Public Policy* 10, no. 2 (1987): 377–380.

43. For a discussion, see, for instance, Jeremy Waldron, "Two Worries about Mixing One's Labour," *The Philosophical Quarterly* 33, no. 130 (1983): 37–44; Clark Wolf, "Contemporary Property Rights, Lockean Provisos, and the Interests of Future Generations," *Ethics* 105, no. 4 (1995): 791–818.

44. Karl Olivecrona, "Locke's Theory of Appropriation," *The Philosophical Quarterly* 24, no. 96 (1974): 225–226.

45. Robert Nozick, *Anarchy, State and Utopia* (New York: Basic Books, 1974), 174–175. See also, Waldron, "Two Worries about Mixing One's Labour."

46. Waldron, "Two Worries about Mixing One's Labour," 44.
47. Stilz, "Why Do States Have Territorial Rights?," 190; Tamar Meisels, *Territorial Rights* (Dordrecht, Netherlands: Springer, 2009), 6; Locke, *Second Treatise of Government*, 27–28 (§45).
48. Steiner, "Territorial Justice," 143.
49. Ibid., 146.
50. Allen Buchanan, "The Making and Unmaking of Boundaries: What Liberalism Has to Say," in *States, Nations, and Borders: The Ethics of Making Boundaries*, ed. Allen Buchanan and Margaret Moore (New York: Cambridge University Press, 2003), 233.
51. Ibid., 234. See also, Cara Nine, "A Lockean Theory of Territory," *Political Studies* 56, no, 1 (2008): 150–151.
52 Nine, "A Lockean Theory of Territory," 151.
53. This view is defended by Hillel Steiner, in Steiner, "Territorial Justice." For Steiner's response to Nine's criticism, see Hillel Steiner, "May Lockean Doughnuts Have Holes? The Geometry of Territorial Jurisdiction: A Response to Nine," *Political Studies* 56, no. 4 (2008): 949–956.
54. Cara Nine, "A Lockean Theory of Territory," 152. On the other hand, if we do not include metajurisdictional authority in the property right, we have to abandon the social-contract element of the theory. For discussion, see ibid., 153–154.
55. Ibid., 153.
56. Cara Nine defends, therefore, a collectivist Lockean theory without reference to property rights or to individual consent. She argues instead that territorial rights help realize other important liberal values, like liberty, desert, and efficiency. Ibid., 154–164.
57. Meisels, *Territorial Rights*, 8.
58. David Miller, *National Responsibility and Global Justice* (Oxford: Oxford University Press, 2007), 218.
59. Meisels, *Territorial Rights*, 124.
60. Stilz, "Nations, States, and Territory," 576–577.
61. Ibid., 577.
62. Miller, *National Responsibility and Global Justice*, 217–218.
63. Ibid., 218–219.
64. Meisels, *Territorial Rights*, 126.
65. Miller, "Secession and the Principle of Nationality," 68.
66. Allen Buchanan, *Secession: The Morality of Political Divorce from Fort Sumter to Lithuania and Quebec* (Boulder, CO: Westview Press, 1991), 109–110.
67. Lea Brilmayer, *Justifying International Acts* (Ithaca: Cornell University Press, 1989), 76–77.
68. Ibid.

69. I borrow this term, as well as the two-staged procedure in assessing territorial claims, from Stilz, "Nations, States, and Territory," 590.

70. Ibid.

71. Leonard Downie Jr., "Plea by Reagan Ignored; Argentina Seizes British Colony," *The Washington Post*, April 2, 1982.

72. "Excerpts from Speeches of Argentine Foreign Minister and British Delegate," *The New York Times*, May 25, 1982.

73. Serb paramilitary forces had taken control of almost one-third of Croatia's territory, primarily in the eastern Krajina region and in Eastern and Western Slavonia.

74. Richard Holbrooke, *To End a War* (New York: Random House, 1998), 45.

75. Richard J. Regan, *Just War: Principles and Cases* (Washington, DC: The Catholic University of America Press, 1996), 60.

76. Ibid.

77. See discussion in, Alexander B. Murphy, "Historical Justifcations for Territorial Claims," *Annals of the Association of American Geographers* 80, no. 4 (1990): 537.

78. Oscar Schachter, "The Lawful Resort to Unilateral Use of Force," *Yale Journal of International Law* 10, no. 2 (1985): 292.

79. Regan, *Just War: Principles and Cases*, 60.

80. Ibid., 61.

81. For a discussion, see Mark W. Zacher, "The Territorial Integrity Norm: International Boundaries and the Use of Force," *International Organization* 55, no. 2 (2001): 215.

82. For a discussion of the demise of the right to conquest, see, Sharon Korman, *The Right of Conquest: The Acquisition of Territory by Force in International Law and Practice* (Oxford: Clarendon Press, 1996).

83. The Kellogg-Briand Pact is more properly known as the General Treaty for the Renunciation of War. The text of this treaty as well as a number of other treaties and documents relating to law and diplomacy are available at: http://avalon.law.yale.edu/.

    cher, "The Territorial Integrity Norm: International Boundaries the Use of Force," 236–237.

    R. Ratner, "Drawing a Better Line: *Uti Possidetis* and the s of New States," *American Journal of International Law* (1996): 593.

    Territorial Acquisition, 120.

    national Court of Justice, Frontier Dispute (Burkina lic of Mali), Judgment December 22, 1986, quoted N. Shaw, *International Law*, 5th ed. (Cambridge: iversity Press, 2003), 448.

88. Ratner, "Drawing a Better Line," 593–601.
89. This view is expressed in Opinion no. 3. The three opinions of the Arbitration Committee are printed as an appendix to Alain Pellet, "The Opinions of the Badinter Arbitration Committee: A Second Breath for the Self-Determination of Peoples," *European Journal of International Law* 3, no. 1 (1992): 182–185.
90. Ratner, "Drawing a Better Line," 591. Despite its purpose, however, the application of the principle has sometimes led to conflict. In Latin America, for instance, border disputes sometimes broke out because one could interpret the principle to mean either *uti possidetis juris* (that legal possession of territory was defined by Spanish legal documents) or *uti possidetis facto* (that legal possession of territory was defined by the land actually held at time of independence). See Beth A. Simmons, *Territorial Disputes and Their Resolution: The Case of Ecuador and Peru*. Peaceworks no. 27 (Washington, DC: United States Institute of Peace, 1999), 4. Available at: http://www.usip.org/publications/territorial -disputes-and-their-resolution.
91. Zacher, "The Territorial Integrity Norm: International Boundaries and the Use of Force," 234–235.
92. Murphy, "Historical Justifcations for Territorial Claims," 533.
93. Ibid., 534.
94. Ibid., 534–357.
95. Ibid., 533.
96. Waldron, "Superseding Historic Injustice," 15–17.
97. Miller, *National Responsibility and Global Justice*, 219.
98. Waldron, "Superseding Historic Injustice," 20.
99. Ibid., 19.
100. Jeff McMahan, "Just Cause for War," *Ethics & International Affairs* 19, no. 3 (2005): 12–13.
101. Ibid.
102. For more on this conflict, see Brian M. Mueller, "The Falkland Islands: Will the Real Owner Please Stand Up?," *Notre Dame Law Review* 58 (1982–83): 616–634; Lowell S. Gustafson, *The Sovereignty Dispute over the Falkland (Malvinas) Islands* (New York and Oxford: Oxford University Press, 1988); Miguel Antonio Sanchez, "Self-Determination and the Falkland Islands Dispute," *Columbia Journal of Transnational Law* 21(1982– 1983): 557–584; Peter Calvert, "Sovereignty and the Falklands Crisis," *International Affairs* 59, no. 3 (1983): 405–413.
103. Samantha Power, *"A Problem from Hell": America and the Age of Genocide* (New York: Harper Perennial, 2003), 247; Marc Tanner, *Croatia: A Nation Forged in War*, 3rd ed. (New Haven, CT: Yale University Press, 2010), 275–278.

104. Zacher, "The Territorial Integrity Norm: International Boundaries and the Use of Force," 224.
105. Mona Fixdal and Ingrid O. Busterud, "The Undiplomatic Diplomat: Peter Galbraith," in *Ways out of War: Peacemakers in the Middle East and Balkans*, ed. Mona Fixdal (New York: Palgrave Macmillan, 2012). Forthcoming.
106. Norman M. Naimark, *Fires of Hatred: Ethnic Cleansing in Twentieth-Century Europe* (Cambridge Harvard University Press, 2001), 174.
107. Holbrooke, *To End a War*, 363.
108. Mark Danner, *Stripping Bare the Body: Politics, Violence, War* (New York: Nation Books, 2009), 301.
109. Sabrina P. Ramet, *Balkan Babel: The Disintegration of Yugoslavia from the Death of Tito to the Fall of Milosevic* (Boulder, CO: Westview Press, 2002), 232.
110. Quoted in Danner, *Stripping Bare the Body: Politics, Violence, War*, 302.
111. Ramet, *Balkan Babel: The Disintegration of Yugoslavia from the Death of Tito to the Fall of Milosevic*, 232.
112. Quoted in, Tanner, *Croatia: A Nation Forged in War*, 299.
113. Danner, *Stripping Bare the Body: Politics, Violence, War*, 302–303; Tanner, *Croatia: A Nation Forged in War*, 298; "Croatia: Impunity for Abuses Committed During 'Operation Storm' and the Denial of the Right of Refugees to Return to the Krajina," Human Rights Watch / Helsinki 8, no. 13 (1996). Available at http://www.hrw.org/sites /default/files/reports/croatia968.pdf.
114. Korman, *Right of Conquest*, 305.
115. Buchanan, "Making and Unmaking of Boundaries," 242.
116. Ibid., 243.
117. Ibid.
118. Henry Shue and David Rodin, Introduction to *Preemption: Military Action and Moral Justification*, ed. Henry Shue and David Rodin (Oxford: Oxford University Press, 2007), 3.
119. This debate was renewed in part because of President Bush's 2003 National Security Statement, which declared that the United States must "stop rogue states and their terrorist clients before they are able to threaten or use weapons of mass destruction against the United States and our allies and friends." Quoted in David Luban, "Preventive War," *Philosophy & Public Affairs* 32, no. 3 (2004): 207.
120. See Kinga Tibori Szabó, *Anticipatory Action in Self-Defense: Essence and Limits under International Law* (The Hague: T.M.C. Asser Press, 2010), 5. While I use the terms interchangeably here, some scholars make a distinction between anticipation and preemption.

See, for instance, W. Michael Reisman, "Assessing Claims to Revise the Laws of War," *The American Journal of International Law* 97, no. 1 (2003): 87.

121. See Michael W. Doyle, "International Law and Current Standards," in *Striking First: Preemption and Prevention in International Conflict*, ed. Stephen Macedo (Princeton: Princeton University Press, 2008), 11–12; Michael Walzer, *Just and Unjust Wars: A Moral Argument with Historical Illustrations*, 3rd ed. (New York: Basic Books, 1977): 74–75.

122. Shue and Rodin, Introduction, 3.

123. Walzer, *Just and Unjust Wars*, 85.

124. See ibid., 82–85.

125. Luban, "Preventive War," 213. Preventive war is much more difficult to justify, both in legal theory and in moral theory. For discussions, see, for instance, ibid; Shue and Rodin, Introduction.

126. Peter Andreas, "Redrawing the Line: Borders and Security in the Twenty-First Century," *International Security* 28, no. 2 (2003): 80–81.

127. Wesley K. Clark, *Waging Modern War: Bosnia, Kosovo, and the Future of Combat* (New York: Public Affairs, 2001), 53–54.

128. Robert Gilpin, *War and Change in World Politics* (Cambridge: Cambridge University Press, 1981), 23.

129. Quoted in Shlomo Ben-Ami, *Scars of War, Wounds of Peace: The Israeli-Arab Tragedy* (Oxford: Oxford University Press, 2006), 122.

130. Yigal Allon, "Israel: The Case for Defensible Borders," *Foreign Affairs* 55, no. 1 (1976): 41.

131. W. W. Harris, "War and Settlement Change: The Golan Heights and the Jordan Rift, 1967–77," *Transactions of the Institute of British Geographers* 3, no. 3 (1978): 309.

132. Michael I. Handel, "The Evolution of Israeli Strategy: The Psychology of Insecurity and the Quest for Absolute Security," in *The Making of Strategy: Rulers, States, and War*, ed. Williamson Murray, Macgregor Knox, and Alvin Bernstein (Cambridge: Cambridge University Press, 1994), 538.

133. In fact, on June 19, ten days after the war was over, the Israeli cabinet voted for a conditional withdrawal from large parts of the territories (but not from the Gaza strip). The proposal, according to Avi Shlaim, was never transmitted to Egypt and Syria. Avi Shlaim, *The Iron Wall: Israel and the Arab World* (New York: W. W. Norton, 2001), 253–254.

134. Ann Mosely Lesch, "Israeli Settlements in the Occupied Territories, 1967–1977," *Journal of Palestine Studies* 7, no. 1 (1977): 26.

135. Ibid. Especially with regard to the West Bank, one cannot claim that the intention of these annexations was their assumed military value.
136. Martin van Creveld, *Defending Israel: A Controversial Plan toward Peace* (New York: Thomas Dunne Books, 2004), 23.
137. Shlaim, *The Iron Wall: Israel and the Arab World*, 254.
138. Ibid.
139. David Rodman, "Review Essay: Israel's National Security Doctrine: An Appraisal of the Past and a Vision of the Future," *Israel Affairs* 9, no. 4 (2003): 120.
140. Ibid., 121.
141. Ibid.
142. van Creveld, *Defending Israel: A Controversial Plan toward Peace*, 8–9.
143. Ibid., 10.
144. Ibid., 20.
145. Ibid., 26.
146. Shlaim, *The Iron Wall: Israel and the Arab World*, 451.
147. Ibid. For further discussion on Palestinian nationalism and the resistance movement, see Yezid Sayigh, *Armed Struggle and the Search for State: The Palestinian National Movement, 1949–1993* (Oxford: Oxford University Press, 1997).
148. Rodman, "Review Essay: Israel's National Security Doctrine: An Appraisal of the Past and a Vision of the Future," 121.
149. van Creveld, *Defending Israel: A Controversial Plan toward Peace*, 108–109.
150. Ben-Ami, *Scars of War, Wounds of Peace*, 130.
151. Andreas, "Redrawing the Line: Borders and Security in the Twenty-First Century," 82.
152. Ibid., 84.

5   OUTCOMES OF WARS OVER GOVERNMENT

1. A caveat is in order here. The choice of political institutions has to be sensitive to the challenges that the particular country faces. Furthermore, institutional design can be a complex and often very technical topic. My discussion will by necessity therefore be quite general.
2. Michael Walzer, *Just and Unjust Wars: A Moral Argument with Historical Illustrations*, 3rd ed. (New York: Basic Books, 1977), 335.
3. Harvey Waterman, "Political Order and the 'Settlement' of Civil Wars," in *Stopping the Killing: How Civil Wars End*, ed. Roy Licklider (New York: New York University Press, 1993), 292.

4. Nicole Ball, "The Challenge of Rebuilding War-Torn Societies," in *Turbulent Peace: The Challenges of Managing International Conflict*, ed. Chester A. Crocker, Fen Osler Hampson, and Pamela Aall (Washington, DC: United States of Peace Press, 2001), 719–721.

5. Roland Paris, *At War's End: Building Peace after Civil Conflict* (New York: Cambridge University Press, 2004), 173.

6. Matthias Stiefel, "Rebuilding after War: Lessons from the War-Torn Societies Project," (Geneva: War-Torn Societies Project & Programme for Strategic and International Security Studies, 1999), 12–13.

7. Ibid., 13.

8. Ian Lustick, "Stability in Deeply Divided Societies: Consociationalism versus Control," *World Politics* 31, no. 3 (1979): 325. The notion of a deeply divided society might be challenged because it paints a picture of national identities as permanent and fixed. But ethnic differences are not set in stone. Rather, they evolve over time. That said, we do not need to accept a view of ethnicity as unchangeable in order to find the notion of a deeply divided society valuable. This concept highlights that deep cleavages as well as a high degree of hatred and intolerance often mark a post–civil war society. For a discussion, see Ian Shapiro and Courtney Jung, "South African Democracy Revisited: A Reply to Koelble and Reynolds," *Politics & Society* 24, no. 3 (1996): 243. See also, Ian Shapiro, "Democratic Innovation: South Africa in Comparative Context," *World Politics* 46, no. 1 (1993): 143. An ethnic groups share many of the same traits as a national group, that is, a common history, a shared language and a culture that sets it apart from other groups. But a nation is often thought to be more self-conscious than an ethnic group, and also have a more clearly defined political identity. See discussion in, Adrian Hastings, *The Construction of Nationhood: Ethnicity, Religion, and Nationalism* (Cambridge: Cambridge University Press, 1997), 2–3.

9. Donald L. Horowitz, *Ethnic Groups in Conflict* (Berkeley: University of California Press, 1985), 12.

10. Fred Charles Ikle, *Every War Must End* (New York: Columbia University Press, 1991), 95.

11. Roy Licklider, "The Consequences of Negotiated Settlements in Civil Wars, 1945–1993," *American Political Science Review* 89, no. 3 (1995): 681.

12. Kofi Annan, "Why Democracy Is An International Issue," Cyril Foster Lecture, Oxford, June 19, 2001. Available at: http://www.un.or /News/ossg/sg/stories/statments_search_full.asp?statID=11.

13. Anna K. Jarstad and Timothy Sisk, introduction to *From War to Democracy: Dilemmas of Peacebuilding*, ed. Anna K. Jarstad and Timothy Sisk (Cambridge: Cambridge University Press, 2008), 3.

14. I am here making the common distinction between procedural fairness and outcome fairness, that is, between "fairness as a procedure that gives an equal chance for each participant to affect the outcome," and "fairness as a tendency of a procedure to produce results that are just." See David Estlund, introduction to *Democracy*, ed. David Estlund (Malden, MA: Blackwell, 2002), 6.

15. Most definitions of democracy will especially emphasize the first two of these three factors, competition for power and the participation of citizens through the electoral system. See Samuel P. Huntington, "The Modest Meaning of Democracy," in *Democracy in the Americas: Stopping the Pendulum*, ed. Robert A. Pastor (New York: Holmes & Meier, 1989), 15–16.

16. Joseph A. Schumpeter, *Capitalism, Socialism and Democracy* (London: George Allen & Unwin, 1976), 269. One of the great empirical advantages of Schumpeter's definition is that it makes it possible to distinguish democracy from other political systems. For a further discussion of advantages and problems with the Schumpeter model of democracy, see Ian Shapiro, *The State of Democratic Theory* (Princeton: Princeton University Press, 2003), 55–64.

17. Shapiro, *The State of Democratic Theory*, 55–58.

18. See discussion in Benjamin Reilly, *Democracy in Divided Societies: Electoral Engineering for Conflict Management* (Cambridge: Cambridge University Press, 2001), 3.

19. Robert A. Dahl, *Democracy and Its Critics* (New Haven, CT: Yale University Press, 1989), 221.

20. Samuel P. Huntington, *The Third Wave: Democratization in the Late Twentieth Century* (Norman: University of Oklahoma Press, 1991), 7.

21. Will Kymlicka, *Contemporary Political Philosophy: An Introduction* (New York: Oxford University Press, 2002), 3–4. Kymlicka builds his argument on suggestions made by Dworkin, for instance, in Ronald Dworkin, *Taking Rights Seriously* (London: Duckworth, 1977), 179–183.

22. Kymlicka, *Contemporary Political Philosophy*, 4. The idea of equality is also closely connected to the idea of liberty. To the extent that we are concerned about promoting people's interests, we must be concerned about securing the liberties that protect these interests. To take Kymlicka's example: if we agree that every person has an important interest in marrying the person of his or her choice, we also have

to protect that interest with a corresponding freedom. Denying a person that liberty would be the same as denying the person's "equal standing as a human being whose well-being is a matter of equal concern." Ibid., 139.

23. Ibid., 4.
24. John Rawls, *A Theory of Justice* (Cambridge, MA: Harvard University Press, 1971), 221.
25. Rawls, *A Theory of Justice*, 223–224.
26. Ibid., 222.
27. James S. Fishkin, *Tyranny and Legitimacy: A Critique of Political Theories* (Baltimore, MD: The Johns Hopkins University Press, 1979), 5.
28. Ibid., 71.
29. Alexander Hamilton or James Madison, "The Federalist No. 51: The Structure of the Government Must Furnish the Proper Checks and Balances between the Different Departments," in *The Federalist Papers*, Alexander Hamilton, James Madison, and John Jay. Edited by Michael A. Genovese (New York: Palgrave Macmillan, 2009), 121.
30. Clearly, not every majority decision is tyrannical. How, then, do we distinguish between majority decisions that are tyrannical and majority decisions that are not? What most approaches to this question agree on is that tyrannical policies violate individuals' essential interests or rights. Thus, Robert Dahl interprets Madison's definition of tyrannical policies to be cases where there are "severe deprivations of natural rights." See, Robert A. Dahl, *A Preface to Democratic Theory* (Chicago: The University of Chicago Press, 1956), 6. But Fishkin believes the concept of "natural rights" is difficult to define precisely, and prefers therefore to define tyrannical policies as those that destroy the essential interests of parts of the population. See, Fishkin, *Tyranny and Legitimacy: A Critique of Political Theories*, 13, 19.
31. For a general overview of this topic, see Katharine Belmont, Scott Mainwaring, and Andrew Reynolds, "Introduction: Institutional Design, Conflict Management, and Democracy," in *The Architecture of Democracy: Constitutional Design, Conflict Management, and Democracy*, ed. Andrew Reynolds (Oxford: Oxford University Press, 2002), 1–11.
32. John McGarry and Brendan O'Leary, "Introduction: The Macro-Political Regulation of Ethnic Conflict," in *The Politics of Ethnic Conflict Regulation*, ed. John McGarry and Brendan O'Leary (London: Routledge, 1993), 23.
33. Other historical examples can be found in Lustick, "Stability Deeply Divided Societies," 330.

34. McGarry and O'Leary, "Introduction: The Macro-Political Regulation of Ethnic Conflict," 23.

35. Majoritarian democracies, which I will discuss more fully below, can also sometimes be described as political systems based on hegemonic control, but in a most of cases, hegemonic control is exercised in political systems that are not democratic. For a fuller discussion of how democracies can be compatible with hegemonic control, see ibid., 24–25.

36. Milton J. Esman, *Ethnic Politics* (Ithaca: Cornell University Press, 1994), 44.

37. Ian Lustick argues that "in particular situations and for limited periods of time, certain forms of control may be preferable to the chaos and bloodshed that might be the only alternative." See, Lustick, "Stability in Deeply Divided Societies," 344.

38. See Arend Lijphart, *Democracy in Plural Societies: A Comparative Exploration* (New Haven and London: Yale University Press, 1977), 227.

39. Arend Lijphart, *Democracies: Pattern of Majoritarian and Consensus Government in Twenty-One Countries* (New Haven, CT: Yale University Press, 1984), 4–9.

40. Reilly, *Democracy in Divided Societies: Electoral Engineering for Conflict Management*, 15.

41. These include the block vote system, which is essentially a FPTP system in multimember districts, and the run-off system, in which voting takes place in two rounds, and the second round is a run-off between the two candidates with most votes from the first round. For a description of these and two other majority systems, see ibid., 15–16.

42. Horowitz, *Ethnic Groups in Conflict*, 83–84.

43. McGarry and O'Leary, "Introduction: The Macro-Political Regulation of Ethnic Conflict," 24.

44. Timothy D. Sisk, *Power Sharing and International Mediation in Ethnic Conflicts* (Washington, DC: United States Institute of Peace, 1996), 33.

45. Andrew Reynolds, "Constitutional Medicine," *Journal of Democracy* 16, no. 1 (2005): 55.

46. Horowitz, *Ethnic Groups in Conflict*, 84.

47. Lijphart, *Democracies: Pattern of Majoritarian and Consensus Government in Twenty-One Countries*, 23.

48. Shapiro, "Democratic Innovation," 125.

49. Sisk, *Power Sharing and International Mediation*, vii.

50. Ibid., 5. Power sharing can be formally incorporated into the constitution or may exist as an informal agreement between elites. See, David A. Lake and Donald Rothchild, "Containing Fear: The

Origins and Management of Ethnic Conflict," *International Security* 21, no. 2 (1996): 59.

51. Donald Rothchild and Philip G. Roeder, "Power Sharing as an Impediment to Peace and Democracy," in *Sustainable Peace: Power and Democracy after Civil Wars*, ed. Philip G. Roeder and Donald Rothchild (Ithaca and London: Cornell University Press, 2005), 35.

52. Horowitz's model has some features in common with consociationalism, such as federalism. But unlike consociationalism, the integrative approach attempts to transcend ethnic group differences. The five main features of this model are: (1) the dispersion of power among the central political institutions; (2) arrangements that decentralize power and make intraethnic competition more important; (3) arrangements that make interethnic cooperation desirable, for instance, through an electoral system such as the alternative vote system (AV) and the single transferable vote system (STV); (4) policies that promote other sources of identification than ethnicity; and (5) politics that reduce differences between ethnic groups and reduce dissatisfaction among the less advantaged groups. For a discussion of these features, see Horowitz, *Ethnic Groups in Conflict*, 597–600; Sisk, *Power Sharing and International Mediation*, 40–45. One problem with this model is that that few countries have the "full packages of all the right institutions." Thus we have limited information about how this political system would work. See ibid., 44.

53. Lijphart develops his model with respect to European countries, in particular the Netherlands. He is aware that there might be problems connected to transporting this essentially European model to countries in Africa and Asia. See Lijphart, *Democracy in Plural Societies*, 21–24. For a further discussion of some of these problems, see Horowitz, *Ethnic Groups in Conflict*, 571–576.

54. Lijphart, *Democracy in Plural Societies*, 25.

55. Ibid., 31.

56. Arend Lijphart, "The Wave of Power-Sharing Democracy," in *The Architecture of Democracy: Constitutinal Design, Conflict Management, and Democracy*, ed. Andrew Reynolds (Oxford: Oxford University Press, 2002), 38–39.

57. Lijphart, *Democracy in Plural Societies*, 36–41.

58. Donald L. Horowitz, *A Democratic South Africa? Constitutional Engineering in a Divided Society* (Berkley and Los Angeles: University of California Press, 1991), 168.

59. Lijphart, *Democracy in Plural Societies*, 41–42. The first and last of these four features—the sharing of executive power group autonomy—are thought to be the least controversial.

discussion, see Lijphart, "The Wave of Power-Sharing Democracy," 38–40.

60. Sisk, *Power Sharing and International Mediation*, 37.

61. McGarry and O'Leary, "Introduction: The Macro-Political Regulation of Ethnic Conflict," 36.

62. Lijphart, *Democracy in Plural Societies*, 238. He stands by that assertion 25 years later. See Lijphart, "The Wave of Power-Sharing Democracy," 37.

63. According to Hartzell and Hoddie, only 1 out of the 38 civil wars in their material that ended in a peace agreement, did not contain some form of power-sharing provision. See, Caroline Hartzell and Matthew Hoddie, "Institutionalizing Peace: Power Sharing and Post–Civil War Conflict Managment," *American Journal of Political Science* 47, no. 2 (2003), 319. It is worth noting that power sharing is here defined more broadly than in Lijphart's consociational model. As Anna Jarstad points out, in democratic theory, power sharing is usually defined in accordance with Lijphart's theory of consociationalism, as I have done here. But in the conflict-resolution literature, power sharing is defined as all types of sharing and dividing power among former enemies. See, Anna K. Jarstad, "Power Sharing: Former Enemies in Joint Government," in *From War to Democracy: Dilemmas of Peacebuilding*, edited by Anna K. Jarstad and Timothy Sisk (Cambridge: Cambridge University Press, 2008), 109.

64. Jarstad, "Power Sharing: Former Enemies in Joint Government," 112.

65. Barbara F. Walter, *Committing to Peace: The Successful Settlement of Civil Wars* (Princeton: Princeton University Press, 2002), 80.

66. For more on the reasons why adversaries want security and political guarantees in the transition from war to peace, see Caroline Hartzell, "Structuring the Peace: Negotiated Settlements and the Construction of Conflict Management Institutions," in *Conflict Prevention and Peacebuilding in Post-War Societies: Sustaining the Peace*, ed. T. David Mason and James D. Meernik (London and New York: Routledge, 2006), 36–38.

67. Matthew Hoddie and Caroline Hartzell, "Power Sharing in Peace Settlements: Initiating the Transition from Civil War," in *Sustainable Peace: Power and Democracy after Civil Wars*, ed. Philip G. Roeder and Donald Rothchild (Ithaca and London: Cornell University Press, 2005), 103. See also, Hartzell, "Structuring the Peace: Negotiated Settlements and the Construction of Conflict Management Institutions," 48.

68. For an outline of these problems, see generally, Rothchild and Roeder, "Power Sharing as an Impediment to Peace and Democracy," 36–41.

69. Anna K. Jarstad, "Dilemmas of War-to-Democracy Transitions: Theories and Concepts," in *From War to Democracy: Dilemmas of Peacebuilding*, edited by Anna K. Jarstad and Timothy Sisk (Cambridge: Cambridge University Press), 35.

70. Paris, *At War's End*, 205.

71. Ibid., 151. Earlier versions of his argument can be found in Roland Paris, "Peacebuilding and the Limits of Liberal Internationalism," *International Security* 22, no. 2 (1997): 54–89; Roland Paris, "Wilson's Ghost: The Faulty Assumptions of Postconflict Peacebuilding," in *Turbulent Peace: The Challenges of Managing International Conflict*, ed. Chester A. Crocker, Fen Osler Hampson, and Pamela Aall (Washington, D.C.: United States Institute of Peace Press, 2001), 765–784.

72. Paris, *At War's End*, 6. Paris argues that the same problems are connected to politices of economic liberalization.

73. Benjamin Reilly, "Post-War Elections: Uncertain Turning Points of Transition," in Jarstad and Sisk, eds., *From War to Democracy: Dilemmas of Peacebuilding*, 157–158, 161.

74. Paris, *At War's End*, 189.

75. Ibid., 188.

76. These elections were to the Bosnia-wide presidency and to the national parliament, as well as to the assembly of the Federation of Bosnia Herzegovina and the National Assembly of the Republika Srpska. The municipal elections, however, were postponed because the situation on the ground was not thought to be ready.

77. Elizabeth Neuffer, "Bosnia Campaign Emphasizes Ethnic Division," *The Boston Globe*, September 13, 1996. For the even more extremist messages of the Serb Radical Party, which was allied with the Serbian Democratic Party (SDS), see Chris Hedges, "Serb Militants Are Running Hard for Posts in Bosnia Election," *The New York Times*, September 1, 1996.

78. See, for instance, Chris Hedges, "Bosnians Vote, But Animosity Is Unrelenting," *The New York Times*, September 14, 1997; Elizabeth Neuffer, "Democracy, Division Clash in Bosnia," *The Boston Globe*, September 13, 1997.

79. International Crisis Group (ICG), *State of the Balkans*, ICG Balkans Report No. 47, Brussels: ICG, November 4, 1998. Quoted in Timothy Donasis, "Division and Democracy: Bosnia's Post-Dayton Elections," in *The Lessons of Yugoslavia*, ed. Metta Spencer (Amsterdam: Elsevier Science, 2000), 248.

80. Benjamin Reilly, "Political Engineering and Party Politics Conflict-Prone Societies," *Democratization* 13, no. 5 (2006): 8

81. For a short discussion of most of these problems, and Arend Lijph response to them, see Donald L. Horowitz, "Constitu

Design: Proposals versus Processes," in *The Architecture of Democracy: Constitutional Design, Conflict Management, and Democracy*, ed. Andrew Reynolds (Oxford: Oxford University Press, 2002), and Lijphart, "The Wave of Power-Sharing Democracy."

82. Esman, *Ethnic Politics*, 257.

83. Reilly, "Political Engineering and Party Politics in Conflict-Prone Societies," 814.

84. Ibid.

85. Ibid., 812.

86. Lijphart, *Democracy in Plural Societies*, 30–31.

87. Horowitz, "Constitutional Design," 20–21; Horowitz, *A Democratic South Africa?*, 140–141.

88. Lee Hockstader, "Bosnian Serb Elections Appear to Deal Setback to Hard-Line Nationalists," *The Washington Post*, December 2, 1997.

89. Chris Hedges, "Muslim Detention of Bosnian Serbs Threatens Truce," *The New York Times*, February 7, 1997. The incident obviously also illustrates the general lack of cooperation between Republika Srpska and the ICTY in The Hague.

90. As Burg notes, lack of elite cooperation must be seen as one of the reasons why Bosnia disintegrated into war. He argues that, "both in their behavior during the electoral campaign, and in their actions upon assuming political power, the leaderships of the three nationalist parties contributed to intensifying the salience of ethnicity for politics, and refused to engage in compromise." Steven L. Burg, "Bosnia Herzegovina: A Case of Failed Democratization," in *Politics, Power, and the Struggle for Democracy in South-East Europe*, ed. Karen Dawisha and Bruce Parrott (Cambridge: Cambridge University Press, 1997), 135.

91. Rothchild and Roeder, "Power Sharing as an Impediment to Peace and Democracy," 41–49.

92. Ibid., 49.

93. Benjamin Reilly has termed this approach "centripetalism," because the hope is to make political competition move to the center, rather than to the periphery. Reilly, "Political Engineering and Party Politics in Conflict-Prone Societies," 816.

94. Ibid., 815–816.

95. Ibid. For a discussion of how this has been done, see ibid., 818–825.

96. Let us assume that there are 100,000 votes to be cast and three candidates, A, B, and C. Each candidate represents one ethnic group; A represents the A's, B represents the B's, and C represents the C's. Let us also assume that A and B have been expressing

hostility towards the other two ethnic groups, but that C has been accommodating and moderate. We might also stipulate that ethnic group A is smaller than the other two. When citizens vote, they express both their first and second preference. In the first count, we can assume that each candidate gets the support from his own ethnic group, so that although A has fewer votes than B or C, no one has the necessary majority to win. In order to win candidates, B and C have to rely on the second preference of the A voters. Since C has been more accommodating and moderate, we can expect that the A voters would list him as their second preference. Therefore the moderate candidate wins. This account is based on an illustration of the alternative vote system from the Australian electoral Commission, reprinted in Reilly, *Democracy in Divided Societies: Electoral Engineering for Conflict Management*, 19. For a description of other ways to encourage vote pooling, see ibid., 17–18.

97. Horowitz, *A Democratic South Africa?*, 196.
98. Sisk, *Power Sharing and International Mediation*, 35, 40. See also, Horowitz, *A Democratic South Africa?*, 154–155, 197.
99. See discussion in, Reilly, "Political Engineering and Party Politics in Conflict-Prone Societies," 820–821; Reilly, *Democracy in Divided Societies: Electoral Engineering for Conflict Management*, 168–169, 171–172.
100. Sisk, *Power Sharing and International Mediation*, 58–59.
101. Reynolds, "Constitutional Medicine," 66.
102. Shapiro, "Democratic Innovation," 147.
103. Robert O. Keohane, "Political Authority after Intervention: Gradations in Sovereignty," in *Humanitarian Intervention: Ethical, Legal and Political Dilemmas*, ed. J. L. Holzgrefe and Robert O. Keohane (Cambridge: Cambridge University Press, 2003), 280–281.
104. For an overview, see Roland Paris, "Post-Conflict Peacebuilding," in *The Oxford Handbook on the United Nations*, ed. Thomas G. Weiss and Sam Daws (Oxford: Oxford University Press, 2007), 407.
105. Roland Paris and Timothy D. Sisk, "Introduction: Understanding the Contradictions of Postwar Statebuilding," in *The Dilemmas of Statebuilding: Confronting the Contradictions of Postwar Peace Operations*, ed. Roland Paris and Timothy D. Sisk (New York: Routledge, 2009), 1.
106. The PIC is the former International Conference on the Form Yugoslavia (ICFY), and consists of 55 governments and inter tional organizations.

107. "Reshaping International Priorities in Bosnia and Herzegovina. Part Two: International Power in Bosnia," (Berlin/Brussels/Sarajevo: European Stability Initiative, March 30, 2000), 25–26. Available at: http://www.esiweb.org/pdf/esI_document_id_8.pdf.
108. Ibid., 26.
109. Ibid., 27.
110. Simon Chesterman, "Whose Strategy, Whose Peace? The Role of International Institutions in Strategic Peacebuilding," in *Strategies of Peace: Transforming Conflict in a Violent World,* ed. Daniel Philpott and Gerard F. Powers (Oxford and New York: Oxford University Press, 2010), 120.
111. United Nations Secretary-General Boutros Boutros-Ghali, in "An Agenda for Peace: Preventive Diplomacy, Peacemaking and Peace-keeping," June 17, 1992, A/47/277—S/24111, paragraph 21. Available at: //www.un.org/Docs/SG/agpeace.html.
    Thus, peacebuilding operations can be distinguished from *peace-keeping operations,* which aim primarily at monitoring ceasefires, and more heavily armed *peace enforcement operations.*
112. Paris and Sisk, "Introduction: Understanding the Contradictions of Postwar Statebuilding," 1.
113. Ibid.
114. Ibid., 2. See also, Francis Fukuyama, "The Imperative of State-Building," *Journal of Democracy* 15, no. 2 (2004): 22.
115. Paris and Sisk, "Introduction: Understanding the Contradictions of Postwar Statebuilding," 14.
116. Stefano Recchia, "Just and Unjust Postwar Reconstruction: How Much External Interference Can Be Justified?," *Ethics & International Affairs* 23, no. 2 (2009): 167.
117. Ibid., 166.
118. Jens Narden, "Dilemmas of Promoting 'Local Ownership': The Case of Postwar Kosovo," in Paris and Sisk, eds., *The Dilemmas of Statebuilding: Confronting the Contradictions of Postwar Peace Operations,* 254–255. Jarstad and Sisk calls the local ownership problem *the systemic dilemma,* that is, the trade-off between international and local control over the peacebuilding and democratization process. See, Jarstad and Sisk, introduction, 11.
119. This is part of what Paris and Sisk refer to as the *dependency dilemmas,* or the problem that host countries become too reliant on external help. See Roland Paris and Timothy D. Sisk, "Conclusion: Confronting the Contradictions," in Paris and Sisk, eds., *The Dilemmas of Statebuilding: Confronting the Contradictions of Postwar Peace Operations,* 308.

120. Jens Narden, "Dilemmas of Promoting "Local Ownership": The Case of Postwar Kosovo," 252.

121. Simon Chesterman, *You, the People: The United Nations, Transitional Administration, and State-Building* (New York: Oxford University Press, 2005), 142.

122. Richard Caplan, "Who Guards the Guardians? International Accountability in Bosnia," *International Peacekeeping* 12, no. 3 (2005): 464. Caplan also distinguishes between vertical accountability, for instance, between a government and its citizens, and horizontal accountability, for instance, between government agencies of equal rank. Ibid.

123. Ibid.

124. Ibid., 463.

125. Parliamentary Assembly of the Council of Europe, Res. 1384, 26 June 2004, Art. 13. Quoted in ibid., 468.

126. Ibid., 465.

127. Paris and Sisk, "Introduction: Understanding the Contradictions of Postwar Statebuilding," 14. See also, Fukuyama, "The Imperative of State-Building."

128. Michael Walzer, *Arguing About War* (New Haven, CT: Yale University Press, 2004), 166.

129. Paris, "Post-Conflict Peacebuilding," 411.

130. Recchia, "Just and Unjust Postwar Reconstruction: How Much External Interference Can Be Justified?," 171. The argument for multilateralism can be made for peacekeeping operations as well. See, for instance, Kimberly Marten Zisk, *Enforcing the Peace: Learning from the Imperial Past* (New York: Columbia University Press, 2004), 157.

131. David Harland, "Legitimacy and Effectiveness in International Administration," *Global Governance* 10, no. 1 (2004): 18.

132. Ibid., 17.

133. Timothy Donasis, "Empowerment or Imposition? Dilemmas of Local Ownership in Post-Conflict Peacebuidling Processes," *Peace & Change* 34, no. 1 (2009): 3.

134. Chesterman, *You, the People: The United Nations, Transitional Administration, and State-Building*, 239.

135. Ibid., 143.

136. Recchia, "Just and Unjust Postwar Reconstruction: How Much External Interference Can Be Justified?," 171.

137. Ibid., 179.

138. Narden, "Dilemmas of Promoting "Local Ownership": The Case of Postwar Kosovo," 278.

139. Ibid., 255.

140. Recchia, "Just and Unjust Postwar Reconstruction: How Much External Interference Can Be Justified?," 175–176.

141. Ibid., 175.

142. This is one aspect of what Jarstad and Sisk describes as the *horizontal dilemma*, that is, the question of which political and societal groups to include in a peacebuilding operation. Jarstad and Sisk, introduction, 11. In Paris and Sisk's terminology, problems related to inclusion of local leaders and groups are referred to as *participation dilemmas*. Paris and Sisk, "Conclusion: Confronting the Contradictions," 307–308.

143. Stephen John Stedman, "Spoiler Problems in Peace Processes," *International Security* 22, no. 2 (1997): 5.

144. See further in Narden, "Dilemmas of Promoting "Local Ownership": The Case of Postwar Kosovo," 260–262.

145. These examples are taken from Caplan, "Who Guards the Guardians? International Accountability in Bosnia," 467.

146. Chesterman, *You, the People: The United Nations, Transitional Administration, and State-Building*, 147.

147. "War Criminals in Bosnia's Republika Srpska: Who Are the People in Your Neighbourhood?," ICG Balkan Report no. 103 (Sarajevo/Washington/Brussels: International Crisis Group, 2000), ii. Available at: http://www.crisisgroup.org/~/media/Files/europe/Bosnia%2039.pdf.

148. Ibid., 3.

149. As Jens Meierhenrich points out, there are important connections between lustrations and occupations. One such connection is provided by Article 43 of the 1907 Hague Convention, which states that an occupant "shall take all the measures in his power to restore, and ensure, as far as possible, public order and safety, while respecting, unless absolutely prevented, the laws in force in the country." This article has been seen to justify criminal justice, because one way to restore "public order" is to prosecute those who undermine it. If criminal justice is justified by the international law of occupations, there is, Meierhenrich argues, a prima facie case for pursuing administrative justice in the form of lustrations. For further discussion, see Jens Meierhenrich, "The Ethics of Lustration," *Ethics & International Affairs* 20, no. 1 (2006): 100.

150. Elmer Plischke, "Denazification Law and Procedure," *The American Journal of International Law* 41, no. 4 (1947): 808, 814.

151. For more, see Mark S. Ellis, "Purging the Past: The Current State of Lustration Laws in the Former Communist Block," *Law and Contemporary Problems* 59, no. 4 (1997): 181–196; Claus Offe, *Varieties of Transitions: The East European and East German*

Experience (Cambridge: Polity Press, 1996), 94–95; "Former Communists: A Phoenix Phenomenon," *The Economist*, February 25, 1995.

152. Eric Schmitt, "Aftereffects: Rumsfeld; Top Baathist Officials to Be Barred from Office," *The New York Times*, May 9, 2003.

153. "De-Ba'athification of Iraqi Society," Coalition Provisional Authority Order Number 1 (CPA/ORD/16 May/01). Available at: http://www.iraqcoalition.org/regulations/20030516_CPAORD_1_De-Ba_athification_of_IraqI_Society_.pdf.

154. Timothy L. O'Brien, "U.S. Bars up to 30,000 Ba'ath Party Members from New Government," *The International Herald Tribune*, May 17, 2003

155. "Disqualification from Public Office," Coalition Provisional Authority Order Number 62 (CPA/ORD/26 Feb 2004/62). Available at: http://www.iraqcoalition.org/regulations/20040301_CPAORD62.pdf.

156. A justification for each of these dismissals are available at the website of the Office of the High Representative: http://www.ohr.int/decisions/removalssdec/archive.asp.Technically the ban of the Serb Radical Party was a result of the OSCE refusing to certify the party before the elections. See discussion in, Sumantra Bose, *Bosnia after Dayton: Nationalist Partition and International Intervention* (Oxford: Oxford University Press, 2002), 276–277; "War Criminals in Bosnia's Republica Srpska," 79.

157. "Report of the Secretary-General on the United Nations Mission in Bosnia and Herzegovina," S/2002/11314 (New York: United Nations, 2002), 2. Available at: http://www.un.org/Docs/sc/reports/2002/sgrep02.htm.

158. Ibid., 3.

159. See Mark Freeman, "Bosnia and Herzegovina: Selected Developments in Transitional Justice," Case Study Series (New York: International Center for Transitional Justice, October 2004), 12–13. Available at: http://ictj.org/sites/default/files/ICTJ-FormerYugoslavia-Bosnia-Developments-2004-English.pdf. A total of 23,751 officers registered for the vetting process, 16,803 were granted provisional authorization, and 15,786 were granted full certification. See, "Report of the Secretary-General on the United Nations Mission in Bosnia and Herzegovina," 3.

160. Freeman, "Bosnia and Herzegovina: Selected Developments in Transitional Justice," 13.

161. As Roger Duthie points out, there is no agreement in the ac demic literature on how these different terms differ from e other. According to Duthie, "purges differ from vetting in

purges target people for their membership in or affiliation with a group rather than their individual responsibility for the violation of human rights." Vetting, on the other hand, describes a screening process of public employees in order to promote state security rather than weed out human rights violators. See Roger Duthie, introduction to *Justice as Prevention: Vetting Public Employees in Transitional Societies*, ed. Alexander Mayer-Rieckh and Pablo de Greiff (New York: Social Science Research Council, 2007), 18.

162. Meierhenrich, "The Ethics of Lustration," 99.

163. Rawls, *A Theory of Justice*, 221–224.

164. For further examples on how vetting can infringe on a person's rights, see Federico Andreu-Guzmán, "Due Process and Vetting," in *Justice as Prevention: Vetting Public Employees in Transitional Societies*, ed. Alexander Mayer-Rieckh and Pablo de Greiff (New York: Social Science Research Council, 2007), 452–454.

165. Roman Boed, "An Evaluation of the Legality and Efficacy of Lustration as a Tool of Transitional Justice," *Columbia Journal of Transnational Law* 37(1998–1999): 392–395.

166. For a discussion of the differences between vetting processes, see Duthie, Introduction, 17–38.

167. Pablo de Greiff, "Vetting and Transitional Justice," in *Justice as Prevention: Vetting Public Employees in Transitional Societies*, ed. Alexander Mayer-Rieckh and Pablo de Greiff (New York: Social Science Research Council, 2007), 523.

168. See, Ruti G. Teitel, *Transitional Justice* (New York: Oxford University Press, 2000), 150.

169. Rawls, *A Theory of Justice*, 223–224.

170. de Greiff, "Vetting and Transitional Justice," 525.

171. Ibid.

172. Teitel, *Transitional Justice*, 150.

173. The reason why this definition of "rule of law" is often called formal, or positivist, is that it involves no judgment on the content of the law. For a discussion, see, Joseph Raz, *The Authority of Law: Essays on Law and Morality* (Oxford: Clarendon Press, 1979), 214.

174. As Hart points out, this means that there also has to be a criterion that determines when cases are alike or different. For instance, the sanity of a person is a relevant factor in murder cases, but the hair color of the offender is not. See H. L. A. Hart, *The Concept of Law* (Oxford: Oxford University Press, 1994), 160.

75. See, Rawls, *A Theory of Justice*, 238–239. The rule of law also implies that laws must provide clear guidelines for prohibited actions and not have retroactive effect. For further discussions of

these principles, see Raz, *The Authority of Law: Essays on Law and Morality*, 214–216; Rawls, *A Theory of Justice*, 236–238.

176. Boed, "An Evaluation of the Legality and Efficacy of Lustration as a Tool of Transitional Justice," 379–380. Boed's article concerns primarily the practice of lustration in the Czech Republic.

177. Stanford Levinson, "Responsibility for Crimes of War," *Philosophy and Public Affairs* 2, no. 3 (1973): 249–250.

178. Andreu-Guzmán, "Due Process and Vetting," 457–458.

179. Boed, "An Evaluation of the Legality and Efficacy of Lustration as a Tool of Transitional Justice," 401.

180. Sean D. Murphy, "Progress and Jurisprudence of the International Criminal Tribunal for the Former Yugoslavia," *The American Journal of International Law* 93, no. 1 (1999): 57; David Wippman, "The Cost of International Justice," *The American Journal of International Law* 100, no. 4 (2006): 861.

181. Murphy, "Progress and Jurisprudence," 59.

182. Gregory L. Naarden, "Nonprosecutorial Sanctions for Grave Violations of International Humanitarian Law: Wartime Conduct of Bosnian Police Officials," *The American Journal of International Law* 97, no. 2 (2003): 343; Alexander Mayer-Rieckh, "Vetting to Prevent Future Abuses: Reforming the Police, Courts, and Prosecutor's Offices in Bosnia and Herzagovina," in *Justice as Prevention: Vetting Public Employees in Transitional Societies*, ed. Alexander Mayer-Rieckh and Pablo de Greiff (New York: Social Science Research Council, 2007), 182–184.

183. The goal of the police reform was not to punish war-crime violators, but to launch a "comprehensive personnel reform in order to build fair and efficient institutions." Ibid., 205.

184. Ibid., 188–189.

185. UNMIBH, Policy on Removal of Provisional Authorization Disqualification of Law Enforcement Personnel in BiH, IPFT-P10/2002, para. 2(h), quoted in ibid., 189.

186. Ibid., 190.

187. Naarden, "Nonprosecutorial Sanctions for Grave Violations of International Humanitarian Law: Wartime Conduct of Bosnian Police Officials," 348. Deauthorization meant that the officer would no longer be allowed to serve as police, and that the Ministry of the Interior would be obliged to initiate a criminal investigation. Ibid.

188. Ibid., 349.

189. Mayer-Rieckh, "Vetting to Prevent Future Abuses: Reforming the Police, Courts, and Prosecutor's Offices in Bosnia and Herzagovina," 190, 193.

190. On the other hand, it seems that the process led to increased public confidence in the police. See, ibid. 102.

191. "The Rule of Law and Transitional Justice in Conflict and Post-Conflict Societies, Report of the Secretary-General," S/2004/616 (New York: United Nations Security Council, 2004), 17–18. Available at; http://www.un.org/Docs/sc/sgrep04.html.

192. In Czechoslovakia, for instance, it was possible to appeal lustration decisions, and most of those who did so were able to clear their names. The attempt to mitigate harm to innocent individuals in Czechoslovakia was further helped by granting individuals the right to file "legal action against the Ministry of Interior for slander." Ellis, "Purging the Past," 182.

193. Naarden, "Nonprosecutorial Sanctions for Grave Violations of International Humanitarian Law: Wartime Conduct of Bosnian Police Officials," 348.

194. James A. McAdams, preface to *Transitional Justice and the Rule of Law in New Democracies*, ed. James A. McAdams (Notre Dame, IN: University of Notre Dame Press, 1997), x. I use the word "legitimacy" here in a descriptive, Weberian, sense. That is, legitimacy refers to the degree to which a population accepts as valid the government and laws. For a discussion, see, for instance, Peter Lassman, "The Rule of Man over Man: Politics, Power and Legitimation," in *The Cambridge Companion to Weber*, ed. Stephen Turner (Cambridge: Cambridge University Press, 2000), 87–88.

195. Teitel, *Transitional Justice*, 150.

196. Arthur L. Stinchcombe, "Lustration as a Problem of the Social Basis of Constitutionalism," *Law & Social Inquiry* 20, no. 1 (1995): 246–247.

197. Neil J. Kritz, "Coming to Terms with Atrocities: A Review of Accountability Mechanisms for Mass Violations of Human Rights," *Law and Contemporary Problems* 59, no. 4 (1996): 139.

198. "War Criminals in Bosnia's Republica Srpska," 3.

199. For a discussion of these and other alternatives, and the goals they serve, see David A. Crocker, "Reckoning with Past Wrongs: A Normative Framework," *Ethics & International Affairs* 13(1999): 43–64; Martha Minow, *Between Vengeance and Forgiveness: Facing History after Genocide and Mass Violence* (Boston: Beacon Press, 1998).

200. de Greiff, "Vetting and Transitional Justice," 528. For a discussion of the relationship between vetting and other transitional justice measures, see, ibid., 527–530.

1. "The Rule of Law and Transitional Justice in Conflict and Post-Conflict Societies, Report of the Secretary-General," 18.

202. Offe, *Varieties of Transitions*, 95. Again, this observation is made in the context of disqualifications in the former Communist countries.

203. The question of ethnic parity has been raised in a similar way with respect to legal proceedings. Here the worry is that the judicial process can be interpreted as a form of victor's justice where only the crimes of the losers are prosecuted. See discussion in, Payam Akhavan, "Justice in the Hague, Peace in the Former Yugoslavia? A Commentary on the United Nations War Crimes Tribunal," *Human Rights Quarterly* 20, no. 4 (1998): 780–781.

204. Offe, *Varieties of Transitions*, 95.

205. Quoted in O'Brien, "U.S. Bars up to 30,000 Ba'ath Party Members from New Government."

206. Edward Wong, "Policy Barring Ex-Baathists from Key Iraq Posts Is Eased," *The New York Times*, April 23, 2004.

207. Quoted in Deborah Pasmanier, "US-Led Coalition Moving to Reform Purge of Baath Party Members in Iraq," *Middle East Online*, April 23, 2004. Available at: http://www.middle-east-online.com /english/?id=9772.

208. Ibid.

CONCLUSION

1. See discussion in Pablo Kalmanovitz, "Justice in Postwar Reconstruction: Theories from Vitoria to Vattel." PhD diss., Columbia University, 2010.

2. Michael Walzer, *Just and Unjust Wars: A Moral Argument with Historical Illustrations*, 3rd ed. (New York: Basic Books, 1977), 21. Jeff McMahan, among others, has challenged this conventional view. See Jeff McMahan, "On the Moral Equality of Combatants," *The Journal of Political Philosophy* 14, no. 4 (2006): 377–393. See also the contributions in David Rodin and David Shue, eds. *Just and Unjust Warriors: The Moral and Legal Status of Soldiers* (Oxford: Oxford University Press, 2008).

3. Avishai Margalit, *On Compromise and Rotten Compromise* (Princeton: Princeton University Press, 2010), 1.

4. Raymond Bonner, "Serbs Said to Agree to Pact with Croatia," *The New York Times*, August 4, 1995. See also, discussion in Mona Fixdal and Ingrid O. Busterud, "The Undiplomatic Diplomat: Peter Galbraith," in *Ways out of War: Peacemakers in the Middle East and Balkans*, ed. Mona Fixdal (New York: Palgrave Macmillan, 2012) Forthcoming.

5. Laura Silber and Allan Little, *Yugoslavia: Death of a Nation*, and updated ed. (New York: Penguin Books, 1997), 360, 388

6. Quoted in Marcus Tanner, *Croatia: A Nation Forged in War*, 3rd ed. (New Haven, CT: Yale University Press, 2010), 298.
7. Only a little over 120,000 of the estimated 300,000 Serbian refugees that left Croatia during the war returned to Croatia in the following decade. Viktor Koska, "Return and Reintegration of Minority Refugees: The Complexity of the Serbian Returnees Experiences in the Town of Glina" *Politička Misao* 45, no. 5 (2008): 200.
8. Margalit, *On Compromise and Rotten Compromise*, 2.

BIBLIOGRAPHY

Akhavan, Payam. "Justice in the Hague, Peace in the Former Yugoslavia? A Commentary on the United Nations War Crimes Tribunal," *Human Rights Quarterly* 20, no. 4 (1998): 737–816.

Albin, Cecilia. *Justice and Fairness in International Negotiation.* Cambridge: Cambridge University Press, 2001.

Alderson, Kai, and Andrew Hurrell, eds. *Hedley Bull on International Society.* Basingstoke, UK: Macmillan, 2000.

Allan, Pierre. "Measuring International Ethics: A Moral Scale of War, Peace, Justice, and Global Care." In *What Is a Just Peace?*, edited by Pierre Allan and Alexis Keller. Oxford: Oxford University Press, 2006; 90–129.

Allan, Pierre, and Alexis Keller. "The Concept of a Just Peace, or Achieving Peace through Recognition, Renouncement, and Rule." In *What Is a Just Peace*, edited by Pierre Allan and Alexis Keller. Oxford: Oxford University Press, 2006, 195–215.

Allman, Mark J., and Tobias L. Winright. *After the Smoke Clears: The Just War Tradition & Post War Justice.* New York: Orbis Books, 2010.

Allon, Yigal. "Israel: The Case for Defensible Borders." *Foreign Affairs* 55, no. 1 (1976): 38–53.

Amnesty International. "Rwanda: The Troubled Course of Justice." April 25, 2000. Available at: http://www.amnesty.org/en/library/info/AFR47/010/2000/en.

Anderson, Jon Lee. "Death of the Tiger: Sri Lanka's Brutal Victory over Its Tamil Insurgents." *The New Yorker*, January 17, 2011: 40–55.

Andreas, Peter. "Redrawing the Line: Borders and Security in the Twenty-First Century." *International Security* 28, no. 2 (2003): 78–111.

Andreu-Guzmán, Federico. "Due Process and Vetting." In *Justice as Prevention: Vetting Public Employees in Transitional Societies*, edited by Alexander Mayer-Rieckh and Pablo de Greiff. New York: Social Science Research Council, 2007, 448–481.

Annan, Kofi "Why Democracy Is An International Issue," Cyril Foster Lecture, Oxford, June 19, 2001. Available at: http://www.un.org/News/ossg/sg/stories/statments_search_full.asp?statID=11.

Anonymous. "Human Rights in Peace Negotiations." *Human Rights Quarterly* 18, no. 2 (1996): 249–258.

Anscombe, G. E. M. "War and Murder." In *Ethics, Religion, and Politics,* The Collected Philosophical Papers of G. M. E. Anscombe, vol. 3. Minneapolis: University of Minnesota Press, 1981, 51–61.

Aquinas, Thomas. *Summa Theologica.* Translated by Fathers of the English Dominican Province. Vol. 2. New York: Benziger Brothers, 1947.

Aristotle. *The Nicomachean Ethics* (Oxford World's Classics). Translated by David Ross. Oxford: Oxford University Press, 1998.

Augustine, Saint. *City of God.* Translated by Henry Bettenson. London: Penguin Books, 1972.

Ball, Nicole. "The Challenge of Rebuilding War-Torn Societies." In *Turbulent Peace: The Challenges of Managing International Conflict,* edited by Chester A. Crocker, Fen Osler Hampson, and Pamela Aall. Washington, DC: United States of Peace Press, 2001, 719–736.

Ballentine, Karen. "Beyond Greed and Grievance: Reconsidering the Economic Dynamics of Armed Conflict." In *The Political Economy of Armed Conflict: Beyond Greed and Grievance,* edited by Karen Ballentine and Jake Sherman. Boulder, CO: Lynne Rienner, 2003, 259–283.

Ballentine, Karen, and Jake Sherman. Introduction to *The Political Economy of Armed Conflict: Beyond Greed and Grievance.* Edited by Karen Ballentine and Jake Sherman. Boulder, CO: Lynne Rienner, 2003, 1–15.

Bass, Gary J. *"Jus Post Bellum." Philosophy and Public Affairs* 32, no. 4 (2004): 384–412.

———. *Stay the Hand of Vengeance: The Politics of War Crimes Tribunals.* Princeton: Princeton University Press, 2000.

Beauchamp, Tom L. *Philosophical Ethics: An Introduction to Moral Philosophy.* 2nd ed. New York: McGraw-Hill, 2001.

Beilin, Yossi. "Just Peace: A Dangerous Objective." In *What Is a Just Peace?,* edited by Pierre Allan and Alexis Keller. New York: Oxford University Press, 2006, 130–148.

Beiner, Ronald S. "National Self-Determination: Some Cautionary Remarks Concerning the Rhetoric of Rights." In *National Self-Determination and Secession,* edited by Margaret Moore. Oxford: Oxford University Press, 1998, 158–180.

Bell, Christine. *On the Law of Peace: Peace Agreements and the Lex Pacificatoria.* Oxford: Oxford University Press, 2008.

Bellamy, Alex J. *Responsibility to Protect: The Global Effort to End Mass Atrocities.* Malden, MA.: Polity Press, 2009.

———. "The Responsibilities of Victory: *Jus Post Bellum* and the Just War." *Review of International Studies* 34, no. 4 (2008): 601–625 .

Belmont, Katharine, Scott Mainwaring, and Andrew Reynolds. "Introduction: Institutional Design, Conflict Management, and Democracy." In *The Architecture of Democracy: Constitutional Design, Conflict Management, and Democracy*, edited by Andrew Reynolds. Oxford: Oxford University Press, 2002, 1–11.

Ben-Ami, Shlomo. *Scars of War, Wounds of Peace: The Israeli-Arab Tragedy*. Oxford: Oxford University Press, 2006.

Beran, Harry. "A Democratic Theory of Political Self-Determination for a New World Order." In *Theories of Secession*, edited by Percy B. Lehning. London: Routledge, 1998, 33–60.

———. "A Liberal Theory of Secession." *Political Studies* 32, no. 1 (1984): 21–31.

Bercovitch, Jacob, J. Theodore Anagnoson, and Donnette L. Wille. "Some Conceptual Issues and Empirical Trends in the Study of Successful Mediation in International Relations." *Journal of Peace Research* 28, no. 1 (1991): 7–17.

Berlin, Isaiah. *The Crooked Timer of Humanity: Chapters in the History of Ideas*. London: John Murray Publishers, 1990.

Billon, Philippe Le. "Angola's Political Economy of War: The Role of Oil and Diamonds, 1975–2000." *African Affairs* 100, no. 398 (2001): 55–80.

Boed, Roman. "An Evaluation of the Legality and Efficacy of Lustration as a Tool of Transitional Justice." *Columbia Journal of Transnational Law* 37 (1998–1999): 357–402.

Bonner, Raymond. "Serbs Said to Agree to Pact with Croatia." *The New York Times*, August 4, 1995.

Bookman, Milica Z. "War and Peace: The Divergent Breakups of Yugoslavia and Czechoslovakia." *Journal of Peace Research* 31, no. 2 (1994): 175–187.

Bose, Sumantra. *Bosnia after Dayton: Nationalist Partition and International Intervention*. Oxford: Oxford University Press, 2002.

———. *Contested Lands: Israel-Palestine, Kashmir, Bosnia, Cyprus, and Sri Lanka*. Cambridge: Harvard University Press, 2007.

Boulding, Kenneth E. *Stable Peace*. Austin: University of Texas Press, 1978.

Boutros-Ghali, Boutros. "An Agenda for Peace: Preventive Diplomacy, Peacemaking and Peace-keeping." June 17, 1992, A/47/277—S/24111. Available at: //www.un.org/Docs/SG/agpeace.html.

———. Introduction to *The United Nations and Rwanda, 1993–1996*. The United Nations Blue Books Series, vol. 10. New York: United Nations, Department of Public Information, 1996, 3–111.

Bregman, Ahron. *A History of Israel*. Basingstoke, UK: Palgrave Macmillan, 2003.

Brilmayer, Lea. "Consent, Contract, and Territory." *Minnesota Law Review* 74, no. 1 (1989–1990): 1–35.

———. *Justifying International Acts.* Ithaca: Cornell University Press, 1989.

———. "Secession and Self-Determination: A Territorial Interpretation." *Yale Journal of International Law* 16 (1991): 177–202.

Buchanan, Allen. "Democracy and Secession." In *National Self-Determination and Secession*, edited by Margaret Moore. New York: Oxford University Press, 1998, 14–33.

———. *Justice, Legitimacy, and Self-Determination: Moral Foundations for International Law.* Oxford: Oxford University Press, 2004.

———. "The Making and Unmaking of Boundaries: What Liberalism Has to Say." In *States, Nations, and Borders: The Ethics of Making Boundaries*, edited by Allen Buchanan and Margaret Moore. New York: Cambridge University Press, 2003, 231–261.

———. *Secession: The Morality of Political Divorce from Fort Sumter to Lithuania and Quebec.* Boulder, CO: Westview Press, 1991.

———. "Self-Determination, Secession, and the Rule of Law." In *The Morality of Nationalism*, edited by Robert McKim and Jeff McMahan. New York: Oxford University Press, 1997, 301–323.

———. "Theories of Secession." *Philosophy and Public Affairs* 26, no. 1 (1997): 31–61.

———. "Toward a Theory of Secession." *Ethics* 101, no. 2 (1991): 322–342.

Buchanan, Allen, and Deborah Mathieu. "Philosophy and Justice." In *Justice: Views from the Social Sciences*, edited by Ronald L. Cohen. New York: Plenum Press, 1986, 11–46.

Buchheit, Lee C. *Secession: The Legitimacy of Self-Determination.* New Haven, CT: Yale University Press, 1978.

Burg, Steven L. "Bosnia Herzegovina: A Case of Failed Democratization." In *Politics, Power, and the Struggle for Democracy in South-East Europe*, edited by Karen Dawisha and Bruce Parrott. Cambridge: Cambridge University Press, 1997, 122–145.

Burg, Steven L., and Paul S. Shoup. *The War in Bosnia-Herzegovina.* Armonk, NY: M.E. Sharpe, 1999.

Bush, George, and Brent Scowcroft. *A World Transformed.* New York: Vintage Books, 1999.

Calvert, Peter. "Sovereignty and the Falklands Crisis." *International Affairs* 59, no. 3 (1983): 405–413.

Caplan, Richard. "Who Guards the Guardians? International Accountability in Bosnia." *International Peacekeeping* 12, no. 3 (2005): 463–476.

rson, Thomas L., and Paul K. Moser. Introduction to *Moral Relativism: A Reader.* Edited by Paul K. Moser and Thomas L. Carson. Oxford: Oxford University Press, 2001, 1–22.

Cashman, Greg. *What Causes War? An Introduction to Theories of International Conflict.* New York: Lexington Books, 1993.

Cassese, Antonio. *International Criminal Law.* Oxford: Oxford University Press, 2003.

Chandhoke, Neera. "Exploring the Right to Secession: The South Asian Context." *South Asia Research* 28, no. 1 (2008): 1–22.

Chapman, Thomas, and Philip G. Roeder. "Partition as a Solution to Wars of Nationalism: The Importance of Institutions." *American Political Science Review* 101, no. 4 (2007): 677–691.

Chesterman, Simon. "Whose Strategy, Whose Peace? The Role of International Institutions in Strategic Peacebuilding." In *Strategies of Peace: Transforming Conflict in a Violent World,* edited by Daniel Philpott and Gerard F. Powers. Oxford and New York: Oxford University Press, 2010, 119–140.

———. *You, the People: The United Nations, Transitional Administration, and State-Building.* New York: Oxford University Press, 2005.

Childress, James F. "Just-War Criteria." In *Moral Responsibility in Conflicts: Essays on Nonviolence, Wars and Conscience.* Baton Rouge: Lousiana State University Press, 1982, 63–94.

Clark, Wesley K. *Waging Modern War: Bosnia, Kosovo, and the Future of Combat.* New York: Public Affairs, 2001.

Clausewitz, Carl von. *On War.* Translated by Michael Howard and Peter Paret. Edited by Michael Howard and Peter Paret. Princeton: Princeton University Press, 1976.

Coates, A. J. *The Ethics of War.* Manchester, UK, and New York: Manchester University Press, 1997.

Cobban, Alfred. *The Nation State and National Self-Determination.* London: Collins, The Fontana Library, 1969.

Collier, Paul. "Doing Well out of War: An Economic Perspective." In *Greed and Grievance: Economic Agendas in Civil Wars,* edited by Mats Berdal and David M. Malone. Boulder, CO: Lynne Rienner, 2000, 91–111.

Coppieters, Bruno. "Conclusion: Just War Theory and the Ethics of Secession." In *Contextualizing Secession: Normative Studies in Comparative Perspective,* edited by Bruno Coppieters and Richard Sakwa. Oxford: Oxford University Press, 2003, 252–279.

"Croatia: Impunity for Abuses Committed during 'Operation Storm' and the Denial of the Right of Refugees to Return to the Krajina." Human Rights Watch/Helsinki 8, no. 13 (1996). Available at: http://www.hrw.org/sites/default/files/reports/croatia968.pdf.

Crocker, David A. "Reckoning with Past Wrongs: A Normative Framework." *Ethics & International Affairs* 13 (1999): 43–64.

Dahl, Robert A. *After the Revolution? Authority in a Good Society.* N Haven, CT: Yale University Press, 1990.

Dahl, Robert A. *Democracy and Its Critics.* New Haven, CT: Yale University Press, 1989.

———. *A Preface to Democratic Theory.* Chicago: The University of Chicago Press, 1956.

Danner, Mark. *Stripping Bare the Body: Politics, Violence, War.* New York: Nation Books, 2009.

"De-Ba'athification of Iraqi Society." Coalition Provisional Authority Order Number 1 (CPA/ORD/16 May/01). Available at: http://www.iraqcoalition.org/regulations/20030516_CPAORD_1_De-Ba_ath ification_of_Iraqi_Society_.pdf.

De Feyter, Koen, Stephan Parmentier, Marc Bossuyt, and Paul Lemmens, eds. *Out of the Ashes: Reparations for Victims of Gross Human Rights Violations.* Antwerp: Intersentia, 2005.

De Greiff, Pablo. "Vetting and Transitional Justice." In *Justice as Prevention: Vetting Public Employees in Transitional Societies*, edited by Alexander Mayer-Rieckh and Pablo de Greiff. New York: Social Science Research Council, 2007, 522–544.

DeVotta, Neil. "The Liberation Tigers of Tamil Eelam and the Lost Quest for Separatism in Sri Lanka." *Asian Survey* 49, no. 6 (2009): 1021–1051.

———. "Sri Lanka's Civil War." In *The Routledge Handbook of Asian Security Studies*, edited by Sumit Ganguly, Andrew Scobell and Joseph Chinyoung Liow. New York: Routledge, 2010, 158–171.

Diehl, Paul F. "What Are They Fighting For? The Importance of Issues in International Conflict Research." *Journal of Peace Research* 29, no. 3 (1992): 333–344.

"Disqualification from Public Office." Coalition Provisional Authority Order Number 62 (CPA/ORD/26 Feb 2004/62). Available at: http://www.iraqcoalition.org/regulations/20040301_CPAORD62.pdf.

Dixon, Jeffrey. "What Causes Civil Wars? Integrating Quantitative Research Findings." *International Studies Review* 11, no. 4 (2009): 707–735.

Donasis, Timothy. "Division and Democracy: Bosnia's Post-Dayton Elections." In *The Lessons of Yugoslavia*, edited by Metta Spencer. Amsterdam: Elsevier Science, 2000, 229–257.

———. "Empowerment or Imposition? Dilemmas of Local Ownership in Post-Conflict Peacebuidling Processes." *Peace & Change* 34, no. 1 (2009): 3–26.

Dos Santos, Anne Noronha. *Military Intervention and Secession in South Asia: The Cases of Bangladesh, Sri Lanka, Kashmir, and Punjab.* Westport, CT: Praeger, 2007.

wnie, Leonard Jr. "Plea by Reagan Ignored; Argentina Seizes British olony." *The Washington Post*, April 2, 1982, A1.

Downs, George, and Stephen John Stedman. "Evaluation Issues in Peace Implementation." In *Ending Civil Wars: The Implementation of Peace Agreements*, edited by Stephen John Stedman, Donald Rothchild and Elizabeth M. Cousens. Boulder, CO: Lynne Rienner Publishers, 2002, 43–69.

Doyle, Michael W. "International Law and Current Standards." In *Striking First: Preemption and Prevention in International Conflict*, edited by Stephen Macedo. Princeton: Princeton University Press, 2008, 7–42.

Doyle, Michael W., and Nicholas Sambanis. "International Peacebuilding: A Theoretical and Quantitative Analysis." *The American Political Science Review* 94, no. 4 (2000): 779–801.

———. *Making War and Building Peace: United Nations Peace Operations*. Princeton: Princeton University Press, 2006.

Druckman, Daniel, and Cecilia Albin. "Distributive Justice and the Durability of Peace Agreements." *Review of International Studies* 37, no. 3 (2010): 1137–1168.

Duthie, Roger. Introduction to *Justice as Prevention: Vetting Public Employees in Transitional Societies*. Edited by Alexander Mayer-Rieckh and Pablo de Greiff. New York: Social Science Research Council, 2007, 17–38.

Dworkin, Ronald. *Taking Rights Seriously*. London: Duckworth, 1977.

Ellis, Mark S. "Purging the Past: The Current State of Lustration Laws in the Former Communist Block." *Law and Contemporary Problems* 59, no. 4 (1997): 181–196.

Esman, Milton J. *Ethnic Politics*. Ithaca: Cornell University Press, 1994.

Estlund, David. Introduction to *Democracy*. Edited by David Estlund. Malden, MA: Blackwell, 2002.

Evans, Mark. "Balancing Peace, Justice and Sovereignty in *Jus Post Bellum*: The Case of 'Just Occupation'." *Millennium — Journal of International Studies* 36, no. 3 (2008): 533–554.

———. "Moral Responsibilities and Conflicting Demands of *Jus Post Bellum*." *Ethics & International Affairs* 23, no. 2 (2009): 147–164.

"Excerpts from Speeches of Argentine Foreign Minister and British Delegate." *The New York Times*, May 25, 1982.

Feinberg, Joel. *Social Philosophy*. Englewood Cliffs, NJ: Prentice-Hall, 1973.

Ferstman, Carla, Mariana Goetz, and Alan Stephens, eds. *Reparations for Victims of Genocide, War Crimes and Crimes against Humanity: Systems in Place and Systems in the Making*. Leiden: Martinus Niihof Publishers, 2009.

Finlan, Alastair. *The Gulf War 1991 (Essential Histories)*. Oxford: Os Publishing, 2003.

Finnie, David H. *Shifting Lines in the Sand: Kuwait's Elusive Frontier with Iraq.* Cambridge: Harvard University Press, 1992.

Fishkin, James S. *Tyranny and Legitimacy: A Critique of Political Theories.* Baltimore, MD: The Johns Hopkins University Press, 1979.

Fixdal, Mona. "Peacemaking in Asymmetrical Conflicts." In *Ways out of War: Peacemakers in the Middle East and Balkans,* edited by Mona Fixdal. New York: Palgrave Macmillan, 2012. Forthcoming.

Fixdal, Mona, and Dan Smith. "Humanitarian Intervention and Just War." *Mershon International Studies Review* 42 (1998): 283–312.

Fixdal, Mona, and Ingrid O. Busterud. "The Undiplomatic Diplomat: Peter Galbraith." In *Ways out of War: Peacemakers in the Middle East and Balkans,* edited by Mona Fixdal. New York: Palgrave Macmillan, 2012. Forthcoming.

"Former Communists: A Phoenix Phenomenon." *The Economist,* February 25, 1995.

Fortna, Virginia Page. *Peace Time: Cease-Fire Agreements and the Durability of Peace.* Princeton: Princeton University Press, 2004.

Fowler, Brenda. "Slovenes to Vote on Independence." *The New York Times,* 23 December 1990, 4.

Freeman, Mark. *Bosnia and Herzegovina: Selected Developments in Transitional Justice.* Case Study Series. New York: International Center for Transitional Justice, October 2004. Available at: http://ictj.org /sites/default/files/ICTJ-FormerYugoslavia-Bosnia-Developments-2004-English.pdf.

Fukuyama, Francis. "The Imperative of State-Building." *Journal of Democracy* 15, no. 2 (2004): 17–31.

Galtung, Johan. "Violence, Peace, and Peace Research." *Journal of Peace Research* 6, no. 3 (1969): 167–191.

Gans, Chaim. *The Limits of Nationalism.* Cambridge: Cambridge University Press, 2003.

Gellner, Ernest. *Nations and Nationalism,* 2nd ed. Ithaca, NY: Cornell University Press, 2006.

George, Alexander L. Foreword to *Stable Peace among Nations.* Edited by Arie M. Kacowicz, Yaacov Bar-Siman-Tov, Ole Elgström, and Magnus Jerneck. Lanham, MD: Rowman & Littlefield, 2000, xi–xvii.

Gilpin, Robert. *War and Change in World Politics.* Cambridge: Cambridge University Press, 1981.

Glaser, Daryl J. "The Right to Secession: An Antisecessionist Defense." *Political Studies* 51, no. 2 (2003): 369–386.

Global Witness. "A Rough Trade: The Role of Companies and Governments in the Angolan Conflict." London: Global Witness, 1998. Available at: http://www.globalwitness.org/sites/default /files/pdfs/A_Rough_Trade.pdf.

Goemans, H. E. *War and Punishment*. Princeton: Princeton University Press, 2000.

Goodin, Robert E. "Enfranchising All Affected Interests, and Its Alternatives." *Philosophy & Public Affairs* 35, no. 1 (2007): 40–68.

Gow, James. *Triumph of the Lack of Will: International Diplomacy and the Yugoslav War*. London: Hurst, 1997.

Greenberg, Melanie C., and Margaret E. McGuinness. "From Lisbon to Dayton: International Mediation and the Bosnia Crisis." In *Words over War: Mediation and Arbitration to Prevent Deadly Conflict*, edited by Melanie C. Greenberg, John H. Barton, and Margaret E. McGuinness. Lanham, MD: Rowman & Littlefield, 2000, 35–75.

Grotius, Hugo. *The Law of War and Peace*. Translated by Francis W. Kelsey. Books 1–3. Indianapolis: Bobbs-Merrill Company, 1925.

Gustafson, Lowell S. *The Sovereignty Dispute over the Falkland (Malvinas) Islands*. New York and Oxford: Oxford University Press, 1988.

Hamilton, Alexander or James Madison, "The Federalist No. 51: The Structure of the Government Must Furnish the Proper Checks and Balances between the Different Departments," in *The Federalist Papers*, Alexander Hamilton, James Madison, and John Jay. Edited by Michael A. Genovese (New York: Palgrave Macmillan, 2009), 119–122.

Hammel, E. A. "Demography and the Origins of the Yugoslav Civil War." *Anthropology Today* 9, no. 1 (1993): 1993: 4–9.

Handel, Michael I. "The Evolution of Israeli Strategy: The Psychology of Insecurity and the Quest for Absolute Security." In *The Making of Strategy: Rulers, States, and War*, edited by Williamson Murray, MacGregor Knox, and Alvin Bernstein. Cambridge: Cambridge University Press, 1994, 534–578.

Harland, David. "Legitimacy and Effectiveness in International Administration." *Global Governance* 10, no. 1 (2004): 15–19.

Harris, W. W. "War and Settlement Change: The Golan Heights and the Jordan Rift, 1967–77." *Transactions of the Institute of British Geographers* 3, no. 3 (1978): 309–330.

Hart, B. H. Liddell. *Strategy*. 2nd rev. ed. New York: Meridian, 1991.

Hart, H. L. A. *The Concept of Law*. Oxford: Oxford University Press, 1994.

Hartzell, Caroline. "Structuring the Peace: Negotiated Settlements and the Construction of Conflict Management Institutions." In *Conflict Prevention and Peacebuilding in Post-War Societies: Sustaining the Peace*, edited by T. David Mason and James D. Meernik. London and New York: Routledge, 2006, 31–52

Hartzell, Caroline, and Matthew Hoddie. "Institutionalizing Peace: Power Sharing and Post-Civil War Conflict Managment." *American Journal of Political Science* 47, no. 2 (2003): 318–332.

Hartzell, Caroline, Matthew Hoddie, and Donald Rothchild. "Stabilizing the Peace after Civil War: An Investigation of Some Key Variables." *International Organization* 55, no. 1 (2001): 183–208.

Hastings, Adrian. *The Construction of Nationhood: Ethnicity, Religion, and Nationalism.* Cambridge: Cambridge University Press, 1997.

Hedges, Chris. "Bosnians Vote, But Animosity Is Unrelenting." *The New York Times*, September 14, 1997.

———. "Muslim Detention of Bosnian Serbs Threatens Truce," *The New York Times*, February 7, 1997.

———. "Serb Militants Are Running Hard for Posts in Bosnia Election." *The New York Times*, September 1, 1996.

Hennayake, Shantha K. "Sri Lanka in 1992: Opportunity Missed in the Ethno-Nationalist Crisis." *Asian Survey* 33, no. 2 (1993): 157–164.

Hensel, Paul R. "Charting a Course to Conflict: Territorial Issues and Interstate Conflict, 1816–1992." *Conflict Management and Peace Science* 15, no. 1 (1996): 43–73.

Hensel, Paul R., Sara McLaughlin Mitchell, Thomas E. Sowers II, and Clayton L. Thyne. "Bones of Contention: Comparing Territorial, Maritime, and River Issues." *Journal of Conflict Resolution* 52, no. 1 (2008): 117–143.

Hockstader, Lee. "Bosnian Serb Elections Appear to Deal Setback to Hard-Line Nationalists." *The Washington Post*, December 2, 1997.

Hoddie, Matthew, and Caroline Hartzell. "Power Sharing in Peace Settlements: Initiating the Transition from Civil War." In *Sustainable Peace: Power and Democracy after Civil Wars*, edited by Philip G. Roeder and Donald Rothchild. Ithaca and London: Cornell University Press, 2005, 83–106.

———. "Signals of Reconciliation: Institution-Building and the Resolution of Civil Wars." *International Studies Review* 7, no. 1 (2005): 21–40.

Hoffmann, Stanley. "Peace and Justice: A Prologue." In *What Is a Just Peace?*, edited by Pierre Allan and Alexis Keller. Oxford: Oxford University Press, 2006: 12–18.

Holbrooke, Richard. *To End a War.* New York: Random House, 1998.

Holsti, Kalevi J. *Peace and War: Armed Conflicts and International Order 1648–1989.* Cambridge: Cambridge University Press, 1991.

———. *The State, War and the State of War.* Cambridge: Cambridge University Press, 1996.

Horowitz, Donald L. "Constitutional Design: Proposals versus Processes" In *The Architecture of Democracy: Constitutional Design, Conflict Management, and Democracy*, edited by Andrew Reynolds. Oxford: Oxford University Press, 2002, 15–36.

———. "The Cracked Foundations of the Right to Secede." *Journal of Democracy* 14, no. 2 (2003): 5–17.

———. *A Democratic South Africa? Constitutional Engineering in a Divided Society.* Berkeley: University of California Press, 1991.

———. *Ethnic Groups in Conflict.* Berkeley: University of California Press, 1985.

Howard, Michael. *The Causes of War.* Cambridge: Harvard University Press, 1984.

Huntington, Samuel P. "The Modest Meaning of Democracy." In *Democracy in the Americas: Stopping the Pendulum,* edited by Robert A. Pastor. New York: Holmes & Meier, 1989, 11–28.

———. *The Third Wave: Democratization in the Late Twentieth Century.* Norman: University of Oklahoma Press, 1991.

Huth, Paul K. *Standing Your Ground: Territorial Disputes and International Conflict.* Ann Arbor: University of Michigan Press, 1996.

Iasiello, Louis V. "*Jus Post Bellum*: The Moral Responsibilities of Victors in War." *Naval War College Review* 57, no. 3/4 (2004): 33–52.

Ikle, Fred Charles. *Every War Must End.* New York: Columbia University Press, 1991.

International Crisis Group (ICG), *State of the Balkans,* ICG Balkans Report No. 47, Brussels: ICG, November 4, 1998.

Jarstad, Anna K. "Power Sharing: Former Enemies in Joint Government." In *From War to Democracy: Dilemmas of Peacebuilding,* edited by Anna K. Jarstad and Timothy Sisk. Cambridge: Cambridge University Press, 2008, 105–133.

———. "Dilemmas of War-to-Democracy Transitions." In *From War to Democracy: Dilemmas of Peacebuilding,* edited by Anna K. Jarstad and Timothy Sisk. Cambridge: Cambridge University Press, 2008, 17–36.

Jarstad, Anna K., and Timothy Sisk. Introduction to *From War to Democracy: Dilemmas of Peacebuilding.* Edited by Anna K. Jarstad and Timothy Sisk. Cambridge: Cambridge University Press, 2008, 1–13.

Jervis, Robert. "Cooperation under the Security Dilemma." *World Politics* 30, no. 2 (1978): 167–214.

Johnson, James Turner. "Comment." *The Journal of Religious Ethics* 26, no. 1 (1998): 219–222.

———. "The Idea of Defense in Historical and Contemporary Thinking about Just War." *Journal of Religious Ethics* 36, no. 4 (2008): 543–556.

———. *Ideology, Reason, and the Limitation of War: Religious and Secular Concepts 1200–1740.* Princeton: Princeton University Press, 1975.

———. "Just War, as It Was and Is." *First Things* 149, January (2005): 14–24.

———. *Just War Tradition and the Restraint of War: A Moral ʠ Historical Inquiry.* Princeton: Princeton University Press, 1981.

230 Bibliography

———. *Morality and Contemporary Warfare*. New Haven, CT: Yale University Press, 1999.

———. *The War to Oust Saddam Hussein: Just War and the New Face of Conflict*. Lanham, MD: Rowman & Littlefield, 2005.

Judah, Tim. *Kosovo: War and Revenge*. New Haven, CT: Yale Nota Bene, 2002.

Kacowicz, Arie M., and Yaacov Bar-Siman-Tov. "Stable Peace: A Conceptual Framework." In *Stable Peace among Nations*, edited by Arie M. Kacowicz, Yaacov Bar-Siman-Tov, Ole Elgström, and Magnus Jerneck. Lanham, MD: Rowman & Littlefield, 2000, 11–35.

Kaldor, Mary. *New and Old Wars*. Stanford, CA: Stanford University Press, 2007.

Kalmanovitz, Pablo. "Justice in Postwar Reconstruction: Theories from Vitoria to Vattel." PhD diss., Columbia University, 2010.

Kapitan, Tomis. "Historical Introduction to the Philosophical Issues." In *Philosophical Perspectives on the Israeli-Palestinian Conflict*, edited by Tomis Kapitan. Armork, NY: M. E. Sharpe, 1997, 3–45.

Kaufmann, Chaim. "Possible and Impossible Solutions to Ethnic Civil Wars." *International Security* 20, no. 4 (1996): 136–175.

———. "When All Else Fails: Ethnic Population Transfers and Partitions in the Twentieth Century." *International Security* 23, no. 2 (1998): 120–156.

Kegley, Charles W. Jr., and Gregory A. Raymond. *How Nations Make Peace*. New York: Worth Publishers, 1999.

Kellogg, Davida E. "*Jus Post Bellum*: The Importance of War Crimes Trials." *Parameters* 32, no. Autumn (2002): 87–99.

Keohane, Robert O. "Political Authority after Intervention: Gradations in Sovereignty." In *Humanitarian Intervention: Ethical, Legal and Political Dilemmas*, edited by J. L. Holzgrefe and Robert O. Keohane. Cambridge: Cambridge University Press, 2003, 275–298.

Keynes, John Maynard. *The Economic Consequences of the Peace*. New York: Harcourt, Brace and Howe, 1920/1988.

Khatchadourian, Haig. "Compensation and Reparations as Forms of Compensatory Justice." *Metaphilosophy* 37, no. 3–4 (2006): 429–448.

King, Iain, and Whit Mason. *Peace at Any Price: How the World Failed Kosovo*. Ithaca, NY: Cornell University Press, 2006.

King, Martin Luther, Jr. "Letter from a Birmingham Jail." In *Approaches to Peace: A Reader in Peace Studies*, edited by David P. Barash. New York: Oxford University Press, 2000, 144–148.

Korman, Sharon. *The Right of Conquest: The Acquisition of Territory by Force in International Law and Practice*. Oxford: Clarendon Press, 1996.

Koska, Viktor. "Return and Reintegration of Minority Refugees: The Complexity of the Serbian Returnees' Experiences in the Town of Glina." *Politička Misao* 45, no. 5 (2008): 191–217.

Krasner, Stephen D., and Carlos Pascual. "Addressing State Failure." *Foreign Affairs* 84, no. 4 (2005): 153–163.

Kriesberg, Louis. *Constructive Conflicts: From Escalation to Resolution.* Lanham, MD: Rowman & Littlefield, 2007.

Kritz, Neil J. "Coming to Terms with Atrocities: A Review of Accountability Mechanisms for Mass Violations of Human Rights." *Law and Contemporary Problems* 59, no. 4 (1996): 127–152.

———, ed. *Transitional Justice: How Emerging Democracies Recon with Former Regimes.* 3 vols. Washington, DC: United States Institute of Peace Press, 1995.

Kymlicka, Will. *Contemporary Political Philosophy: An Introduction.* New York: Oxford University Press, 2002.

Lake, David A., and Donald Rothchild. "Containing Fear: The Origins and Management of Ethnic Conflict." *International Security* 21, no. 2 (1996): 41–75.

Lassman, Peter. "The Rule of Man over Man: Politics, Power and Legitimation." In *The Cambridge Companion to Weber,* edited by Stephen Turner. Cambridge: Cambridge University Press, 2000, 83–98.

Lesch, Ann Mosely. "Israeli Settlements in the Occupied Territories, 1967–1977." *Journal of Palestine Studies* 7, no. 1 (1977): 26–47.

Levinson, Stanford. "Responsibility for Crimes of War." *Philosophy and Public Affairs* 2, no. 3 (1973): 244–273.

Licklider, Roy. "The Consequences of Negotiated Settlements in Civil Wars, 1945–1993." *American Political Science Review* 89, no. 3 (1995): 681–690.

———. "Ethical Advice: Conflict Management vs. Human Rights in Ending Civil Wars." *Journal of Human Rights* 7, no. 4 (2008): 376–387.

Lijphart, Arend. *Democracy in Plural Societies: A Comparative Exploration.* New Haven and London: Yale University Press, 1977.

———. *Democracies: Pattern of Majoritarian and Consensus Government in Twenty-One Countries.* New Haven, CT: Yale University Press, 1984.

———. "The Wave of Power-Sharing Democracy." In *The Architecture of Democracy: Constitutinal Design, Conflict Management, and Democracy,* edited by Andrew Reynolds. Oxford: Oxford University Press, 2002, 37–54.

Locke, John. *Second Treatise of Government.* Edited by C. B. Macpherson. Indianapolis: Hackett Publishing Company, 1980.

Luard, Evan. *War in International Society: A Study in International Sociology.* New Haven, CT: Yale University Press, 1986.

Luban, David. "Preventive War." *Philosophy & Public Affairs* 32, no. 3 (2004): 207–248.

Lustick, Ian. "Stability in Deeply Divided Societies: Consociationali Versus Control." *World Politics* 31, no. 3 (1979): 325–344.

Lyons, David. "The New Indian Claims and Original Rights to Land." *Social Theory and Practice* 4, no. 3 (1977): 249–272.

Mackie, J. L. *Ethics: Inventing Right and Wrong*. London: Penguin Books, 1977.

Malcolm, Noel. *Bosnia: A Short History*. Rev. ed. New York: New York University Press, 1996.

———. *Kosovo: A Short History*. New York: Harper Perennial, 1999.

Malnes, Raino. *National Interests, Morality and International Law*. Oslo: Scandinavian University Press, 1994.

Mamatey, Victor S. *The United States and East Central Europe, 1914–1918: A Study in Wilsonian Diplomacy and Propaganda*. Princeton: Princeton University Press, 1957.

Margalit, Avishai. *On Compromise and Rotten Compromise*. Princeton: Princeton University Press, 2010.

Marks, Sally. *The Illusion of Peace: International Relations in Europe 1918–1933*. New York: St. Martins Press, 1976.

Mayer-Rieckh, Alexander. "Vetting to Prevent Future Abuses: Reforming the Police, Courts, and Prosecutor's Offices in Bosnia and Herzagovina." In *Justice as Prevention: Vetting Public Employees in Transitional Societies*, edited by Alexander Mayer-Rieckh and Pablo de Greiff. New York: Social Science Research Council, 2007, 180–220.

McAdams, James A. Preface to *Transitional Justice and the Rule of Law in New Democracies*, edited by James A. McAdams. Notre Dame, IN: University of Notre Dame Press, 1997, ix–xvii.

McGarry, John, and Brendan O'Leary. "Introduction: The Macro-Political Regulation of Ethnic Conflict." In *The Politics of Ethnic Conflict Regulation*, edited by John McGarry and Brendan O'Leary. London: Routledge, 1993, 1–40.

McGrath, Sarah. "Moral Disagreement and Moral Expertise." In *Oxford Studies in Metaethics: Volume 3*, edited by Russ Shafer-Landau. Oxford: Oxford University Press, 2008, 87–107.

McMahan, Jeff. "Aggression and Punishment." In *War: Essays in Political Philosophy*, edited by Larry May. New York: Cambridge University Press, 2008: 67–84.

———. "Just Cause for War." *Ethics & International Affairs* 19, no. 3 (2005): 1–21.

———. "On the Moral Equality of Combatants." *The Journal of Political Philosophy* 14, no. 4 (2006): 377–393.

Meierhenrich, Jens. "The Ethics of Lustration." *Ethics & International Affairs* 20, no. 1 (2006): 99–120.

Meisels, Tamar. *Territorial Rights*. Dordrecht, The Netherlands: Springer, 2009.

Miller, David. *National Responsibility and Global Justice*. Oxford: Oxford University Press, 2007.

————. *On Nationality*. Oxford: Oxford University Press, 1995.

-————. "Secession and the Principle of Nationality." In *National Self-Determination and Secession*, edited by Margaret Moore. Oxford: Oxford University Press, 1998, 62–78.

————. "Territorial Rights: Concept and Justification. *Political Studies* 60, no. 2 (2012). Forthcoming.

Miller, Richard B. "Aquinas and the Presumption against Killing and War." *The Journal of Religion* 82, no. 2 (2002): 173–204.

————. *Interpretations of Conflict: Ethics, Pacifism, and the Just-War Tradition*. Chicago: Chicago University Press, 1991.

Miller, Richard B. *Interpretations of Conflict: Ethics, Pacifism, and the Just-War Tradition*. Chicago: University of Chicago Press, 1991.

Minow, Martha. *Between Vengeance and Forgiveness: Facing History after Genocide and Mass Violence*. Boston: Beacon Press, 1998.

Moore, Margaret. *The Ethics of Nationalism*. Oxford: Oxford University Press, 2001.

————. "The Ethics of Secession and a Normative Theory of Nationalism." *Canadian Journal of Law and Jurisprudence* XIII, no. 2 (2000): 225–250.

————. "The Ethics of Secession and Postinvasion Iraq." *Ethics and International Affairs* 20, no. 1 (2006): 55–78.

————. Introduction to *National Self-Determination and Secession*. Edited by Margaret Moore. New York: Oxford University Press, 1998, 1–13.

————. "The Territorial Dimension of Self-Determination." In *National Self-Determination and Secession*, edited by Margaret Moore. Oxford: Oxford University Press, 1998, 134–157 .

Mueller, Brian M. "The Falkland Islands: Will the Real Owner Please Stand Up?" *Notre Dame Law Review* 58 (1982–83): 616–634.

Murphy, Alexander B. "Historical Justifcations for Territorial Claims." *Annals of the Association of American Geographers* 80, no. 4 (1990): 531–548.

Murphy, Sean D. "Progress and Jurisprudence of the International Criminal Tribunal for the Former Yugoslavia." *The American Journal of International Law* 93, no. 1 (1999): 57–97.

Naarden, Gregory L. "Nonprosecutorial Sanctions for Grave Violations of International Humanitarian Law: Wartime Conduct of Bosnian Police Officials." *The American Journal of International Law* 97, no. 2 (2003): 342–352.

Naimark, Norman M. *Fires of Hatred: Ethnic Cleansing in Twentiet* Century Europe. Cambridge: Harvard University Press, 2001.

Narden, Jens. "Dilemmas of Promoting "Local Ownership": The of Postwar Kosovo." In *The Dilemmas of Statebuilding: Confr the Contradictions of Postwar Peace Operations*, edited by Roland Paris and Timothy D. Sisk. New York: Routledge, 2009, 252–283.

Neuffer, Elizabeth. "Bosnia Campaign Emphasizes Ethnic Division." *The Boston Globe*, September 13, 1996.

———. "Democracy, Division Clash in Bosnia." *The Boston Globe*, September 13, 1997.

Nine, Cara. "A Lockean Theory of Territory." *Political Studies* 56, no. 1 (2008): 148–156.

———. "Superseding Historic Injustice and Territorial Rights." *Critical Review of International Social and Political Philosophy* 11, no. 1 (2008): 79–87.

Norman, Wayne. "The Ethics of Secession as the Regulation of Secessionist Politics." In *National Self-Determination and Secession*, edited by Margaret Moore. New York: Oxford University Press, 1998, 34–61.

Nozick, Robert. *Anarchy, State and Utopia*. New York: Basic Books, 1974.

O'Brien, Timothy L. "U.S. Bars up to 30,000 Ba'ath Party Members from New Government." *The International Herald Tribune*, May 17, 2003.

Offe, Claus. *Varieties of Transitions: The East European and East German Experience*. Cambridge: Polity Press, 1996.

Olivecrona, Karl. "Locke's Theory of Appropriation." *The Philosophical Quarterly* 24, no. 96 (1974): 220–234.

Orend, Brian. "*Jus Post Bellum*." *Journal of Social Philosophy* 31, no. 1 (2000): 117–137.

———. "*Jus Post Bellum:* The Perspective of a Just-War Theorist." *Leiden Journal of International Law* 20, no. 3 (2007): 571–591.

———. "Justice after War." *Ethics & International Affairs* 16, no. 1 (2002): 43–56.

———. *Michael Walzer on War and Justice*. Cardiff: University of Wales Press, 2000.

———. *The Morality of War*. Peterborough, Ont.: Broadview Press, 2006.

———. *War and International Justice: A Kantian Perspective*. Waterloo, Ont.: Wilfrid Laurier University Press, 2000.

Orentlicher, Diane F. "Separation Anxiety: International Responses to Ethno-Separatist Claims." *Yale Journal of International Law* 23 (1998): 1–78.

Owen, David. *Balkan Odyssey*. San Diego: Harcourt Brace, 1995.

Paris, Roland. *At War's End: Building Peace after Civil Conflict*. New York: Cambridge University Press, 2004.

———. "Peacebuilding and the Limits of Liberal Internationalism." *International Security* 22, no. 2 (1997): 54–89.

———. "Post-Conflict Peacebuilding." In *The Oxford Handbook on the United Nations,* edited by Thomas G. Weiss and Sam Daws. Oxford: Oxford University Press, 2007, 404–426.

———. "Wilson's Ghost: The Faulty Assumptions of Postconflict Peacebuilding." In *Turbulent Peace: The Challenges of Managing International Conflict,* edited by Chester A. Crocker, Fen Osler Hampson, and Pamela Aall. Washington, DC: United States Institute of Peace Press, 2001, 765–784.

Paris, Roland, and Timothy D. Sisk. "Conclusion: Confronting the Contradictions." In *The Dilemmas of Statebuilding: Confronting the Contradictions of Postwar Peace Operations,* edited by Timothy D. Sisk. New York: Routledge, 2009, 304–315.

———. "Introduction: Understanding the Contradictions of Postwar Statebuilding." In *The Dilemmas of Statebuilding: Confronting the Contradictions of Postwar Peace Operations,* edited by Roland Paris and Timothy D. Sisk. New York: Routledge, 2009, 1–20.

Pasmanier, Deborah. "US-Led Coalition Moving to Reform Purge of Baath Party Members in Iraq." *Middle East Online,* April 23, 2004. Available at: http://www.middle-east-online.com/english/?id =9772.

Pateman, Carole. *The Problem of Political Obligation: A Critique of Liberal Theory.* Berkeley: University of California Press, 1985.

Patten, Alan. "The Autonomy Argument for Liberal Nationalism." *Nations and Nationalism* 5, no. 1 (1999): 1–17.

Pellet, Alain. "The Opinions of the Badinter Arbitration Committee: A Second Breath for the Self-Determination of Peoples." *European Journal of International Law* 3, no. 1 (1992): 178–186.

Philpott, Daniel. "In Defense of Self-Determination." *Ethics* 105, no. 2 (1995): 352–385.

———. "Self-Determination in Practice." In *National Self-Determination and Secession,* edited by Margaret Moore. New York: Oxford University Press, 1998, 79–102.

Plischke, Elmer. "Denazification Law and Procedure." *The American Journal of International Law* 41, no. 4 (1947): 807–827.

Power, Samantha. *"A Problem from Hell": America and the Age of Genocide.* New York: Harper Perennial, 2003.

Premdas, Ralph R. "Secessionist Movements in Comparative Perspective." In *Secessionist Movements in Comparative Perspective,* edited by Ralph R. Premdas, S. W. R. de A. Samarasinghe, and Alan B. Anderson. London: Pinter, 1990, 12–29.

Ramet, Sabrina P. *Balkan Babel: The Disintegration of Yugoslavia from the Death of Tito to the Fall of Milosevic.* Boulder, CO: Westview Press, 2002.

Ramet, Sabrina P. "Slovenia's Road to Democracy." *Europe-Asia Studies* 45, no. 5 (1993): 869–886.

Randle, Robert. *Issues in the History of International Relations.* New York: Praeger, 1987.

Ratner, Steven R. "Drawing a Better Line: *Uti Possidetis* and the Borders of New States." *American Journal of International Law* 90, no. 4 (1996): 590–624.

Ratner, Steven R., and Jason S. Abrams. *Accountability for Human Rights Atrocities in International Law: Beyond the Nuremberg Legacy.* 2nd ed. Oxford: Oxford University Press, 2001.

Rawls, John. *The Law of Peoples.* Cambridge, MA: Harvard University Press, 1999.

———. *A Theory of Justice.* Cambridge, MA: Harvard University Press, 1971.

Raz, Joseph. *The Authority of Law: Essays on Law and Morality.* Oxford: Clarendon Press, 1979.

Recchia, Stefano. "Just and Unjust Postwar Reconstruction: How Much External Interference Can Be Justified?" *Ethics & International Affairs* 23, no. 2 (2009): 165–187.

Reed, Wm. Cyrus. "Exile, Reform, and the Rise of the Rwandan Patriotic Front." *The Journal of Modern African Studies* 34, no. 3 (1996): 479–501.

Regan, Richard J. *Just War: Principles and Cases.* Washington, DC: The Catholic University of America Press, 1996.

Reichberg, Gregory M., Henrik Syse, and Endre Begby, eds. *The Ethics of War: Classic and Contemporary Readings.* Oxford: Blackwell Publishing, 2006.

Reilly, Benjamin. *Democracy in Divided Societies: Electoral Engineering for Conflict Management.* Cambridge: Cambridge University Press, 2001.

———. "Political Engineering and Party Politics in Conflict-Prone Societies." *Democratization* 13, no. 5 (2006): 811–827.

———. "Post-War Elections: Uncertain Turning Points of Transition." In *From War to Democracy: Dilemmas of Peacebuilding,* edited by Anna K. Jarstad and Timothy Sisk. Cambridge: Cambridge University Press, 2008, 157–181.

Reisman, W. Michael. "Assessing Claims to Revise the Laws of War." *The American Journal of International Law* 97, no. 1 (2003): 82–90.

"Report of the Secretary-General on the United Nations Mission in Bosnia and Herzegovina." S/2002/1314. New York: United Nations, 2002. Available at: http://www.un.org/Docs/sc/reports/2002/sgrep02.htm.

eshaping International Priorities in Bosnia and Herzegovina. Part Two: International Power in Bosnia." Berlin/Brussels/Sarajevo: European

Stability Initiative, March 30, 2000. Available at: http://www.esiweb
.org/pdf/esi_document_id_8.pdf.

Reynolds, Andrew. *The Architecture of Democracy: Constitutinal Design,
Conflict Management, and Democracy*. Oxford: Oxford University
Press, 2002.

———. "Constitutional Medicine." *Journal of Democracy* 16, no. 1
(2005): 54–68.

Rieff, David. *Slaughterhouse: Bosnia and the Failure of the West*. New
York: Touchstone, 1995.

Roberts, Adam. "Just Peace: A Cause Worth Fighting For." In *What Is a
Just Peace?*, edited by Pierre Allan and Alexis Keller. Oxford: Oxford
University Press, 2006, 52–89.

Roberts, Adam, and Richard Guelff. *Documents on the Laws of War*. 3rd
ed. Oxford: Oxford University Press, 2000.

Rodin, David. "The Ethics of Asymmetric War." In *The Ethics of War:
Shared Problems of Different Traditions*, edited by Richard Sorabji and
David Rodin. Aldershot, Hampshire, UK: Ashgate, 2006, 153–168.

———. "The Moral Inequality of Soldiers: Why *Jus in Bello* Asymmetry
Is Half Right." In *Just and Unjust Warriors: The Moral and Legal
Status of Soldiers*, edited by David Rodin and David Shue. Oxford:
Oxford University Press, 2008, 44–68.

Rodin, David, and David Shue, eds. *Just and Unjust Warriors: The Moral
and Legal Status of Soldiers*. Oxford: Oxford University Press, 2008.

Rodman, David. "Review Essay: Israel's National Security Doctrine: An
Appraisal of the Past and a Vision of the Future." *Israel Affairs* 9, no.
4 (2003): 115–140.

———. "Two Emerging Issues of *Jus Post Bellum*: War Termination and
the Liability of Soldiers for Crimes of Aggression." In *Jus Post Bellum:
Towards a Law of Transition from Conflict to Peace*. Edited by Carsten
Stahn and Jann K. Kleffner. The Hague: T.M.C. Asser Press, 2008,
53–75.

———. *War and Self-Defense*. Oxford: Oxford University Press, 2002.

Rothchild, Donald, and Philip G. Roeder. "Power Sharing as an
Impediment to Peace and Democracy." In *Sustainable Peace: Power
and Democracy after Civil Wars*, edited by Philip G. Roeder and
Donald Rothchild. Ithaca and London: Cornell University Press,
2005, 29–50.

Rothstein, Robert L. "In Fear of Peace: Getting Past Maybe." In *After the
Peace: Resistance and Reconciliation*, edited by Robert L. Rothstein.
Boulder, CO: Lynne Rienner Publishers, 1999, 1–25.

"The Rule of Law and Transitional Justice in Conflict and Post-Conflic
Societies, Report of the Secretary-General." S/2004/616. New Yo
United Nations Security Council, 2004. Available at: http://w
.un.org/Docs/sc/sgrep04.html.

Samarasinghe, S. W. R. de A. Introduction to *Secessionist Movements in Comparative Perspective.* Edited by Ralph R. Premdas, S. W. R. de A. Samarasinghe, and Alan B. Anderson. London: Pinter, 1990: 1–9.

Sambanis, Nicholas, and Jonah Schulhofer-Wohl. "What's in a Line? Is Partition a Solution to Civil Wars?" *International Security* 34, no. 2 (2009): 82–118.

Sanchez, Miguel Antonio. "Self-Determination and the Falkland Islands Dispute." *Columbia Journal of Transnational Law* 21 (1982–1983): 557–584.

Sanders, John T. "Justice and the Initial Acquisition of Property." *Harvard Journal of Law and Public Policy* 10, no. 2 (1987): 369–399.

Sassòli, Marco. "Reparation." In *Post-Conflict Peacebuilding: A Lexicon,* edited by Vincent Chetail. Oxford: Oxford University Press, 2009, 279–290.

Sayigh, Yezid. *Armed Struggle and the Search for State: The Palestinian National Movement, 1949–1993.* Oxford: Oxford University Press, 1997.

Sayre-McCord, Geoffrey. "Contractarianism." In *The Blackwell Guide to Ethical Theory,* edited by Hugh LaFollette. Oxford: Blackwell Publishers, 2000, 247–267.

Schabas, William A. *The UN International Criminal Tribunals: The Former Yugoslavia, Rwanda and Sierra Leone.* Cambridge: Cambridge University Press, 2006.

Schachter, Oscar. "The Lawful Resort to Unilateral Use of Force." *Yale Journal of International Law* 10, no. 2 (1985): 291–294.

Schmitt, Eric. "Aftereffects: Rumsfeld; Top Baathist Officials to Be Barred from Office." *The New York Times,* May 9, 2003.

Schumpeter, Joseph A. *Capitalism, Socialism and Democracy.* London: George Allen & Unwin, 1976.

Shapiro, Ian. "Democratic Innovation: South Africa in Comparative Context." *World Politics* 46, no. 1 (1993): 121–150.

———. *The State of Democratic Theory.* Princeton: Princeton University Press, 2003.

Shapiro, Ian, and Courtney Jung. "South African Democracy Revisited: A Reply to Koelble and Reynolds." *Politics & Society* 24, no. 3 (1996): 237–247.

Sharma, Surya P. *Territorial Acquisition, Disputes and International Law.* The Hague: Kluwer Law International, 1997.

Shastri, Amita. "Ending Ethnic Civil War: The Peace Process in Sri Lanka." *Commonwealth & Comparative Politics* 47, no. 1 (2009): 76–99.

Shaw, Malcolm N. *International Law.* 5th ed. Cambridge: Cambridge University Press, 2003.

Shlaim, Avi. *The Iron Wall: Israel and the Arab World.* New York: W. W. Norton, 2001.

Shue, Henry, and David Rodin. Introduction to *Preemption: Military Action and Moral Justification,* edited by Henry Shue and David Rodin. Oxford: Oxford University Press, 2007, 1–22.

Silber, Laura, and Allan Little. *Yugoslavia: Death of a Nation.* Rev. and updated ed. New York: Penguin Books, 1997.

Simmons, Beth A. *Territorial Disputes and Their Resolution: The Case of Ecuador and Peru.* Peaceworks No. 27. Washington: United States Institute of Peace, 1999. Available at: http://www.usip.org /publications/territorial-disputes-and-their-resolution.

Sisk, Timothy D. *Peacemaking in Civil Wars: Obstacles, Options, and Opportunities.* Occasional Paper Series No. 20:OP:2. Notre Dame, IN (The Joan B. Kroc Institute for International Peace Studies), 2001.

———. *Power Sharing and International Mediation in Ethnic Conflicts.* Washington, DC: United States Institute of Peace, 1996.

Smith, Dan. "Trends and Causes of Armed Conflicts." In *Tranforming Ethnopolitical Conflict—The Berghof Handbook,* edited by Alex Austin, Martina Fisher, and Norbert Roberts. Wiesbaden: VS Verlag, 2004, 111–127.

Snow, Donald M. *Uncivil Wars: International Security and the New Internal Conflicts.* Boulder, CO: Lynne Rienner Publishers, 1996.

Snyder, Jack, and Leslie Vinjamuri. "Trials and Errors: Principle and Pragmatism in Strategies of International Justice." *International Security* 28, no. 3 (2003/04): 5–44.

Spector, Bertram I. "Negotiating with Villains Revisited: Research Note." *International Negotiation* 9, no. 1 (2003): 613–621.

Stedman, Stephen John. Introduction to *Ending Civil Wars: The Implementation of Peace Agreements.* Edited by Stephen John Stedman, Donald Rothchild, and Elizabeth M. Cousens. Boulder, CO: Lynne Rienner Publishers, 2002, 1–40.

———. "Spoiler Problems in Peace Processes." *International Security* 22, no. 2 (1997): 5–53.

Steiner, Hillel. "May Lockean Doughnuts Have Holes? The Geometry of Territorial Jurisdiction: A Response to Nine." *Political Studies* 56, no. 4 (2008): 949–956.

———. "Territorial Justice." In *National Rights, International Obligations,* edited by Simon Caney, David George, and Peter Jones. Boulder, CO: Westview Press, 1996, 139–148.

Stiefel, Matthias. "Rebuilding after War: Lessons from the War-Torn Societies Project." Geneva: War-Torn Societies Project & Programme for Strategic and International Security Studies, 1999.

Stilz, Anna. "Nations, States, and Territory." *Ethics* 121, no. 3 (2011): 572–601.

———. "Why Do States Have Territorial Rights?" *International Theory* 1, no. 2 (2009), 185–213.

Stinchcombe, Arthur L. "Lustration as a Problem of the Social Basis of Constitutionalism." *Law & Social Inquiry* 20, no. 1 (1995): 245–273.

Suárez, Francisco. *Selections from Three Works of Francisco* Suárez. Vol. 2. Translated by Gwladys L. Williams, Ammi Brown, and John Waldron. Oxford: Clarendon Press, 1944.

Suganami, Hidemi. *On the Causes of War.* Oxford: Clarendon Press, 1996.

Szasz, Paul C. "The Dayton Accord: The Balkan Peace Agreement." *Cornell International Law Journal* 30, no. 3 (1997): 759–768.

Tambiah, Stanley Jeyaraja. *Sri Lanka: Ethnic Fratricide and the Dismantling of Democracy.* London: I. B. Tauris, 1986.

Tamir, Yael. *Liberal Nationalism.* Princeton: Princeton University Press, 1993.

Tanner, Marcus. *Croatia: A Nation Forged in War.* 3rd ed. New Haven, CT: Yale University Press, 2010.

Teitel, Ruti G. *Transitional Justice.* New York: Oxford University Press, 2000.

Thatcher, Margaret. *The Downing Street Years.* London: HarperCollins, 1993.

———. "Speech in a Debate on the Falkland Islands in the House of Commons, 3 April 1982." In *The Collected Speeches of Margaret Thatcher*, edited by Robin Harris. London: HarperCollins 1997, 149–157.

Themnér, Lotta, and Peter Wallensteen. "Appendix 2a. Patterns of Major Armed Conflicts, 2001–10." In *SIPRI Yearbook 2011: Armaments, Disarmament and International Security.* Oxford: Oxford University Press, 2011, 61–76.

———. "Armed Conflict, 1946–2010." *Journal of Peace Research* 48, no. 4 (2011): 524–536.

Tibori Szabó, Kinga. *Anticipatory Action in Self-Defense: Essence and Limits under International Law.* The Hague: T.M.C. Asser Press, 2010.

Toft, Monica Duffy. *Securing the Peace: The Durable Settlement of Civil Wars.* Princeton: Princeton University Press, 2010.

Trachtenberg, Mark. *Reparations in World Politics: France and European Economic Diplomacy, 1916–1923.* New York: Columbia University Press, 1980.

Trahan, Jennifer. "The Rome Statute's Amendment on the Crime of Aggression: Negotations at the Kampala Review Conference." *International Criminal Law Review* 11, no. 1 (2011): 49–104.

Uyangoda, Jayadeva. "Sri Lanka in 2009: From Civil War to Political Uncertainties." *Asian Survey* 50, no. 1 (2010): 104–111.

Van Creveld, Martin. *Defending Israel: A Controversial Plan toward Peace.* New York: Thomas Dunne Books, 2004.

Vasquez, John A. "Understanding Peace: Insights from International Relations Theory and Research." In *A Natural History of Peace*, edited by Thomas Gregor. Nashville and London: Vanderbilt University Press, 1996, 273–296.

———. *The War Puzzle Revisited*. Cambridge: Cambridge University Press, 2009.

Vasquez, John A., and Brandon Valeriano. "Classification of Interstate Wars." *The Journal of Politics* 72, no. 2 (2010): 292–309.

———. "Territory as a Source of Conflict and a Road to Peace." In *The Sage Handbook of Conflict Resolution*, edited by Jacob Bercovitch, Victor Kremenyuk, and I. William Zartman. London: Sage Publications, 2009, 193–209.

Vitoria, Francisco de. *Political Writings*, edited by Anthony Pagden and Jeremy Lawrence. Cambridge: Cambridge University Press, 1991.

Waldron, Jeremy. "Enough and as Good Left for Others." *The Philosophical Quarterly* 29, no. 117 (1979): 319–328.

———. "Superseding Historic Injustice." *Ethics* 103, no. 1 (1992): 4–28.

———. "Two Worries About Mixing One's Labour." *The Philosophical Quarterly* 33, no. 130 (1983): 37–44.

Walter, Barbara F. *Committing to Peace: The Successful Settlement of Civil Wars*. Princeton: Princeton University Press, 2002.

———. "Explaining the Intractability of Territorial Conflict." *International Studies Review* 5, no. 4 (2003): 137–153.

Walzer, Michael. *Arguing About War*. New Haven, CT: Yale University Press, 2004.

———. *Just and Unjust Wars: A Moral Argument with Historical Illustrations*. 3rd ed. New York: Basic Books, 1977.

"War Criminals in Bosnia's Republika Srpska: Who Are the People in Your Neighbourhood?" ICG Balkan Report no. 103. Sarajevo/Washington/Brussels: International Crisis Group, 2000. Available at: http://www.crisisgroup.org/~/media/Files/europe/Bosnia%2039.pdf.

Waterman, Harvey. "Political Order and the 'Settlement' of Civil Wars." In *Stopping the Killing: How Civil Wars End*, edited by Roy Licklider. New York: New York University Press, 1993, 292–302.

Weller, Marc. "The International Response to the Dissolution of the Socialist Federal Republic of Yugoslavia." *The American Journal of International Law* 86, no. 3 (1992): 567–607.

Wellman, Christopher Heath. *A Theory of Secession: The Case for Political Self-Determination*. New York: Cambridge University Press, 2005.

White, George W. *Nationalism and Territory: Constructing Group Identity in Southeastern Europe*. Lanham, MD: Rowman & Littlefield, 2000.

Williams, Robert E. Jr., and Dan Caldwell. "*Jus Post Bellum*: Just War Theory and the Principles of Just Peace." *International Studies Perspectives* 7, no. 4 (2006): 309–320.

Wippman, David. "The Cost of International Justice," *The American Journal of International Law* 100, no. 4 (2006): 861–881.

Wolf, Clark. "Contemporary Property Rights, Lockean Provisios, and the Interests of Future Generations." *Ethics* 105, no. 4 (1995): 791–818.

Wolf, Susan. "Two Levels of Pluralism." *Ethics* 102, no. 4 (1992): 785–798.

Wong, Edward. "Policy Barring Ex-Baathists from Key Iraq Posts Is Eased." *The New York Times*, April 23, 2004.

Woodward, Susan. *Balkan Tragedy: Chaos and Dissolution after the Cold War*. Washington, DC: The Brookings Institution, 1995.

Zacher, Mark W. "The Territorial Integrity Norm: International Boundaries and the Use of Force." *International Organization* 55, no. 2 (2001): 215–250.

Zartman, I. William, Daniel Druckman, Lloyd Jensen, Dean G. Pruitt, and H. Peyton Young. "Negotiations as a Search for Justice." *International Negotiation* 1, no. 1 (1996): 79–98.

Zisk, Kimberly Marten. *Enforcing the Peace: Learning from the Imperial Past*. New York: Columbia University Press, 2004.

INDEX